Africville

DATE DUE
DATE DE RETOUR

Africville

*The Life and Death of a
Canadian Black Community*

Third Edition

Donald H. Clairmont

and

Dennis William Magill

Canadian Scholars' Press   Toronto   1999

Africville: The Life and Death of a Canadian Black Community
Donald H. Clairmont and Dennis William Magill

First published in 1974 by
McClelland and Stewart Limited
25 Hullinger Road
Toronto, Ontario

Canadian Cataloguing in Publication Data

Clairmont, Donald H. (Donald Hayden), 1938–
    Africville : the life and death of a Canadian black community

3rd ed.
Includes bibliographical references.
ISBN 1-55130-093-1

1. Relocation (Housing) – Nova Scotia – Halifax. 2. Black Canadians –
Nova Scotia – Halifax – Social conditions.* 3. Black Canadians – Nova
Scotia – Halifax – Relocation.* 4. Africville (Halifax, N.S.). I. Magill,
Dennis William, 1939–   . II. Title.

FC2346.9.B6C58 1999   971.6'22500496   C97-930984-0
F1039.5.H17C58 1999

Page layout and cover design by Brad Horning

With love and thanks we dedicated the first edition of this book to

Anne Clairmont
and
James and Alberta Magill

The revised edition is dedicated to the late Guy Henson
who is remembered fondly

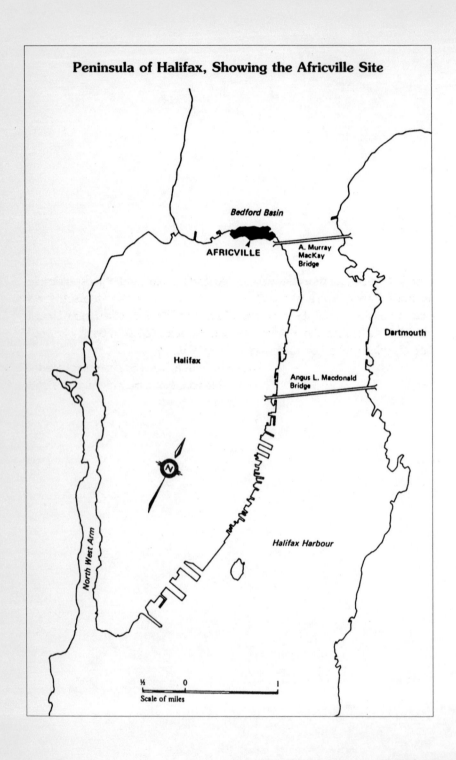

Peninsula of Halifax, Showing the Africville Site

Bedford Basin

AFRICVILLE

A. Murray
MacKay
Bridge

Dartmouth

Halifax

Angus L. Macdonald
Bridge

North West Arm

Halifax Harbour

½   0   1
Scale of miles

I think the man got what he wanted—that [Africville] land. It was as simple as that. People were allowed to stay there the same as black folks anywhere; they could stay until the white man decided. Okay, now I want my land back. And the time came, and he said, 'Okay nigger, get out!' And the black folks had to get out.

Interview with a Nova Scotian black leader
Halifax, Nova Scotia, August 1969

Table of Contents

List of Tables

List of Photographs and Maps

Photographs

Maps

Preface to the 1974 Edition

This book spans a significant period in the personal lives of its authors. Between the time when the study of Africville was conceived (1967) and the present (1974), we have experienced occupational, residential and attitudinal change. Not the least important has been the change in our thinking with regard to planned social change in general and to the Africville relocation in particular. The proposal for the Africville study, written by Clairmont in 1967, was prefaced with an observation that the organization and rhetoric of the Africville relocation might well be a model to follow in future planned social change. The more we studied the relocation and the history of Africville, the more critical we became of the way that the City of Halifax related to Africville residents and the more sceptical we became of the liberal-welfare model of planned social change, of which the Africville relocation appeared to be particularly illustrative. This change was consonant with other changes in attitude associated with our growing apprehension of society's ever-increasing tendency to centralization and technocracy.

Throughout this book we have endeavoured to situate the Africville relocation in an historical and comparative perspective. We are convinced that one can assess the relocation, and its value as a guide to future social change, only if one understands the historical development of Africville and its relationships with the broader society and also understands the alternatives to the specific relocation program. Readers should not attempt to single out as "villains in the piece" individual persons or agencies; rather they should evaluate the relocation in terms of mechanisms that were operating within a complex social system. "How does a community or an area become ripe for relocation?" or, "How can advocacy bearing on the interests of poor and marginal members of society be mobilized effectively?" are questions too vital to be lost in a fog of personal blame or praise.

The Africville research was patterned after the 1967 research proposal; subsequently, our mutual exchange of ideas led to new research directions. Our research and writing responsibilities followed our respective sociological interests: Clairmont was concerned with the relocation phenomenon, changes in Africville's social structure, the relocation from the perspective of the Africville residents, and life after the relocation; Magill focused on the decision-making and bureaucratic dimensions of the relocation and the relocation from the perspective of political administrative individuals. Throughout the book, however, the analysis is the result of an intimate and rewarding collaborative effort expanding over seven years.

In expressing our acknowledgements, we state first deep appreciation to the Africville relocatees; this book would have been impossible without their cooperation and assistance. Our research assistants, John E. De Roche, Bernard MacDougall, and Harry Wells must be singled out for their work. Many other persons and agencies, far too many to personally thank, contributed in various ways to the success of the research project. In addition, we acknowledge the following persons and organizations that gave permission to reprint written and photographic works: C.R. Brookbank; Bob Brooks; Central Mortgage and Housing Corporation; Dennis Harvey, Editor, *Star Weekly*; A.M. Savage, Managing Editor, the *Halifax Herald Limited*; David Lewis Stein; C.A. Ward, former City Manager, City of Halifax; and Wamboldt-Waterfield Photography Limited. The 1964 map of the Africville area is reprinted by Mr. Ward's permission.

Special acknowledgement is due the Institute of Public Affairs, Dalhousie University, for providing resources and administrative assistance; the book's completion has depended upon Institute moral and financial support. Thanks are extended to Kell Antoft, Guy Henson, and Marjorey Walters. Our greatest debt is to Donald F. Maclean who read the entire manuscript and whose numerous criticisms prevented many errors of judgment and imperfections in style. The unsung heroines are the Institute's secretarial staff. Deserving special mention are Angela Martin, the project secretary during the 1969 fieldwork phase; Margaret Dingley, who made many constructive criticisms in editing the manuscript; Jeanne Arsenault, who assisted with the artwork; Sandra Cashen and Linda Ede, who completed much of the typing; and Joan Embrey who supervised the preparation of the final draft manuscript.

For their patience in accepting unavoidable delays in finishing the manuscript, we extend our appreciation to the editorial staff of McClelland and Stewart Limited. Linda McKnight, Paul Audley, and Ross Baker provided us with important editorial advice. In numerous ways, this book reflects Paul Audley's and Ross Baker's careful and critical reading.

Finally, we express our gratitude to the funding agencies that supported this research project: the Nova Scotia Department of Public Welfare and the Federal Department of Health and Welfare (Project No. 522-21-2). Additional financial support was given through small research grants from Dalhousie University and from the Humanities and Social Sciences Committee, the Research Board, University of Toronto.

Donald H. Clairmont
Bedford, Nova Scotia

Dennis William Magill
Toronto, Ontario
June 9, 1973

Preface to the 1987 Edition

Thirteen years after the initial publication of *Africville* by McClelland and Stewart and almost seventeen years after the last resident was cajoled into moving to a decrepit city-owned house, the word Africville continues to have powerful meaning for many of the former residents and indeed for Nova Scotia blacks in general. Where Africville once stood there is now the Seaview Memorial Park (named after Africville's Seaview African United Baptist Church), a tidy but underutilized and kind of eerie facility. To the north of the park is the Fairview Cove Terminal where transatlantic ships disgorge their valuable cargo without having to brook the quizzical stares of the area's former long-time settlers and the unslightliness of the sprawling open dump which once bridged the community and the cove. Arching high above the former Africville site is the A. Murray Mackay Bridge linking the cities of Dartmouth and Halifax, its approaches and roads on the Halifax side securely rooted at the inland boundary of the community. What remains physically in the area is clean, tidy, technologically sophisticated. Gone are the people, their community, their — and especially others' — debris. Yet Africville still generates warm memories and purposive identity for its relocated people and their children and is still a rallying symbol in the black subculture.

Beyond the park designation Africville's continued existence has no official basis. The Seaview Credit Union referred to in the first edition collapsed a decade ago. There is no agency, program or fund which specifically serves Africville people. It still thrives however in the hearts and minds of the many relocatees. As recently as February 1987 a regional CBC television production focused upon the relocatees' remembrances and current feelings, highlighting the sense of the family, community, and continuity they associate with Africville and detailing their continued efforts to "keep it alive and pass it along" through song, summer gatherings "out home" in the park under the auspices of their own genealogical society, and by ensuring that the young generation know the Africville story. Of course the story as told may be somewhat mythical in its romanticization of community life and its unqualified conspiratorial allegation as regards city officials, but it reflects a coherent, valid position even if it is not the only possible valid story.

As indicated in the first edition, the symbolic significance and connotation of Africville for the Nova Scotian black community changed dramatically over the years. Subsequent to the relocation, Africville became a kind of red alert, signalling danger to black communities and traditions in the guise of city development projects, area upgrading, and gentrification, i.e., the "yuppie" invasion of low-cost housing areas. It still has that salience. Recently, as the federal and provincial governments announced a five to seven million dollar revitalization of Uniacke Square, the public housing project in Halifax built in the 1960s to accommodate many Africville relocatees and others, the executive director of the Black United Front of Nova Scotia warned that "another Africville-type relocation" may be in the works. He feared that the project's residents — both black and white, Africville and non-Africville descendants — might lose their homes as "yuppies" moved in to replace existing low-income families in the upgraded facilities.

Why does Africville continue to be so meaningful for its former residents? One might contend that it is because they never did get the new start promised them in the relocation liberal-welfare rhetoric. Many indeed are still suffering from socio-economic disadvantage and live in crowded and "bureaucratic" public housing. But this cannot be the sole or perhaps even the most important factor since some of the socio-economically successful relocatees (or their offspring) grieve the loss of community identity. One sometimes encounters such feelings among migrants from other well-known Canadian 'tough areas' such as Point St. Charles in Montreal or the Northend in Hamilton, areas that were not sanitized nor homogeneous but exhibited a wholeness of life — the good and the bad, the steady, and the sliders. Such communities had a rich texture and life; there was not just a "one two, one two" blandness. Certainly in modern society, as many observers have noted, relationships are usually temporal, functional, and without depth, hardly the stuff of rich identity and meaning. The former Africville residents who meet annually "out home" at reunions sponsored by the Africville Genealogy Society emphasize its continuing significance for their sense of self and their roots. And the fact that the community was taken away from them rather than they themselves migrating from it adds a profundity to their grievance. One relocatee at the 1986 reunion remarked, "I don't want my kids to lose sight of where I came from. It could have been their home too" (*The Daily News*, July 30, 1986). Another said, "The reunion is important to the descendants because it gives them a place to come back to and remember. And it's important to teach the children . . . we hope that they learn from what has happened" (*The Mail-Star*, August 2, 1986).

The continued salience of Africville in the wider black community is evident in the recent remarks of one local black leader: "When you're a minority you need to stick together. They [the Africville people] lost that." Africville has rich symbolic value for black organizations charged with the mandate of fostering black culture and development and fighting racism and shallow promises. "Remember Africville" is a phrase that has numerous meanings such as "stand together," "don't let your community get run-down," and "beware glib talk of progress." The depth and diversity of Africville's symbolic connotations ensure its future.

Beyond the relocatees and the Nova Scotia black community, Africville has symbolic significance as one of the last of a species, namely the large-scale relocation of persons from communities or neighbourhoods chiefly into fairly densely populated public housing complexes with an accompanying liberal-welfare rhetoric of progress. In the first edition we observed that such large-scale upheavals, being carried out presumably for the relocatees' own good, were common throughout the 1960s. Also we envisaged the liberal-welfare rationale being somewhat superceded by a more political rhetoric whereby such upheavals would be more clearly seen to require the mobilization of the communities or groups in order that the potential relocatees' values and interests be fully incorporated in the developments. Certainly the liberal-welfare model has gone, but then so too has the more political approach. Wholesale uprooting of communities, large public housing complexes, grand projects of 'people' development are all passé. What we have now is a largely market-driven and house-specific change. Issues of community and social equality rarely receive acknowledgement. As for housing itself, issues concerning housing tenure, access, and affordability of course are of considerable importance especially to low-income Canadians who — like many Africville relocatees and their descendants — face high-cost housing, the gentrification process, and a *sauve qui peut* social mentality with only limited employment opportunities and a pared-to-the-bone social-housing policy available to them.

The 1974 and 1987 Editions

Both editions are highly condensed versions of the authors' *Africville Relocation Report* published in 1971 by the Institute of Public Affairs, Dalhousie University. The 1987 edition contains new material which enriches the 1974 analysis.

Donald H. Clairmont
Bedford, Nova Scotia

Dennis William Magill
Toronto, Ontario

April, 1987

Preface to the 1999 Edition

It has been thirty-four years since the first Africville person left the community under the Africville Relocation Program. Yet Africville has continued to be a major referent point for the definition of the black experience in Nova Scotia if not for the black diaspora more generally. As one black writer has observed (Saunders, 1994) it has the status of an icon in the Afro-Canadian social construction of Canadian society. It is a tangible and immediate symbol to many persons with ties to the community, providing memories, social networks and even possibilities and dreams for the future. It is concretized in the Seaview Memorial Park and in the organization and activities of the Africville Genealogical Society which continues to sponsor annual summer get-togethers and to pursue legal action against the City of Halifax. It remains a powerful presence in local politics, as attested to by numerous newspaper headlines and Council discussions up to the present day, where the Africville interests, channelled by the Africville Genealogical Society, continue to clash with the positions of City politicians and bureaucrats.

Since the 1987 edition of this book there have been several significant events pertinent to the Africville experience. In the fall of 1989 an exhibition entitled 'Africville: A Spirit That Lives On' was successfully launched at Mount Saint Vincent University in Halifax. The exhibition subsequently went across Canada receiving critical acclaim and drawing large crowds; after the tour it was provided a permanent home at the Black Cultural Centre of Nova Scotia. A number of important events were held in association with the Halifax debut, including a church service, an evening of artistic celebration, the reassembling of some of the key relocation decision-makers to provide their perspective on the Africville Relocation Program, and a day of moving responses and testimonials from former Africville residents. In 1991 the award-winning film documentary, Remembering Africville, which was inspired by the exhibition, was released by the National Film Board.

There was more than mere celebration of Africville as remembrance. In 1991 the symbolic Africville won a zoning battle rarely achieved by the historic Africville when the Government of Nova Scotia, after protest from the Africville Genealogical Society and others, ordered the re-routing of a major truck route encroaching upon the Seaview Memorial Park that was being proposed by the Halifax Port Corporation. A second commercial proposal allowing CN Rail to construct a multi-building, intermodal freight terminal would have meant much great commercial encroachment on the Seaview parkland. It had received City staff support on the grounds that it would benefit the Halifax economy and ease traffic flow but it too was shelved after Halifax aldermen raised the red flag; one alderman commented that Nova Scotia's black community would be even more upset with CN's proposal than it was with the Port Corporation's one, adding "If they were wild over the last one—look out". In 1992 the sod was turned for the construction of a replica of the Seaview United Baptist Church - the Africville church—within the Seaview Memorial Park; actual construction has yet to take place.

Many songs, poems, and short stories have been written about Africville over the years, supplementing the many graduate theses, newspaper articles, radio and television documentaries. Two significant happenings occurred in 1993/94, namely the publication of The Spirit of Africville, a multi-authored compilation of history and interpretation which was selected as the editor's choice in the Toronto Globe and Mail, and the premiere of a major jazz piece entitled the Africville Suite. The book, like the NFB film, was inspired by the 1989 exhibition and combined scholarly writings and creative interpretation of life in pre-location Africville. The Africville Suite written by jazzman Joe Sealey in tribute to his father who was born in Africville, premiered in Halifax in 1994.

There were developments too on the 'political' front. In 1993 negotiations were resumed between representatives of the Africville Genealogical Society and the City of Halifax. While negotiations were in progress, in the summer of 1994 two middle-aged brothers, former residents of Africville, began their live-in protest ('tent-in') in Seaview Park, a protest aimed at getting the City to respond to their demands for significant compensation if not re-establishment at the old Africville site. A month later the new Halifax city manager held an open meeting with former Africville residents and other interested citizens at the North Branch Library to have a dialogue on possible negotiated agreements. The meeting was generally deemed unsuccessful, in large part because the City's position was that there would be no individual compensation of any kind, whether monetary or housing. City staff issued an assessment of the Africville relocation and some recommendations in the fall of 1994. The six page report in effect argued that relocatees had been adequately compensated at the time of relocation and recommended only the establishment of a modest educational fund (a fund of $100,000 with scholarships provided from its accrued interest) and that the City donate a hectare of land adjacent to Seaview Park for a lasting Africville memorial (i.e., the building of the Seaview church replica in commemoration of Africville). After a short period of negotiation between the politicians (elected Council members) and representatives of the Genealogical Society a negotiated agreement was unanimously approved by City Council. The agreement called for the educational fund and the donated land as specified in the staff report but also allowed the Genealogical Society access to municipal records to see if a legal claim could be made against the City; the mayor commented that "if there is a legal basis for a claim, they can still pursue it and we won't hold them up". Concurrently the Genealogical Society received funding from Heritage Canada to undertake the pertinent research. The live-in protest by the two brothers continued until late spring 1995 when under legal pressure they moved to a site just outside the fenced parkland. The sit-in never did become a rallying point for Africville-centred protest.

In 1996 events happened which ensured that the Africville-Halifax City continuing confrontation would outlast the physical demise of both parties. Halifax merged with the rest of Halifax County to constitute a new municipality. For a variety of reasons, including tactical ones, the organization of former Africville residents launched legal action just prior to the official amalgamation, action which is pending. Meanwhile plans are being laid for the annual summer Africville reunion and at least three new theses and two radio documentaries are being prepared on Africville. While former residents and their offspring have received virtually nothing in the way of material benefits since the relocation and the demise of the Seaview Credit Union established by the City and the Province to provide modest post-relocation financial relief, they continue to keep a high profile, to celebrate their history and identity, 'to keep the spirit alive and pass it along', and Africville continues to exert a major presence for Afro-Canadians and in Nova Scotian life.

The 1999 Edition

To update recent events since the publication of the 1987 edition, Chapter Nine was written in order to "deconstruct" the community twenty-nine years after the last resident was relocated from Africville.

Donald H. Clairmont
Bedford, Nova Scotia

Dennis William Magill
Toronto, Ontario

January, 1999

The Relocation Phenomenon and the Africville Study

> To seek social change, without due recognition of the manifest and latent functions performed by the social organization undergoing change, is to indulge in social ritual rather than social engineering.[1]
>
> — Robert K. Merton

Halifax, the foundation city of English-speaking Canada, experienced much change during its first two hundred years of existence. Yet the facelift and redevelopment it has undergone since the late 1950s have effected a change as dramatic as the 1917 explosion that levelled much of the city. Stimulated by the Stephenson Report of 1957,[2] urban renewal and redevelopment have resulted in the relocation of thousands of people, the demolition of hundreds of buildings, and the construction of impressive business and governmental complexes. The Africville relocation was part of the larger redevelopment pattern; Africville residents constituted some eight to ten percent of the people affected by approved urban renewal schemes in the city of Halifax during the relocation years.

Africville was a black community within the city of Halifax, inhabited by approximately four hundred people, comprising eighty families, many of whom were descended from settlers who had moved there over a century ago. Tucked away in a corner of the city, relatively invisible, and thought of as a "shack town," Africville was a depressed community both in physical and in socio-economic terms. Its dwellings were located beside the city dump, and railroad tracks cut across the one dirt road leading into the area. Sewerage, lighting, and other public services were conspicuously absent. The people had little education, very low incomes, and many were underemployed. Property claims were in chaos. Only a handful of families could establish legal title; others claimed squatter rights; and still others rented. Africville, long a black mark against society, had been designated for future industrial and harbour development. Many observers reported that despite these liabilities there was a strong sense of community and that some residents expressed satisfaction with living in Africville.

In 1964 the small black ghetto of Africville began to be phased out of existence. By that time most residents of Halifax, black and white, had come to think of Africville as "the slum by the dump." Most Haligonians, including some Africville residents, did not regard the community as viable and recognized a need for planned social change. The relocation plan announced by the city of Halifax, which purported to be more than simply a real estate operation, appeared to be a response to this need. The plan emphasized humanitarian concern, included employment and education programs, and referred to the creation of new opportunities for the people of Africville. To the general public, the proposed relocation was a progressive step.

In addition to official pronouncements, there were other indications that the Africville program would be more humane and progressive than the typical North American urban relocation. Halifax city council had adopted recommendations contained in a report submitted by a noted Canadian welfare specialist experienced in urban renewal. There was much preliminary discussion of the relocation by city officials among themselves, with Africville residents, and with a "caretaker" group of black and white progressionals associated with the Halifax Human Rights Advisory Committee. Relocation plans were not *ad hoc* and haphazard. City officials were required to articulate their policies well and in detail; many implications and alternatives were considered.

There were also indications in the relocation decision-making structure that the Africville program might realize its official rhetoric. A social worker was appointed by the city to take front-line responsibility for the varied aspects of the relocation and to act as liaison between the city administration and the relocatees. The social worker, who was on loan from the Nova Scotia Department of Public Welfare, had a measure of autonomy vis-à-vis the city and an independent contingency fund to meet day-to-day emergencies and opportunities with a minimum of bureaucratic delay. In negotiating the real estate aspects of relocation, the social worker brought proposed agreements before a special advisory committee consisting of aldermen and several members of the Halifax Human Rights Advisory Committee.

In terms of its rationale, public rhetoric, and organizational structure, the Africville relocation seemed worthy of study. The plan was *liberal-oriented* (that is, aimed at ending segregation and providing improved opportunities for the disadvantaged), *welfare-oriented* (that is, it hoped to coordinate employment, educational, and rehabilitative programs with the rehousing of people), and run by *experts* (that is, the planning, execution, and advice were provided by professionals). An examination of the Africville relocation could be expected to yield greater fundamental insight into planned social change than would a study of typical relocation programs that were accomplished by administrative fiat and stressed primarily the physical removal of persons. It seemed important to study and evaluate the Africville relocation both in its particularity and against the background of general relocation issues.

There were additional reasons for studying the Africville relocation. First, Africville was part of a trend in the 1960s for governmental initiative in relocation programs, and there was reason to expect that other tentative relocations in Nova Scotia and elsewhere would be patterned after the Africville experience. Second, Africville had attracted national and even international notice, and there was broad public interest in the relocation. Third, accounts of pre-relocation social conditions and attitudes were available. Two surveys had been conducted[3] and other material was available in city records. Finally, in 1968 the Africville relocation had already been acclaimed locally as a success. One city alderman noted:

> The social significance of the Africville program is already beginning to show positive results as far as individual families are concerned. The children are performing more satisfactorily in school and they seem to take more of an interest in their new surroundings. This report is not intended to indicate that the program has been 100 percent successful; however I believe it can be said that it has been at least 75 percent, judging by the comments of the relocated families.[4]

Private communication with city officials and relocation officials in the United States and Canada brought forth praise for the organization and rhetoric of the Africville relocation.

Was the Africville relocation a success? If so, from whose perspective? To what extent? What accounted for the success or lack of it? It is hoped that answers to these and related questions will contribute to an appreciation of the Africville relocation and of relocation generally.

The Relocation Phenomenon

Relocation must be seen in the context of a general North American mobility pattern, and certain distinctive features should be noted. The most important distinction is that relocation is part of planned social change carried out, or at least approved, by public agency. The initiation of relocation, as seen by the relocatees, is usually involuntary and an immediate function of the political process. Our present concern is with relocation as it pertains to private residences, involves neighbourhoods or communities, and is a function of comprehensive programs of social change. This kind of relocation accounts for but a small measure of the mobility noted in Canada and the United States, but it was significant because it was distinctive. It was noted earlier that the Africville relocation was itself part of a much larger redevelopment project in the city of Halifax. In terms of the sweep of lifestyle change, even such large urban projects have been dwarfed by post-Second World War Canadian relocation projects in the Arctic and in Newfoundland. In 1953, Newfoundland, with 6000 miles of coastline and approximately 1150 settlements, undertook a program to move people from the small outposts to larger viable communities which could be serviced efficiently. Between 1965 and 1970 over 3250 households were moved.[5]

As many low-income Americans and Canadians can testify, urban renewal is a prime example of forced relocation. Urban renewal legislation began in the 1940s in both countries. By 1968 approximately forty-five Canadian urban redevelopments had been initiated at a cost of 270 million dollars for 1500 cleared acres.[6] While the scope of urban renewal in Canada was quite small in the light of American experience, the Canadian program was significant enough that one can complain that there were too few Canadian studies looking into the politics, issues, and human consequences of renewal programs. To overcome this lack of knowledge and to place the Africville relocation in perspective, more comprehensive themes will be discussed in this introduction.

From a political-administrative perspective there are four relocation models: the traditional, development, liberal-welfare, and political. The Africville project is the best Canadian example of the liberal-welfare type of relocation. As shown in Table I.1, the appendix to this Introduction, these models vary along six dimensions: (1) ideological premises; (2) formulation of policy; (3) implementation of policy; (4) intended beneficiaries; (5) central actors and organizational units; and (6) key problems. These models are ideal types to which actual relocation programs correspond to a greater or lesser degree.

The Development Model

The development model was the most prevalent political-administrative approach to relocation in North America. This type of relocation was usually justified in terms of supposed benefits for the system as a whole, whether the system is society, the city, etc. It was usually initiated by order of political authorities and administered by bureaucrats; it was not anticipated that relocatees would benefit other than indirectly. The underlying ideology of the development model was system-oriented and neo-capitalist; an accurate statement of its premise in urban renewal has been offered by Wallace: "[it considers] renewal, as a public activity, to be intervention in a market and competitive system and to be justified by the need to make up for imperfections in the market mechanism that impede the adjustment process, to eliminate conditions which are economic or social liabilities."[7] In the context of contemporary urban renewal, the development model incorporated the usual city-design approach, focusing on questions of beautification, zoning, and structure,[8] and was usually intended to increase the city tax base and achieve civic pride or attract industry.

The development model can be illustrated by past urban renewal programs in Toronto. Ignoring relocatees as viable interest groups the programs operated implicitly on the basis of certain ideological premises: to correct imperfections in the social system (removal of so-called slums) and overall system development (economic growth), or both. As is the case in many Canadian cities, Toronto's past development policy was closely linked to the businesses and commercial-property industry which provided homes, apartment buildings, shopping centres, and industrial complexes. Thus the elimination of "blight areas" and construction of highrise apartment and office buildings generated an important source of urban revenue. Referring to this policy of "dollar planning," Fraser observed:

> As long as Toronto, [in 1972] like all other municipalities
> in Canada has to depend upon property taxes as its sole

source of income, the overwhelming power of development interests in determining the direction and quality of Toronto's growth will remain unchallenged.

> ...the key to a municipality's prosperity remains its rate of growth; Toronto planners have been consistently ignored by city councils that have been over the years almost exclusively uninterested in any discussions about the quality of that development.[9]

A non-urban example of the development model of relocation has been described by John Matthiasson, in his study of the forced relocation of a band of Cree Indians in Northern Manitoba. The Cree were relocated to make way for a gigantic power project; they were not involved in the project planning and despite their displeasure "they accepted in a fatalistic manner the announcement of the relocation. They believed that the decision had been made by higher authorities, and that they had neither the right nor power to question it."[10]

The development model of relocation had its limitations. In particular, its econocentric and "undemocratic" features were criticized. The assumption that relocatees benefit indirectly from relocation was challenged, as was the premise that the system as a whole somehow redistributed fairly the benefits accruing from forcing people to move and facilitating the development of private industry. Some critics argued that if one included social-psychological factors in one's conception of costs, the relocatees could be seen as subsidizing the rest of the system. The criticism had some effect, and the liberal-welfare model became increasingly common.[11] One official explained:

> In the fifteen years since [urban renewal's] inception, we have seen a progressive broadening of the concept and a strengthening of tools. We have seen, increasingly, both the need for, and realization of, rapprochement between physical and social planning, between renewal and social action. But the fully effective liaison of the two approaches has almost everywhere been frustrated by the absence of the tools to deal as effectively with the problems of human beings as with the problems of physical decay and blight.[12]

Another writer has observed,

> social welfare can no longer be treated as the responsibility
> of private and more or less bountiful ladies and gentlemen
> or as the less respected branch of the social welfare
> community and the city government. Tied as it is to the
> concerns as dear to the heart of the country as economic
> prosperity it merits a place in the inner sanctum, particularly
> of planning commissions.[13]

The Liberal-Welfare Model

The "rediscovery" of poverty,[14] the war on poverty, the increasing
pressure "from below" upon the development model, and the broadening
definition of urban renewal led to the widespread emergence of the liberal-
welfare-oriented approach. The liberal-welfare model, like the development
model, emphasized expertise and technical knowledge in its operation and
administration, and invariably was initiated by public authority. The principal
difference is that the liberal-welfare model purported to benefit the
relocatees primarily and directly. Under this model, welfare officials often
saw themselves as "caretakers" for the relocatees; one relocation official
has said, "the department of relocation is the tenants' advocate."[15] The
liberal-welfare model of relocation was characterized by a host of social
welfare programs supplemental to housing policies and was regarded as
an opportunity for a multifaceted attack on poverty and other problems.
It was this liberal-welfare model and its assumptions that shaped the rhetoric
underlying the 1963-64 decision to relocate Africville.

Ideologically, the liberal-welfare model was much like the development
model in that it tended to operate with a consensus model of society and
posited a basic congruency between the interests of relocatees and those
of society as a whole. It was "undemocratic" in the same sense as the
development model; the low-status relocatees were accorded little attention,
either as participants in the implicit political process or as contributors to
specific policies or plans of action. There was an effort, however, to
persuade rather than to ignore the relocatees. Criticism of the liberal-welfare
model of relocation was related primarily to the ideological level. Some
writers noted that liberal welfarism had become part of the establishment
of contemporary North American society.[16] Its proponents were presumed
to be handmaidens of strong vested interests, reconciling the disadvantaged

and patching up the symptoms of social malaise. Critics pointed out that the special programs associated with the liberal-welfare model of relocation tended to be short-term and unsuccessful. The welfare rhetoric often diverted attention from the gains and benefits accruing to the middle-income and elite groups in society. The critics attacked the liberal-welfare model on the premise that the social problems to which it is ostensibly directed could be solved only through profound structural change effecting a redistribution of resources, and by providing relocatees with the consciousness and resources to restructure their own lives.

The liberal-welfare model is best illustrated by the Africville relocation, discussed at length in this book. The community of Africville was defined as a social problem, and relocation was regarded as an intervention strategy designed to help solve the "social and economic problems of Africville residents." The central actors in the formation and implementation of relocation policy were politicians, bureaucrats, experts, and middle-class caretakers; there was no meaningful *collective* participation by Africville residents. The relocatees were to be major beneficiaries through compensation, welfare payments, and rehabilitative retraining programs. The major problem with the relocation was that, although rooted in liberal-welfare rhetoric, it failed to achieve its manifest goals.

The Political Model

The liberal-welfare model of relocation was revised and developed both as a response to criticism at the ideological level and in reaction to its lack of operational success. There was a growing interest in citizen participation in all phases of relocation; in the firmer acceptance, structurally and culturally, of the advocacy function of relocation officials; in the co-ordination of relocation services; and in the provision of resources. It is difficult to assess how far this interest has been translated into fact. There appeared to be a shift in the 1970s, at least conceptually, to the political model of relocation and a frank recognition that relocation usually entailed a conflict of interest, for example, between the relocatees and the city. There was an attempt to structure the conflict by providing relocatees with resources to develop a parallel structure to that of the government. Although society and the relocatee were considered to benefit equally, this political perspective assumed that relocatees benefited both directly and indirectly; directly in terms of, say, housing and other welfare services, and indirectly by participating in the basic decision-making and the determination of their life situation. The political model of relocation was based on the premise that social problems were political problems and emphasized solutions through political action; relocation was approached primarily as a situation in which problems were solved not by the application of expertise but by the resolution of conflicting interests.

Beyond the considerable costs (the dollar cost is less hidden than in the other relocation model) and administrative difficulties entailed, there were other grounds for criticism of the political model. There was a tendency to overemphasize the solidarity and common interests of relocatees, to exaggerate the multiplying effects of political participation in relocation,[17] and to raise serious questions about how far government could proceed or would proceed in fostering extra-parliamentary political action.

Citizen participation, a core element in the political model, was institutionalized in the United States by the community action programs of the 1964 Economic Opportunity Act. Numerous books and articles, far too many to cite, have discussed the reasons, operations, and failures of "maximum feasible participation" of the poor in the war on poverty.[18] Citizen participation was also part of the United States model city programs, which required that local residents be involved in the planning process and implementation of changes in their neighbourhoods. Contrasted with the United States, Canada has relatively few examples of related social-animation projects. The rise of "militant" citizen groups was a phenomenon which developed later in Canada. The public outcry against the community work of the Company of Young Canadians and the subsequent governmental intervention to close this organization may be an indication of the limits of this perspective. The only Canadian publication illustrating the political model of a relocation is Fraser's study of Toronto's Trefann Court. Trefann Court residents successfully fought off a development-type relocation project; subsequently, the conflict arising from different interests was recognized as an integral part of the city's social organization. Despite internal community conflict between homeowners and tenants, a number of community residents, leaning heavily on outside "resource people," developed a cohesive organization and set up a working committee (a parallel structure) to establish a conceptual scheme for community change in conjunction with the existing city bureaucracy. The Trefann Court case also pointed to a key problem in the political model, that of assessing the representativeness of any one group of citizens to speak, argue, or vote for an entire community. With the establishment of "parallel structures," many citizens grow frustrated with the tedious detail involved in committee work. In Fraser's words:

> The fact that the Working Committee operated under formal rules of order, dominated by minutes, reports, rules of procedure and legislative decorum widened the gap between the committee and the community. As debates became more lengthy, detailed and technical, the meetings became harder to follow for the ordinary Trefann resident who might drop in.[19]

The Traditional Model

Finally, there is the traditional model of relocation in North American society. This is a limiting type of relocation carried out under governmental auspices, for it is a form of planned social change characterized by self-help and self-direction. It is the neighbourhood or community leaders, often indigenous minority-group leaders working through indigenous social organizations, who plan and carry out the relocation, generally with official support and some resource commitment by government agencies. The traditional model entails a largely laissez-faire strategy whereby the relocatees benefit directly and technical expertise is used to advise rather than to direct. Criticism of this approach contends that, without political action, neither the available resources nor the generation of initiative can be effective in the case of low-status groups.

There are numerous examples of the traditional model of relocation. Group settlement and resettlement in various parts of Canada have been common. The relocation of Beechville, a black community on the outskirts of Halifax, is an example within the Halifax metropolitan area. Community leaders, anticipating a government attempt to relocate the residents, organized themselves into a co-operative housing association, received funds from Central Mortgage and Housing Corporation, and reorganized their community partly on their own terms. The scope available for traditional relocation models lessens as society becomes more technocratic and centralized.

Conceptual Framework

Throughout this book our emphasis will be on the liberal-welfare model of planned social change and its implementation during the Africville relocation. During the analysis we focus on questions of power and exchange among the various participants of the relocation. Thus, from the perspective of power and exchange,[20] we can examine the power resources and relationships among the individual persons and groups involved in the relocation, the historical evolution of these social facts, the goals held by the different parties, and the strategies and tactics employed in establishing the terms of the relocation "contract." We can also analyse the role of outsiders, experts, and community "leaders" and focus on questions such as the mobilization of advocacy, relocation resistances and alternatives, and the relation of rhetoric to action. It is vital in the Africville case to have a larger historical view, observing the historical exchange patterns between the city and the Africville people and tracing the implications of these patterns in making Africville "ripe for relocation" and in influencing the relocation decision-making and mechanics.

An aspect of this perspective concerns the context of negotiations and the bargaining strategies developed by the parties involved. Accordingly, attention was devoted to probing the relocatees' knowledge about the relocation; their strategies (use of lawyers, co-operation with fellow relocatees, and development of special arguments in dealing with city officials), and their perceptions of the city's goals, strategies, and resources. The relocation social worker completed a questionnaire concerning each relocated family which paid considerable attention to his negotiations with relocatees and his perception of their goals, strategies, and resources. This perspective included the concepts of rewards, costs, profits, and distributive justice. It would appear, for instance, that relocatees would have been satisfied with the relocation if rewards exceeded costs and if they thought that the city and other relocatees would not "get a better deal." Information concerning rewards, costs, sense of distributive justice, and satisfaction was obtained through the questionnaires, the interviews, and the case studies.

Despite problems in measuring each relocatee's perception of the relative profit accruing to himself or herself, other relocatees, and the city of Halifax, and problems occasioned by differences between long-term and short-term effects, this power and exchange approach is significant for the relocation literature which often appears to keep aloof from the "blood and guts" of relocation transaction. Equally important, by placing the Africville relocation within a typology of relocation models, it is possible to explore the domain consensus (that is, the basic terms of reference held in common and prerequisite to any exchange) associated with the liberal-welfare approach, and especially how such domain consensus (for example, "disadvantaged communities or people have few intrinsically valuable resources and need to be guided by sympathetic experts") develops and how it sets the limits and context of bargaining and reciprocity.

Research Strategies

The methods employed in this study were varied: questionnaires, in-depth interviews, historical documents, newspapers, case studies, and "bull sessions" with relocatees. A useful baseline source of data was the survey of Halifax blacks, including Africville, conducted in 1959 by the Institute of Public Affairs, Dalhousie University. The original questionnaires were available for re-analysis, an important consideration since many of the data were not published and the published material contained several significant inaccuracies.[21] The 1959 survey questionnaire provided basic demographic data as well as information concerning mobility aspirations, employment, education, and social life.

The collection of data for this study began in 1968. The researchers arranged for two students from the Maritime School of Social Work to prepare twenty case studies.[22] A review of the students' case studies and field notes, guided by the perspective developed by the researchers, aided the drafting of a questionnaire. In 1968 current addresses of the relocatees were also traced and brief acquaintance interviews were conducted.

The most intensive data collection period was June to December 1969. One of the researchers (D.W.M.) conducted in-depth, tape-recorded interviews with individual people associated with the relocation decision-making and implementation: politicians, city officials, middle-class caretakers, the relocation social worker, consultants, and Africville relocatees involved in the decision-making. During these interviews an open-ended interview guide[23] was used to explore knowledge of Africville and awareness of pre-1964 relocation attempts and also the actual relocation decision-making and mechanics. Each of the approximately two-hour interviews was transcribed and analysed for patterns. Many quotations used in this book are taken from these tape-recorded interviews.

Concurrently, the other researcher (D.H.C.), with two assistants, was meeting informally with the relocatees, individually and in "bull sessions." On the basis of these experiences and the case studies, we drafted and pre-tested an extensive questionnaire. From September to December, 1969, the questionnaire was employed by interviewers hired and trained by the researchers. The lengthy questionnaire[24] asked about the relocatee's background characteristics: life in Africville, personal knowledge of relocation decision-making processes, relocation strategies, negotiations, costs, rewards, and post-relocation conditions. The questionnaire was given to all household heads and spouses who had lived in Africville and had received a relocation settlement of any kind. Approximately 140 persons were interviewed, several in places as far distant as Winnipeg and Toronto.

In June, 1969, the relocation social worker spent eight days answering a questionnaire[25] on the relocatees' background characteristics, his relocation bargaining with each relocatee, and his perception of the latter's rewards, costs, and strategies. Such data enabled us to analyse more precisely the relationships among parties to the relocation, for similar data from the relocatees and their perception of the relocation social worker were obtained from the relocatee questionnaire.

Two other research tactics were employed at the same time as the interviews were conducted. One of our assistants was conducting in-depth, tape-recorded interviews with black leaders in the Halifax area concerning their assessment of Africville and the implications of relocation. Another assistant was gathering historical data and interviewing selected Africville relocatees concerning the historical development of the community. Important sources of historical data were the minutes of Halifax City Council (read from 1852 to 1969), reports of the Board of Halifax School Commissioners, the Nova Scotia Public Archives, files in the Registry of Deeds, the Halifax *Mail-Star* library, and the minutes of the Halifax Human Rights Advisory Committee. In all phases of research, the Africville files in the Social Planning Department, City of Halifax were of especial value.

Phases of the Africville Study

The Africville Relocation Report, in addition to being an examination of relocation and planned social change and a contribution to the sparse literature on blacks in Nova Scotia, represents a fusion of research and action. The researchers did not begin the study until virtually all the

Africville people had been relocated, and the research strategy resulted in the study being more than an evaluation.[26] The process of obtaining collective as well as individual responses, and of establishing a meaningful exchange with relocatees, fostered collective action from former Africville residents. Some local government officials objected to what they have referred to as the researchers' "activist" bias. The researchers maintain, however, that exchanges had to be worked out with the subjects of research as well as with the funding agencies. The liberal ethic posits informed voluntary consent as fundamental to adult social interation; informed voluntary consent requires, in turn, meaningful exchange among the participants.

The study began in October, 1968 with a meeting of relocated Africville people. This was the first time since relocation that former residents of Africville had met collectively. This stormy meeting, called by the researchers, was a public airing of relocatee grievances and led to relocatee support of the proposed study. Subsequent talk of forming committees to press grievances with the city of Halifax was an important result of the meeting. The researchers encouraged this tendency, for the expressed grievances appeared legitimate, and the researchers considered that it would be both possible and important to tap a collective or group dimension in the relocation process as well as to study the usual social-psychological considerations.

Later in the same week, at a meeting that the researchers had arranged with city officials, relocation caretakers, and civic leaders, the researchers related the expressed grievances of the relocatees and urged remedial action. General support for the proposed study was obtained at this second meeting, and the pending reconsideration of relocation by the city's newly created Social Planning Department was crystallized.

During the winter and spring of 1969, as the present study was being planned in detail, the action-stimulus of the researchers' early efforts was bearing fruit. Social Planning Department officials were meeting with the relocatees and, as it were, planning the second phase (not initially called for) of the Africville relocation. With provincial and municipal grants totalling seventy thousand dollars, the Seaview Credit Union was organized to assist relocatees experiencing financial crises; in addition, plans were formulated to meet housing and employment needs, and special consideration was to be given to former Africville residents whose needs could be met within the city's existing welfare system. A relocatee was hired to manage the credit union and to assist with other anticipated programs.

During the main data-gathering period, the summer of 1969, and in line with a decision to obtain collective as well as individual responses, the researchers met with informed groups of Africville relocatees to discuss current and future remedial action. It became apparent that the so-called second phase of the relocation would be inadequate to meet the people's needs. There was little identification with the credit union and it was floundering, for many relocatees who became members were either unable or unwilling to repay loans. Other anticipated programs and action promised by the city were delayed or forgotten due to bureaucratic entanglements and to lack of organization and pressure on the part of the relocatees.

The relocatees still had legitimate grievances related to unkept promises made at the time of relocation and later. With the formation of the Africville Action Committee, a third phase of the relocation began in the fall of 1969 and winter of 1970. The task of this new committee, developed from group discussions held between the researchers and relocatees, was to effect governmental redress through organized pressure. Several position papers were developed by the Africville Action Committee and negotiations were reopened with the city of Halifax. Although numerous meetings of relocatees were held during the first half of 1970, problems within the Africville Action Committee and the absence of resource people until the fall of 1970 hindered progress. With the committee stumbling along, and the credit union and other city-sponsored projects either ineffectual or nonexistent, the relocation process appeared to have petered out. The action committee was reactivated when one of the authors (D.H.C.) returned to Halifax permanently in the fall of 1970 and groups of relocatees were subsequently reinvolved in reading and criticizing a draft of the present study and in evaluating the relocation and the remedial action taken. Since the fall of 1970, the Africville Action Committee was active. Widespread support for its claims was obtained from community organizations, subcommittees were established to deal with questions of employment, housing, and financial compensation; and city council authorized the establishment of a city negotiating team to meet with representatives of the action committee.

In 1974, at the time of publication of the first edition of this book, the Africville Action Committee, to all intents and purposes, had ceased to function. Although it could claim some credit for a special employment training program through which a number of unemployed Africville relocatees had found jobs, the action committee fell far short of its goals.

The city's lack of a positive imaginative response and the internal organizational problems of the action committee hindered other proposals. What remained in 1974 was a reorganized credit union, a modest base for further redress and group action. However, by 1999 the Seaview Credit Union was no longer in existence; it had collapsed over two decades ago. However, the community is not dead. As noted in the preface of this revised [1999] edition, Africville still thrives in the hearts and minds of many of the relocatees. In addition, Africville still has rich symbolic value for fostering black consciousness in Nova Scotia.

Postscript

Throughout the study, we consciously and deliberately attempted to achieve a viable fusion of research and social responsibility. The research focussed on the collective responses of the group as well as on individual responses. At each stage in the study (conception, data gathering, data analysis, and preparation for publication) the collective and individual inputs that gave the study an action potential were obtained from relocatees. Drafts of appropriate chapters were sent for critical comment to officials and others involved in the relocation. The study became a stimulus to action because the normal researcher-subject exchanges could be worked out in concrete, actual terms. This was preferable to the usual research situation where, in effecting exchanges with the people being studied, the researcher typically makes vague references to the possible benefit of the study and does little or nothing to follow up implied promises of action.[27] But of course, our research strategy has its weakness too. It is difficult to feel satisfied that the kind of exchange relations that we established had productive consequences. Despite our involvement (in the early 1970s) with petitions, committee work, and attempts at rational problem solving, little redress of the inadequacies of the relocation program was achieved and the manifest goals of the liberal-welfare rhetoric of the relocation remain, in large measure, unrealized.

Notes

[1] *Social Theory and Social Structure* (Glencoe, Ill.: The Free Press, 1949), p. 80.

[2] Gordon Stephenson, *A Redevelopment Study of Halifax, Nova Scotia* (Halifax, N.S.: City of Halifax, 1957).

3   *The Condition of the Negroes of Halifax City, Nova Scotia* (Halifax: Institute of Public Affairs, Dalhousie University, 1962); and G. Brand, *Interdepartmental Committee on Human Rights: Survey Reports* (Halifax, N.S.: Nova Scotia Department of Welfare, Social Development Division, 1963).

4   Minutes of the Halifax City Council, Halifax, N.S., September 14, 1967.

5   The Government of Newfoundland initiated the program in 1953. In 1965 a joint federal-provincial program was initiated under a resettlement act. In 1970 the program was placed under the direction of the Federal Department of Regional Economic Expansion. For an overview of the resettlement program, see Noel Iverson and D. Ralph Matthews, *Communities in Decline: An Examination of Household Resettlement in Newfoundland*, Newfoundland Social and Economic Studies, No. 6, (St. John's, Nfld.: Memorial University of Newfoundland, Institute of Social and Economic Research, 1968). For a critical assessment of studies of the resettlement program, see Jim Lotz, "Resettlement and Social Change in Newfoundland," *The Canadian Review of Sociology and Anthropology* 8 (February, 1971): 48-59.

6   See Table 4, "Completed Redevelopment Projects" in *Urban Renewal* (Toronto: Centre for Urban and Community Studies, University of Toronto, 1968). Reprinted from *University of Toronto Law Journal*, 18, No. 3 (1968): 243.

7   David A. Wallace, "The Conceptualizing of Urban Renewal," *Urban Renewal* (Toronto: Centre for Urban and Community Studies, University of Toronto, 1968), 251.

8   An example of such a project is one reported by Thurz in southwest Washington, D.C. Little was done for the relocatees, but the relocation was widely acclaimed for its futuristic redevelopment design. For a critique of this approach, see Daniel Thurz, *Where Are They Now* ? (Washington, D.C.: Health and Welfare Council of the National Capital Area, 1966). See also, Jane Jacobs, *The Death and Life of Great American Cities* (New York: Random House, 1961).

9   Graham Fraser, *Fighting Back: Urban Renewal in Trefann Court* (Toronto: Hakkert, 1972), p. 55.

10   John Matthiasson, "Forced Relocation: An Evaluative Case Study," paper presented at the annual meeting of the Canadian Sociology and Anthropology Association, Winnipeg, 1970.

11   In recent years some minor progressive modifications have been introduced with reference to the development model; these deal with advance notice and public hearings, relocation compensation, and the availability of housing stock. See, Robert P. Groberg, *Centralized Relocation* (Washington, D.C.: National Association of Housing and Redevelopment Officials, 1969).

12 William L. Slayton, "Poverty and Urban Renewal," quoted in Hans B.C. Spiegal, "Human Considerations in Urban Renewal," *Urban Renewal,* op. cit., 311.

13 Elizabeth Wood, "Social Welfare Planning," quoted in Spiegel, op. cit., 315.

14 For a discussion of this, see Kenneth Craig, "Sociologists and Motivating Strategies," M.A. Thesis, University of Guelph, Department of Sociology, 1971.

15 Groberg, op. cit., p. 172.

16 See Alvin W. Gouldner, *The Coming Crisis of Western Sociology* (New York: Basic Books, 1970), pp. 500-502.

17 Relocation is a short-term consideration, for most services brought to bear on relocatee problems rarely extend beyond rehousing. A more general critique of the multiplying effect of citizens' involvement in relocation is given by S.M. Miller and Frank Riessman, *Social Class and Social Policy* (New York: Basic Books Inc., 1968).

18 The historical antecedents and reasons for the legislation are discussed in Daniel Moynihan, *Maximum Feasible Misunderstanding* (New York: Free Press, 1970). For an alternative interpretation, see Francis Fox Piven and Richard A. Cloward, *Regulating the Poor: The Functions of Public Welfare* (New York: Random Vintage Books, 1972), pp. 248-284. The operation of the program is discussed by Ralph M. Kramer, *Participation of the Poor: Comparative Community Case Studies in the War on Poverty* (Englewood Cliffs, N.J.: Prentice Hall, 1969).

19 Fraser, op. cit., p. 262.

20 For a discussion of this theoretical perspective, see Peter M. Blau, *Exchange and Power in Social Life* (New York: Wiley, 1964); and George Caspar Homans, *Social Behavior: Its Elementary Forms* (New York: Harcourt, Brace and World, 1961).

21 *The Condition of the Negroes of Halifax City, Nova Scotia,* op. cit.

22 Sarah M. Beaton, "Effects of Relocation: A Study of Ten Families Relocated from Africville, Halifax, Nova Scotia," Master of Social Work Thesis, Maritime School of Social Work, Halifax, N.S., 1969; and Bernard MacDougall, "Urban Relocation of Africville Residents," Master of Social Work Thesis, Maritime School of Social Work, Halifax, N.S., 1969.

23 The interview guide is published in Donald H. Clairmont and Dennis W. Magill, *Africville Relocation Report* (Halifax, N.S.: Institute of Public Affairs, Dalhousie University, 1971), pp. A131-A135.

24 Ibid., pp. A97-A128.

25 Ibid., pp. A83-A96.

26 Some relocation studies have been carried out as part of the relocation decision-making, see William H. Key, *When People are Forced to Move* (Topeka, Kansas: Menninger Foundation, 1967), mimeographed; others have been concurrent with the relocating of people, see Herbert J. Gans, *The Urban Villagers: Group and Class in the Life of Italian Americans* (New York: The Free Press, 1962). The present study is unique in that it fostered collective action carried out after the relocation.

27 See Craig, op. cit.

Table I.1
Models of Relocation

Dimensions	Traditional Method	Development Model	Liberal-Welfare Model	Political Model
Ideological premise	Society is a mosaic of groups, each of which can, within limits, structure its life conditions. Government facilitates these actions, although self-help (and self-organization) is most important.	Operating with a consensus model of society, this perspective is holistic and systems-oriented. Relocation programs represent interventions designed to correct imperfections in the social system and to achieve system development.	Society is based on a consensus of values, in terms of which social problems are defined. Some groups are the focal point of many problems. These groups need special attention. Relocation is an intervention designed to deal with the peculiar problems of particular groups.	Structured conflict is endemic in society because of different interests associated with different classes, strata, and other groupings. Society is based on the management of such conflict. This management has negative (prevent war) and positive (ensure groups have real opportunity to express their interests) aspects. Relocations entail a clash of interests and/or an opportunity to develop political consciousness and participation.
Formulation of Policy	Done primarily by indigenous group leadership within limits set by government policy.	By politicians and bureau-technocrats. Community-oriented citizens are sometimes co-opted.	By politicians and bureaucrats primarily. Varying degree of consultation with relocatees. Community-oriented citizens sometimes are co-opted.	Co-operative effort between indigenous leaders (who draw on resource people) and politicians and bureaucrats.

Dimensions	Traditional Method	Development Model	Liberal-Welfare Model	Political Model
Implementation of policy and control of administrative resources	Largely in the hands of the group being relocated	Control by bureaucrats-technocrats	By bureaucrats, although some resources may be distributed in the event that relocatees and community-oriented citizens are co-opted	Co-operation and negotiation through parallel structures representing relocatees on the one hand and government on the other. Resources usually provided relocatees by government.
Intended beneficiary	The group being relocated	The system as a whole, success being measured in terms of some indicator of system growth or development.	Relocatees primarily, although society benefits in that social problems become attenuated	Reciprocal benefits: to relocatees the benefit of meaningful political participation as well as relocation advantages; to society the benefit of a more informed and active citizenry
Central actors and organizational units	The indigenous leader; local organization or community associations	Technocrats and experts; government bureaucracy	Bureaucratics, relocatee advocates, and caretakers; government bureaucracy and citizen groups	Politicians, bureaucrats, indigenous leaders and resource people; government bureaucracy and relocatee organizations

Appendix: Table I.1: Models of Relocation   23

Dimensions	Traditional Method	Development Model	Liberal-Welfare Model	Political Model
Key problems	Lack of resources among many groups; decline of opportunity in centralized planned technocratic	Exploitation of and inattention to low-status relocatees; lack of participation by relocatees in the structuring of their life situation	Lack of success in achieving manifest goals; failure to effectively incorporate relocatee interests; lack of participation of relocatees in the structuring of their life conditions	The extent to which the government can or will proceed in developing extra-parliamentary parallel structures, problems of representativeness, legitimacy, and organization among potential relocatees

Black Immigration to Nova Scotia and the Settlement of Africville

There is no accurate historical memory in Canada of British
North America's own experience with the Negro and even
a clouded awareness of an earlier Negro presence is slight.[1]
—Robin W. Winks

With few exceptions,[2] only in recent years have scholars interested
themselves in the settlement and historical development of blacks in Nova
Scotia. Nova Scotian blacks, as a result of their educational deprivation,
scattered population, and lack of a rich subcultural tradition, have been
neither particularly conscious of their own settlement and development nor
able chroniclers. Much superficial material is available, but few facts are
known and most of what is known is mythical or erroneous. For instance,
Africville has been referred to as a community of transients;[3] in fact, most
Africville residents had ancestral roots reaching back almost a century and
a half.

The history of blacks in Nova Scotia has not been pleasant. Blacks
have been poorer than the average white Nova Scotian who, in turn, over
the past hundred years has been poorer than the average Canadian.
Throughout their settlement in Nova Scotia, blacks have had to carry a
special burden, the burden of the white person's prejudice, discrimination,
and oppression. The result is that Nova Scotian blacks became marginal
people in a relatively depressed region.[4] One of the best indicators of the
marginal status of blacks is the fact that throughout the years most have
been clustered in isolated rural areas or on the fringes of white towns and
cities; generally, their housing has been inferior and lacking public services.

A Slave Society

It is impossible to understand either the contemporary socio-economic conditions of black Nova Scotians or the peculiar development of Africville without recognizing that Nova Scotia was at one time a "slave society" and appreciating the conditions of migration and settlement of free blacks in Nova Scotia. Slavery was never instituted by statute in Nova Scotia,[5] yet slavery was practised in Halifax a year after the city was founded and, over the next five decades, it was not uncommon in other parts of the province. Although lack of agricultural potential in the uneven and rocky terrain of Nova Scotia prevented slavery from developing on a plantation scale, the number of slaves in Nova Scotia continued to grow. At the outbreak of the American Revolution, there were approximately 500 slaves, many of whom had come with their New England masters in the late 1750s after the expulsion of the Acadians. Slave-holding Loyalist immigrants increased the number by approximately 1000.[6]

Many observers have pointed out that slavery cannot exist without a slave society; that is, without a society whose values at least tolerate slavery. Although popular opinion and the benevolence of the courts were responsible for eliminating slavery at a relatively early date in Nova Scotia (after 1800 it became rapidly more and more difficult to retain slaves), slavery survived for over half a century. The major undermining influence was not so much a public outcry against slavery; rather, it was the obsolescence of slave labour following the arrival of many hundreds of free Loyalist blacks and whites whose services could be had for little more than it had cost earlier to house and feed slaves.

The groundwork for the subordination of the blacks as a people in Nova Scotia was laid by the early existence of a slave society. Insidious social-psychological concomitants of institutionalized oppression included attitudes of white superiority, which remain deeply rooted,[7] and a form of self-hatred and race-hatred among the blacks themselves. There are clear indications of change in the attitudes of blacks in Nova Scotia, but one is still able to find traces of the historical style of identification with subordination. We found, for instance, a number of blacks arguing that Africville was not a slum because "whites lived there, too."

Free Loyalist Blacks

Most of the blacks migrating to Nova Scotia after the American Revolution were free, for the most part having been freed by the British as an inducement to encourage them to leave their revolutionary masters. Free blacks were promised equal treatment with their white peers, but these promises were not fulfilled. The minority of black Loyalists who did obtain land grants found themselves settled on small and usually barren lots on the periphery of white Loyalist townships or in the more remote sections of the province.[8] Moreover, very few blacks received the provisions that the British government promised to the Loyalists. Loyalist immigrants outnumbered the resident population of Nova Scotia, and the problems of settling and supplying so many people were so great that many white settlers also experienced wretched deprivation. Predictably, deprivation among blacks was both more intensive and more extensive. In order to survive, a number of blacks were forced to sell themselves or their children into slavery or long-term indenture. In contrast with whites of equivalent class level, blacks were disproportionately represented among the sharecropping, domestic service, and indentured occupations.[9]

In addition to petitioning the Imperial government to fulfil its promises concerning land and provisions, and indenturing themselves to local whites, many blacks reacted by migrating from Nova Scotia when the opportunity arose. When an agent of the Sierra Leone Company came recruiting among the blacks of the province in 1792, some 1200 accepted his company's offer and sailed to Africa. Undoubtedly more of the free blacks, described by the agent as "deceived and ill-treated through life," would have responded if the emigration offer had been adequately communicated.[10] Nevertheless, as Winks observed, "When the 1792 migration of free Negroes to Sierra Leone took place, this left more Negro slaves than free Negroes in Nova Scotia."[11] Additional migrations took place, in 1800 to Sierra Leone and in 1821 to Trinidad.

The Maroons

After the departure of Loyalists to Sierra Leone a small group of blacks settled temporarily on the lands vacated by the black Loyalists in the Preston area. In 1796 some 550 Maroons, deported from Jamaica, were settled on the lands vacated by the black Loyalists at Preston. The Maroons, with their different customs, were well-treated officially but encountered some local prejudice and discrimination. In 1800 virtually all the Maroons (at most, a handful may have been assimilated into the black Nova Scotian population) were shipped to Sierra Leone where, ironically enough, they helped to suppress a rebellion by the former black Loyalists.[12]

Refugee Blacks

When the War of 1812 broke out, the British followed the strategy that they had used in the American Revolutionary War and offered freedom to every American-owned slave who would run away from his master and join the British. Thus, by 1815, another 2000 free blacks arrived in Nova Scotia in anticipation of freedom, land, and wages. These refugees appear to have received better official reception and more food, clothing, and medicine than had their Loyalist predecessors, although the land received was similarly rocky and barren. Nearly all the refugee blacks were settled within a short distance of Halifax, principally at Preston, which was depopulated due to the emigration of black Loyalists to Sierra Leone, and at Hammonds Plains. They were settled on small lots of rocky soil and scrubby forest, ranging from eight to ten acres in size.

Willson aptly characterized the subsequent situation of the refugee blacks as privileged "to enjoy the comforts of political freedom and physical starvation under the British flag in Nova Scotia."[13] In the first year after settlement, province-wide crop failures made 1815 the "year without summer." Crops failed repeatedly, woodlots were exhausted quickly, and, during most years, wage labour in Halifax was scarce in summer and non-existent in winter. The government experimented with phasing out its assistance to the refugees but, for well over thirty years, was forced by their starvation to issue numerous welfare grants.[14] The government's initial hope that the refugee settlers would supply the Halifax market with vegetables appears absurd in retrospect. Lacking a resource base, it required the black settlers' most vigorous efforts merely to survive. To build for the future was impossible, for there was no surplus to accumulate.

Refugee blacks had an additional problem concerning their grants of land. Presumably to protect the refugees against unscrupulous white landgrabbers,[15] the government had given them only "licences of occupation," rather than full grants; the licences allowed all the rights of property save those of sale or conveyance. It had promised that full grants would be issued after three years to those who had developed their holdings, and most black settlers fulfilled this stipulation; however, for twenty-five years the grants were not forthcoming. The delay rendered the blacks immobile, for they could not move elsewhere without abandoning their investment, and also contributed to the perception of blacks as second-class citizens.

As the situation remained bad and no agreeable migration plan was developed,[16] the refugee blacks further petitioned the government for full grants, more land, better land, and welfare assistance. In 1839 heavy relief costs finally convinced a reluctant British government to empower the local government to give blacks portions of unoccupied Crown lands in the province. The refugees disliked the government's plan of dispersing them by giving land to a few families in each of several counties in the province; they preferred to resettle in large community groups.[17] The proposal also provided for licences of occupation rather than full grants. The plan was never implemented. In 1842 the government finally issued an order of true grants to the refugee blacks at Preston so that although these blacks remained on essentially the same barren land obtained twenty-five years earlier, now they could know that the land was unquestionably theirs.

With the permanent establishment of the refugee blacks, the basic settlement pattern of blacks in Nova Scotia was drawn. Apart from the immigration of groups of West Indian blacks around the turn of the twentieth century and during the 1920s to work in the coal-steel complex of Cape Breton, emigration and immigration were henceforth on an individual or family basis.[18] The establishment of churches and schools in the segregated black communities laid the basis for possible growth of a genuine black Nova Scotian subculture. The basis was also laid for years of deprivation and hardship; after release from a slave subculture, the refugee blacks joined the remnants of Loyalist blacks and former slaves in a continuing state of subsistence poverty.

The condition of subsistence poverty and marginality of Nova Scotian blacks in the 1840s has continued into the present day. Since the early 1960s and especially after the Africville relocation, change has accelerated, particularly at the level of group consciousness and identification, but over the past two decades newspaper articles have presented intermittent accounts of scandalous socio-economic conditions among blacks.[19] To account for the continuing oppression and deprivation and for the belated realization of a distinctive subculture, it is necessary to refer to racism, the sluggish regional economy,[20] and the "migrate or accommodate" response of blacks.[21]

First Africville Settlers[22]

The Halifax lands that eventually became known as Africville comprised the first three of the sixteen five-acre lots in Division "Letter K" of the original land-grant survey of the Halifax peninsula.[23] All lots of Division "Letter K" were initially owned by whites, although it appears that whites

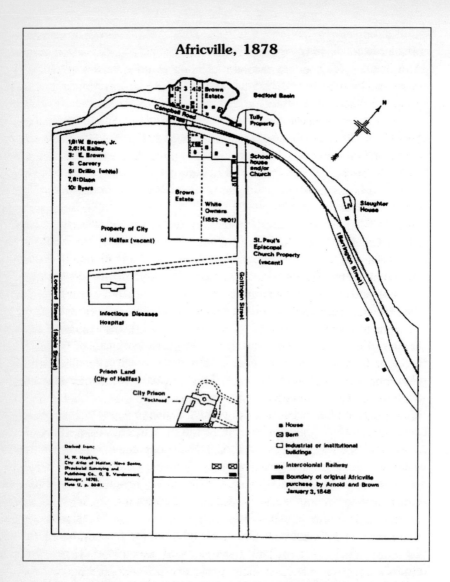

Africville, 1878

Bedford Basin

Brown Estate

Campbell Road

Tully Property

1,9: W. Brown, Jr.
2,6: H. Bailey
3: E. Brown
4: Carvery
5: Drillio (white)
7,8: Dixon
10: Byers

School house and/or Church

Brown Estate

White Owners (1852 -1901)

Property of City of Halifax (vacant)

St. Paul's Episcopal Church Property (vacant)

Slaughter House

(Barrington Street)

Gottingen Street

Longard Street (Robie Street)

Infectious Diseases Hospital

Prison Land (City of Halifax)

City Prison "Rockhead"

Derived from:

H. W. Hopkins, City Atlas of Halifax, Nova Scotia, Provincial Surveying and Publishing Co. O. S. Vandervoort, Manager, 1878). Plate U, p. 80-81.

■ House
⊠ Barn
☐ Industrial or institutional buildings
▬▬ Intercolonial Railway
▬▬ Boundary of original Africville purchase by Arnold and Brown January 3, 1848

did not occupy the lots. These owners were, for the most part, "merchants and gentlemen," at least several of whom possessed slaves and two of whom dealt in slavery.[24] The first Africville settlers were refugee blacks who came to Nova Scotia after the War of 1812 and moved, not earlier than 1835 and probably during the 1840s, from the outlying communities of Preston and Hammonds Plains. The earliest Africville deeds indicate that in 1848 William Brown and William Arnold purchased separate parts of lots 1 through 3 of Division "Letter K."[25] The combined purchase established the basic boundaries within which Africville developed (see map, Africville, 1878). There is evidence, however, that Brown and Arnold and other blacks may have been living in the Africville area prior to their purchase of land there.[26]

From early Africville deeds and a list of the first church officers, it is possible to identify eight original families: Brown, Carvery, Dixon, Arnold, Hill, Fletcher, Bailey, and Grant. The first three names designate major Africville families over the following century; the other names disappeared from the community at a relatively early date, presumably through marriage, migration, or death. The origins of these eight families can be traced to Hammonds Plains and Preston, with the possible exception of Dixon, whose former place of residence is not certain.

William Brown Sr. is regarded in Africville lore as the founder of the community. His original purchase, and that of William Arnold (about six acres of land each), marked the establishment of the settlement. For years the Browns were the principal owners of land and were among the community's elite. Although various community myths surrounded William Brown, the facts are clear. His father, Perry Brown, one of the blacks brought from Chesapeake Bay during the War of 1812, settled at Hammonds Plains. He was active in church affairs and protested against the dire economic straits of refugee blacks in the area. A census of households at Hammonds Plains in 1835 indicated that a William Brown occupied a lot owned by another black, but the name of William Brown is not among those householders who received food allowances in 1837 nor among householders recorded in the census of 1838. The 1838 census shows Perry Brown and W. Brown, both "men of colour," in Halifax. Unfortunately, the latter census makes no explicit reference to place of residence. The Africville site was within the town limits, and it is possible that Brown had already settled there but had not yet purchased land.

Isaac Grant and Henry Bailey occupied neighbouring lots at Hammonds Plains. Numerous citings of their names appear in documents and they and their families are listed in the 1838 census. The next documentary evidence of their whereabouts is mention of them, in 1849, as church officers at Africville. Both the Grant and Bailey families disappeared from Africville before 1900. The 1861 census lists Isaac Grant as living alone, a very old man. According to interviewees, the Baileys were part of the large black migration from Nova Scotia to the United States in the last quarter of the nineteenth century.

William Arnold came from Hammonds Plains and retained real estate there after he settled in Africville. He was probably not a young man when he bought his land at Africville; the census of 1851 lists him as being over fifty and a widower. He died in 1852, leaving his estate to his son Charles, a mariner, who promptly sold the property, and the surname Arnold does not appear again in the records of Africville.

Eppy Carvery, Henry Hill, and Bennett Fletcher may have moved together from Preston to Africville. In 1848 they bought an acre in common from William Arnold. A map of Preston dated 1816 shows that the original Hill and Fletcher land grants were adjacent, on Lake Echo. In 1824 Henry Hill and Bennett Fletcher jointly petitioned the government, stating that they had been issued land in a section of the Preston community that "is so rocky and sterrile [sic] that it is unfit to settle on," and requesting permission to settle on some of the more favourable nearby lots that had been abandoned. Eppy Carvery, too, was a dissatisfied landowner at Preston. He was one of the signers of an early Preston petition requesting that land grants be made final. In 1842 both Hill and Carvery received title to lots at Preston. Since Carvery, Hill, and Fletcher bought land from William Arnold within a week of the latter's own purchase, it is possible that they may have been living in Africville prior to 1848. Through the years, the name Carvery became common in Africville; that of Hill, and later Fletcher, disappeared. In 1858 Eppy Carvery bought out Hill and Fletcher. The Fletcher name reappears in deed transfers in 1882 and 1901, but Hill is not cited in later Africville documents. The Fletchers and Hills also may have been part of the large migration to the United States in the late nineteenth century.

Allen Dixon, a refugee black who migrated to Nova Scotia during the period 1813-1816, initially settled in the Preston area; however, by 1849 he had moved to Africville, where he was listed as an officer of the community church. He was the forefather of one of the larger Africville families.

Factors in Africville's Settlement

The original Africville settlers were, then, former residents of the refugee settlements at Preston and Hammonds Plains who moved to Africville in order to escape the economic hardships encountered on rocky and barren land. Local tradition offers no account of the motivation that led to migration from Hammonds Plains and Preston; almost every interviewed resident of Africville believed that Africville had been founded under the auspices of royalty by former slaves from the United States. In the 1840s the Africville site offered several advantages. It was not significantly more arable but, located on Bedford Basin, it was convenient for fishing and, most important, it was convenient for wage labour in the Halifax area. Around 1839, with the establishment of a steamship line for mail service, Halifax received a long-awaited economic boom.[27] The following decade was characterized by economic expansion, a flourishing wholesale trade, development of new docking facilities, and increased shipbuilding. It required only the Reciprocity Treaty of 1854 with the United States to consolidate the favourable economic status of Halifax by setting off a boom in the trade with New England.[28]

Apart from the fact of general economic growth in the Halifax area, it is difficult to identify other particular factors accounting for the migration to Africville. It has been suggested that some of the settlers may have been employed in the construction of Campbell Road, which was built in 1836 around the northeastern end of the peninsula as an alternative to the main thoroughfare between the town of Halifax and the outlying communities. There is no evidence to support this suggestion, although the Africville settlement was formed around the Campbell Road area of Bedford Basin and for many years the community itself was known as Campbell Road. It has also been suggested that blacks settled at Africville while laying track for the Intercolonial Railroad, which was to run through the community; however, the railroad was begun in 1854, several years after the Africville community was established.[29] There is a further suggestion that the black settlers may have been attracted by the Bedford Basin shoreline, which provided a fine setting for mass baptisms. MacKerrow, familiar with the history of the Nova Scotia African Baptist Association, mentioned "the placid waters of Bedford Basin, beneath whose surface Brothers Burton, Preston [etc.]…have buried in the likeness of Christ many willing converts in the ordinance of Baptism."[30] Since the Rev. Mr. Burton died in 1838, this reference is either erroneous or indicates that there were baptisms at the Africville site before 1838. If the latter, it could have been the Bedford Basin exposure that drew black settlers to the Africville area.[31]

In the final analysis, however, it appears that the key pull factor in the migration to the Africville area was economic opportunity, although there may have been additional incentives affecting the precise location of the first homes. The migration push factor appears to have been the hardships of life in Preston and Hammonds Plains. Numerous examples of the plight of refugee settlers in the Preston area have been cited. Although true land grants were made final in 1842, significant improvement did not take place in living conditions. Extensive potato-crop failure occurred in 1847 and again in 1848. Legislative Assembly proceedings indicate that throughout this period grants had to be given in order to prevent starvation. In February, 1851 a petition from the "Teacher at the African School at Hammonds Plains on behalf of the people of colour at that place, was presented..., setting forth the great destitution prevailing in a number of families in that Settlement, and praying relief."[32]

Land Conveyance and Myths of Settlement

Many Africville relocatees believed that their community was among the original refugee black settlements established by Crown grant, but evidence does not support this belief. The principal reason for the myth is that, between the 1840s and the time of relocation, the original Africville acreage was subject to a series of complicated and often unrecorded purchases and sales.

In addition to difficulties encountered in tracing the initial land purchases of some Africville settlers, there are numerous problems in determining land conveyance over the years. Many landowners died intestate; often land was conveyed informally, especially to children and in-laws. This created a situation in which eventually only a fraction of Africville families held true title to land that they occupied, although many others believed that their ownership was established through their family's long-standing possession and occupancy of the land.

During a period of roughly 125 years, the Africville land underwent various changes. Three systems of railway tracks were built through the community, necessitating expropriation of land and relocation homes, and expansion of railway facilities resulted in a further shuffle of property. In addition to the occasional seizure of land for non-payment of tax arrears, the city of Halifax purchased several Africville properties as potential sites for municipal institutions and in anticipation of waterfront redevelopment.[33] Other institutional purchasers of Africville lands included the Nova Scotia Light and Power Company, which obtained land for construction of a tower. The shoreline itself also changed, for some properties were diminished by soil erosion and others were extended by fill. To these changes in land and land use was added a new factor, the absentee landlord. The city, the railway, and other institutions occasionally leased land to Africville residents, usually at a nominal rental. The city owned the land on which the Africville school was built and leased land for the site of the Africville church.[34] In the 1950s both the railway and the city leased property to residents who were displaced and homeless,[35] but in some instances, Africville residents squatted on government-owned land. This had been the practice for many years, but until the end of the Second World War there was little opposition to this for the number of squatters was relatively small and the land was not being used by its owners.[36]

The Africville population increased almost tenfold between 1850 and 1964. By 1964 there were approximately eighty families living in an area no larger than that originally purchased by Brown and Arnold. It was common for offspring to establish their own households on parental land, and property in Africville was usually divided equally among the immediate heirs although the land was not conveyed by formal instrument. There was, consequently, a substantial decline in the size of individual land-holdings over the years, land shortage developed, and disputes concerning land ownership were not uncommon among close relatives. Many family lines terminated through death, migration, and lack of offspring, creating further ambiguity in land ownership. As a result of far-reaching kinship ties among most Africville residents, there were multiple claims on many pieces of property.[37]

Because of these factors of population pressure on land, informal conveyance of property, inclusive patterns of inheritance, extensive kinship ties, profound changes in land use, unrecorded original purchases, and occasional squatting, it was difficult to unravel property claims in Africville and to discount speculation concerning Crown grants. These difficulties were more pronounced given the sense of historical continuity possessed by residents and the absence of diaries and other written materials available to demolish most of the myths associated with the settlement and development of Africville. Certainly the public image of Africville as a community of transients and squatters can be rejected as there was little squatting in the sense of random occupation of land by rootless in-migrants. To equate the absence of legal title with squatting would be misleading in the Africville context.

The major myth was that Africville was an original refugee black settlement. Although the principal myth of settlement held by Africville residents was that their forefathers had escaped from slavery in the United States and were granted Africville land by Queen Victoria,[38] there were various other myths. Some residents held that black slaves escaping from the United States settled inland to avoid recapture; that Africville was settled first and other nearby black communities followed later. The fact is that black refugees were told by government officials where they could settle. A more prevalent myth held that Africville families were descended from the Maroons deported to Halifax from Jamaica in 1796. One version of this myth centred on Prince Edward, father of Queen Victoria, who during his tenure as commander-in-chief of the armed forces, resided at an estate on the shore of Bedford Basin. Purportedly, Prince Edward had a black servant named William Brown; pleased with his service, the Prince saw to it, upon his recall to England, that Brown and others were granted land at Bedford Basin. In fact, however, the Prince left Nova Scotia prior to the War of 1812 and there is little likelihood that the name of William Brown can rightly be linked with his. As for being descended from Maroons, records indicated that while some did live near Bedford Basin for a short period, virtually all the Maroons sailed to Sierra Leone in 1800[39] and the original Africville settlers came from refugee settlements elsewhere in Halifax County.

The myths held by Africville residents concerning the settlement of their community are none the less significant and merit attention. In essence, they served to reinforce claims to land, which was an important consideration in the face of the frequent absence of deeds and other legal title. In the myths, land is granted in common; accordingly, every individual who could establish hereditary right through descent or marriage would have a claim on the land. In the myths, too, land is granted by royal personages who are considered more powerful and significant authorities than city and other governmental officials. The myths, by holding forth a special association with royalty, not only established a common bond among residents but underlined the real marginality felt by Africville people vis-à-vis other Haligonians, and perhaps provided a cultural weapon against oppressors.

Although the myths of settlement existed apart from the relocation experience, it is useful to consider them in relation to the relocation negotiations. Many white Haligonians also believed the myth of a Queen-given grant to blacks at Africville. The relocation social worker, charged with the task of negotiating the real-estate aspects of relocation, did not discount the possibility of such a grant. He was, however, scarcely in a position to undertake more than a casual examination of historical materials. The director of welfare suggested that the Development Department had sent a representative to England to determine whether the myth was valid. One of the research directors (D.W.M.) interviewed the development director about this possibility:

> I asked him [the development director] if they had ever investigated whether the Africville land had been granted by Queen Victoria. He stated that they had not discovered any intensive historical research. They did just enough to convince themselves that the deeds were in chaotic order. When I told him that the director of welfare reported that he, the director of development, had sent people to England to see if Africville land was a grant from the Queen, he laughed and said: 'That is the most absurd thing I ever heard.'[40]

It appears that, despite some second thoughts, city officials did not investigate thoroughly the possibility of a Crown grant to Africville settlers. Information was presumably sought by the city from the provincial archivist who, in 1962, requested information from the Director of Crown Lands, Nova Scotia Department of Lands and Forests. The director replied, "We do not find that William Brown was a grantee in the district. Neither do we know of any records of any unusual circumstances in regards the granting of land in Africville." The provincial archivist surmised: "I suppose that the Negroes either purchased land from previous owners or squatted on it."

What difference would it have made if the myth of a Crown grant could have been substantiated? It would not have added legal weight to the claims of Africville residents beyond that of ownership through purchase or inheritance, for all land derives ultimately from a Crown grant. The legal aspects of relocation negotiations might have been quite different, however, if the land had been granted in common to Africville residents. Certainly a grant in common, direct from the Crown, would have been considered as lending a more powerful moral thrust to the relocatees' claims.

The Name "Africville"

The black settlement of Africville was named first after the road around which it grew: Campbell Road. This name remained until around the turn of the century, when "Africville" became current. During interviews, only the very oldest residents intimated that they had in their youth commonly referred to the community as "Campbell Road," although most respondents, regardless of age, were acquainted with the earlier appellation.

The earliest documentary use of "Africville" is found in a petition from William Brown, dated March 21, 1860, stating "That your Petitioner is the owner of a lot of land situate at Africville in the City of Halifax..." Yet in a petition for aid to establish a school, dated one day earlier, residents referred to themselves as "Nine Families of Colour residing on Campbell Road, West of the Rail Road Terminus." Early deed transfers referred to the Africville site as "Richmond" or "Campbell Town in the north suburbs of the City of Halifax." The first land deed to use the form "Africville" is dated 1866.

In the early nineteenth century, both "African" and "Men of Colour" were common descriptive terms. In their report of 1858 the railway commissioners listed an expenditure "for material and labour in removing and fixing up buildings at African village." A railway compensation deed of 1861 also called the community "African Village." Railway officialdom may have been responsible for making common the name "Africville;" on the other hand, "Africville" may have been a popular designation used in Halifax, descriptively at first, and later as a proper name. City council minutes refer to the community as "Campbell Town," in 1852; the "Black Settlement," in 1854; and "Africville," in 1867.[41] The relocatees speculated about the origin of "Africville," and indicated mixed feelings about the term. There was a consensus that it had been imposed by white Haligonians, "since our forefathers came from Africa." One elderly relocatee, very conscious of her people's ancestry in American slavery, was scornful of the African designation: "It wasn't Africville out there. None of the people came from Africa; you want to believe it. It was part of Richmond,[42] just the part where the coloured people lived." Another lady of advanced years was favourably disposed to the name "Africville" and hostile towards those "meddlers" who would have it otherwise.

By the twentieth century, the name "Africville" was firmly established. Some residents attempted to refer to their community as "Seaview," but this name never stuck. Perhaps it did not resonate well with the deprivation which increasingly became the lot of the people there. In the years ahead, mail would be sent to persons in "Africville;" local athletic teams would bear the name, as would the small segregated school. At the time of relocation the appellation had not only a common geographical reference but a widely shared connotation as a deviant slum community.

Notes

1. "The Canadian Negro," *Journal of Negro History*, 53, No. 4 (October, 1968): 290.

2. The exceptions include publications emanating from the Public Archives of Nova Scotia and publications written by members of the Oliver family. For a bibliography, see Donald H. Clairmont and Dennis W. Magill, *Nova Scotian Blacks: An Historical and Structural Overview* (Halifax, N.S.: Institute of Public Affairs, Dalhousie University, 1970). See also, Francis Henry, *Forgotten Canadians: The Blacks of Nova Scotia* (Toronto: Longman Canada, 1973); J.W. Walker, "The Establishment of a Free Black Community in Nova Scotia," in R. Rotberg and M. Kilson (eds.) *African Diaspora: Interpretative Essays* (Boston: Harvard University Press, 1974); and J.W. Walker, *A History of Blacks in Canada* (Ottawa: Canadian Government Publishing Centre, 1980); Donald Clairmont and Fred Wein, "Blacks and Whites: The Nova Scotia Race Relations Experience," in Douglas F. Campbell (ed.) *Banked Fires—The Ethnics of Nova Scotia* (Port Credit: The Scribblers' Press, 1978).

3. See C.R. Brookbank, "Afro-Canadian Communities in Halifax County, Nova Scotia," M.A. Thesis, University of Toronto, 1949.

4. Marginality denotes here a lack of influence in societal decision-making and a low degree of participation in the mainstream of political or economic life. For a general causal model of black marginality see Clairmont and Magill, *Nova Scotian Blacks*.

5. J.F. Krauter, "Civil Liberties and the Canadian Minorities," unpublished Ph.D. dissertation, University of Illinois, 1968.

6. T. Watson Smith, *The Slave in Canada*, Vol. X of *Collections of the Nova Scotia Historical Society* (Halifax, N.S.: Nova Scotia Printing Company, 1899), p. 32. Black slaves were brought to Nova Scotia by many whites. Smith observed that "the names of proprietors owning but one or two 'servants' are too many for repetition," (p. 24).

7. For references see Clairmont and Magill, *Nova Scotian Blacks,* p. 7.

8. The Tracadie-Sunnyville area of Guysborough County is an example of a remote black Loyalist settlement which still exists.

9. Thomas C. Haliburton, *An Historical and Statistical Account of Nova Scotia*, Vol. II (Halifax, N.S.: Joseph Howe, 1829), p. 280; and C.B. Wadstrom, An Essay on Colonization, Vol. II (London: Darton and Harvey, 1794), pp. 220-224.

10. For references concerning the Sierra Leone migration, see Clairmont and Magill, *Nova Scotian Blacks,* pp. 10-13.

11 Robin W. Winks, "The Negro in Canada: An Historical Sketch," p. 42, draft for the *The Blacks in Canada* (New Haven: Yale University Press, 1971).

12 See Haliburton, op. cit., 280-292. Winks provides an excellent overview of the Maroon migration. *The Blacks in Canada*, pp. 79-95.

13 Beckles Willson, *Nova Scotia: A Province That Has Been Passed By* (London: Constable, 1911), p. 53.

14 For documentation, see Clairmont and Magill, *Nova Scotian Blacks*, p. 14.

15 Black Loyalist settlers at Birchtown had had problems of this kind with whites. See Ida Greaves, *The Negro in Canada: National Problems of Canada* (McGill University, Department of Economics and Political Science, n.d.), p. 22.

16 Numerous migration plans, which blacks did not trust, were suggested by officials. Some of the plans, such as returning the blacks to their former masters if pardons could be obtained, were callous.

17 P.A.N.S., Vol. 115, pp. 56-57, August 25, 1837; and Vol. 77, pp. 21-28, January 8, 1839. Local government officials appeared to believe that blacks, if scattered, might be found useful as 'Labourers;' moreover, it was believed that they might be more industrious if they were settled farther from the town of Halifax.

18 Winks also mentions the migration of several carloads of blacks from Alabama around the turn of the century to work in the burgeoning industrial area of Cape Breton. See Winks, *The Blacks in Canada*, p. 300.

19 See A. Westell's account ("Shocking Poverty in Nova Scotia," *Detroit Free Press*, June, 1969) of a visit by the Minister of National Health and Welfare to one of the black communites in Nova Scotia, June, 1969. See also Edna Staebler, "Would You Change the Lives of These People?" *Maclean's Magazine*, May 12, 1956, p. 30. For more substantive treatments of black poverty and oppression see *The Condition of the Negroes of Halifax City, Nova Scotia*, op. cit.; and Donald H. Clairmont in collaboration with K. Scott Wood, George Rawlyk, and Guy Henson, *A Socio-Economic Study and Recommendations: Sunnyville, Lincolnville and Upper Big Tracadie, Guysborough County, Nova Scotia* (Halifax, N.S.: Institute of Public Affairs, Dalhousie University, 1965).

20 The regional economy did not generate much economic opportunity for blacks. Even in the "Golden Age" of Nova Scotia in the mid-nineteenth century, blacks did not benefit significantly from economic prosperity.

21 Blacks did protest racism and oppression and did petition for change. The history of Africville is testimony to this. There is also evidence of strong efforts to organize Nova Scotian blacks into a cohesive interest group

through the African Baptist Association and the Anglo-African Mutual Improvement and Aid Association. Yet little was achieved and blacks remained powerless and frustrated.

22 For much of this section we are indebted to the work of our research assistant, John DeRoche.

23 Haliburton, op. cit., p. 21.

24 Several of the white men owning land in the area in the eighteenth century, such as Joseph Gerrish, Joseph Fairbanks, and Joshua Mauger, owned slaves (Smith, op. cit., pp. 10, 13, 15, 84). Mauger, a prominent merchant who imported and sold slaves, had large land dealings with Richard Jacobs.

25 William Arnold purchased his part (about six acres) from the estate of James Fullerton, as did William Brown. The purchases were made on January 3, 1848 (Registry of Deeds, Book 90, p. 323, and Book 92, p. 255). Fullerton had purchased the three lots from Godfrey Jacobs in 1818 (Registry of Deeds, Book 44, p. 339).

26 A church was organized at Africville in 1849. This suggests that blacks may have been living there prior to 1848, when the first purchases by blacks were recorded.

27 Stephenson, op. cit., p. 2. See also J.S. Martell, "Halifax During and After the War of 1812," The Dalhousie Review 23 (1943-44).

28 This period of economic growth ushered in what has been termed the "Golden Age" of Nova Scotia. The boom was centred in Halifax. For a discussion of the economy at this time, see Stanley B. Ryerson, Unequal Union: Confederation and the Roots of Conflict in the Canadas, 1815-1873 (Toronto: Progress Books, 1968), pp. 237, 242 et passim.

29 A report of the exploration survey of routes between Halifax and Quebec was presented to the legislature in 1848 (Nova Scotia Legislative Assembly, Journal and Proceedings of the House of Assembly, 1848, Appendix 64); actual construction did not get under way at Halifax until 1854.

30 P.E. MacKerrow, A Brief History of the Coloured Baptists of Nova Scotia, 1832-1895, (Halifax, N.S.: Nova Scotia Printing Co., 1895), p. 33.

31 Given the absence of any other reference linking Burton to Campbell Road, we believe that MacKerrow may have erred.

32 N.S.L.A., Journal and Proceedings, 1851, p. 681.

33 Part of the original Arnold property was subsequently owned by two white people, then sold in 1901 to a West Indian who settled in Africville and married a granddaughter of William Brown (Registry of Deeds, Book 324, p. 494). When this family moved to Boston, the entire lot (perhaps three acres) may have been sold to the city; the site was occupied until spring, 1971 by the city-operated Basinview Home for the aged.

[34] After the school was closed in the early 1950s the school building itself was leased by the city at one dollar per year as a community hall for Africville residents. The church property was also leased by the city, beginning in 1916.

[35] The city leased a property in 1951 to an Africville resident who had been squatting on Dominion government property and had been forced to vacate. The rental was set at an amount equal to the annual tax payable on the property (Minutes of the Committee on Works, City of Halifax, May 3, 1951). It appears that, in 1956, the railway leased a small lot to an employee who was also a resident of Africville.

[36] Around the turn of the century there were complaints voiced at meetings of the Halifax City Council concerning squatters in the Africville area.

[37] In several instances land was transferred to trustees charged with processing and validating the multiple claims (Registry of Deeds, p.. 577; Book 338, p. 24; and Book 1153, p. 61).

[38] Perhaps an explanation for this myth arises from the fact that true grants issued to refugee settlers in the Preston area always began with the conventional greeting: "*Victoria* by the grace of God of the United Kingdom of Great Britain and Ireland Queen defender of the Faith and of the United Church of England and Ireland on earth the Supreme Head. To all to whom these Presents shall come *Greeting*" (The Preston grant, 1842, C. Bruce Fergusson, *A Documentary Study of the Establishment of the Negroes in Nova Scota*, Bulletin No. 8 (Halifax, N.S.: Public Archives of Nova Scotia, 1948). An association between land grants and the Queen was easy to elaborate; and extrapolation from the black community of Preston to the black community of Africville was all that was needed to root the myth.

[39] Another myth linking Africville to the Maroons posits that the land was obtained by blacks in exchange for their work on the construction of the Halifax Citadel. The Maroons did participate in the construction, but there is, of course, no evidence of a link between the Maroons and the Africville residents.

[40] Research diary, July, 1969. There was clearly a failure of communication between the directors of the welfare and development departments. During the relocation, all welfare dealings with the Africville population were handled by the Development Department. The director of welfare publicly criticized the relocation program; see "Says City Falling Down on Africville Project: Welfare Director Says Relocation not Necessary," *The Mail-Star,* Halifax, N.S., April 26, 1965.

[41] *Minutes of the Halifax City Council,* October 27, 1852, p. 283; January 11, 1854; and late 1867.

[42] Richmond was the name given to the northerly part of Halifax in the nineteenth century.

Africville's Social Structure

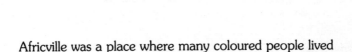

Africville was a place where many coloured people lived
together trying to do the best they could.
—Interview, Africville relocatee, 1969.

One of the most significant facets of Africville is its long history. One social
scientist has described Africville as follows: "There are no roots here; it is
almost a community in suspension, a stepping-stone in the pattern of a
population movement from the rural settlements to the larger cities of
Montreal and Boston."[1] On the contrary, compared with many urban areas
that are being redeveloped in Canada and the United States, the historical
character of the community and its people stands out. We have noted
already that Africville was established before 1850 and that at the time
of relocation most of the inhabitants were descendants of a small group
of founders, refugee blacks who first fled slavery in the United States and,
later, starvation and dire poverty at Preston and Hammonds Plains.
Migrants to Africville who had taken up residence there as long as thirty
years prior to the relocation remained acutely conscious of their migrant
status. One of our research assistants noted in his field report:

> Mrs. _____ was not born in Africville. She was born in
> New Glasgow. To start off with, she said that even though
> she lived in Africville for over twenty years, she still had a
> stigma of being an outsider and although she has some
> feelings towards the place, her feelings could never match
> up to the people who were born there.

Such historicity is unusual, for in most urban areas of Canada and the United States the pattern of invasion and succession has meant that continuous waves of immigrants and rural poor have replaced earlier arrivals as the latter have climbed the ladder of social success.[2] The redevelopment areas in cities such as Topeka, Philadelphia, Cleveland, Toronto, and Winnipeg have usually had populations with an average residence of less than ten years.[3] Africville inhabitants, however, in addition to being among the poorest of the poor, were black; accordingly, other poor and immigrants did not replace them but rather "jumped over" them. These others had enough trouble overcoming their own marginality and obtaining a full and equal share of the social wealth without becoming mixed with blacks in a society where racist attitudes lingered from slavery days.[4]

Rural Life Style

An important factor in Africville's historicity was that it was isolated from Halifax proper. Africville was set apart from the rest of the city, situated on Bedford Basin and flanked by the railway. Although almost since its first settlement Africville has been linked to Halifax proper by a railway and an unpaved road, it was traditionally more a rural community than an urban neighbourhood.

Africville used to be separated from the rest of the city by bush and rock; one elderly relocatee recalled that, prior to the First World War, "all the rest around [Africville] there was a lot of bush, nothing but bush." Long-time residents mentioned the many farm animals (chickens, horses, goats) in Africville around the turn of the century, and a local observer, referring to the same period, has written that the community boasted some of the largest piggeries in the Halifax area.[5] Africville residents never had rich enough soil or sufficient land to engage in substantial farming, but relative isolation and the general ecology of the community did allow them to maintain a meaningful rural image until the First World War. Non-commercial fishing was another traditional activity that contributed to Africville's bucolic character. One Africville relocatee referred to the fishing as follows:

> The fishing! It really hurts to go down to the grocery store
> and pay really high prices for fish. That really makes me
> sick. We used to catch almost every kind of fish there is in
> the Atlantic, right here in Bedford Basin—haddock, cod,

mackerel, perch, eels, clams. The only kind of fish we didn't get was smelts.

As the city of Halifax grew in population and in industry,[6] Africville became cluttered with railway tracks and industry and city service depots such as the city dump. By the decade preceding relocation, Africville's rural image had little meaning. City ordinances and the encroachment of industry and government has led to the disappearance of farm animals,[7] and pollution of Bedford Basin has virtually eliminated fishing. Yet, even as late as the early 1960s, the editor of a Halifax newspaper felt able to refer to Africville as the "last rural remnant in Halifax peninsula,"[8] and several Africville residents could welcome the relocation because, as one relocatee put it, "I'm a city woman." By this time, however, Africville's ruralness was largely a matter of being located "off the beaten path" and lacking standard city services. This sprawling community of approximately thirteen acres, with its dwellings, sheds, and outdoor privies haphazardly positioned and built, possessed few urban facilities. Residents had to do without paved roads (or even dust deterrent), convenient public transportation, sewerage, water, or garbage collection. The neglect of Africville by city officials was such that, according to one elderly relocatee, "For many years, Africville people were led to believe they were in the County—outside the city limits. It was only when the younger generation came along that we found we were within the city."[9]

Kinship and Fluid Social Structure

Both the sense of historical continuity possessed by Africville residents[10] and the rural characterization of the community by outsiders (and by some residents as well) were congruent with community structure. The population of Africville was always small. In 1851 there were fifty-four blacks living in the area; in 1964, at the time of relocation, the population was approximately 400.[11] Much of Africville's population growth took place during the last thirty to forty years of its existence.[12] The majority of this small population were bound together through numerous kinship ties. Approximately seventy-five percent of the relocated population were associated, either by blood or marriage, with at least one of the five principal families in Africville, families that could trace their Africville ancestry back one hundred years.[13] It is not surprising, under these circumstances, that the social structure of Africville can be characterized as "fluid"[14]—in the sense that kinship and family systems were adaptable and there was a certain interchangeability of personnel. It was common for an older couple to "take in" a grandchild or nephew, and there were numerous instances of adoption, fosterage, and step- and half-kin relationships. The use of intimate kinship terms, such as "ma," "pa," and "aunt," to refer to more distant relatives, and even to non-relatives, was common. This structural fluidity and intimacy was compounded, in the several decades preceding the relocation, by an increasing degree of cohabitation and the presence of illegitimate offspring,[15] and was accentuated by the widespread use of nicknames. Haligonians who knew Africville well could often identify its residents by nicknames only; even some of the indigenous leaders were hard-pressed to identify the proper names of some Africville residents.[16] To the outsider (especially to many white Haligonians, welfare workers, city officials, and relocation caretakers) the Africville population appeared to be "jumbled."[17]

The Seaview African United Baptist Church

An important component of Africville's social structure was the church, and the roles and organizations that it engendered. The church was as old as the community itself and embodied much of Africville's sense of historical continuity. The Seaview African United Baptist Church contained within itself the principal formal organizations in the community. Through religious services, youth and auxiliary organizations, and a missionary society, it provided residents with a collective identity and fostered sentiments of solidarity. As one Africville resident put it:

> Sunrise Service on Easter morning…that was a great thing. You get up on Easter morning at five o'clock and go to church there. You hear some of the loveliest things you ever wanted to hear, the spirituals; most of the people from Preston, Hammonds Plains, and right in the city here, you hear them say, 'If you want to get the spirit, you go to Africville for Sunrise Service on Easter morning, and when you come away from there, you are either lifted up or you're dead!' To tell the truth, when they tore that church down, I cried.[18]

Through the church, Africville residents were linked by traditions to other black communities in Halifax County and to white congregations in the city. Pastors and lay preachers were exchanged and visiting and other social gatherings were frequent.

Since Africville was not large or wealthy enough to support a resident pastor, leadership and management of the church was left to church members themselves. Involvement in church affairs provided one with status in the community, and the church elders — the deacons, trustees, and leading "sisters" — constituted, as it were, the official representatives. They received communiqués from city officials, petitioned for needed services on behalf of Africville residents, and acted as the vehicle through which philanthropic and other voluntary organizations entered the community.[19]

Community Organizations

Africville possessed, in addition to the church, other institutions and roles characteristic of small rural communities. It had a school, a post office, a neighbourhood store, midwives, and political party agents. As early as 1860, Africville residents had petitioned the provincial government for financial aid to support a qualified teacher.[20] Older respondents reported that, prior to 1883, a community resident had taught Africville children in the old Africville church. In 1883 a school was established under the jurisdiction of the city government.[21] This school continued to function until 1953, when it was closed by the city and the children were transferred to larger, racially integrated schools elsewhere in Halifax. Over the years most of the schoolteachers were blacks who resided elsewhere in Halifax.

Since 1936 Africville had its own sub-post office; the two postmistresses (one served from October 3, 1936 to March 31, 1944; the other, from 1944 to October 31, 1967) were Africville residents. The small neighbourhood stores were a feature of this relatively isolated community since at least early in this century. These stores were owned and operated by community residents who derived from them a modest supplement to family income.[22] At the time of relocation in 1964, two very small stores were operating in Africville. Several Africville women, a few of whom were licensed, carried out the duties of midwife and general "therapist" in the community. These women enjoyed considerable status and were usually proud of their record and their special remedies and techniques.[23] As Africville became less remote from the rest of the city in the decades preceding relocation, and as city health services expanded and local expectations rose, such traditional roles diminished in importance. Like other small communities in Nova Scotia, Africville had its political party agents. They were residents who had established ties with the provincial political parties and who were especially active at election time.[24] Both male and female residents acted as political captains who were responsible for "getting out the vote."

A Segregated Black Community

That Africville was a black community is important in explaining how part of the city could develop with the particular characteristics that Africville had and in understanding the changes in social structure that took place during the last thirty to forty years of its existence. Although Africville was always physically part of Halifax, socially it was just an appendage. In this respect it was similar to most of the other black settlements in Nova Scotian towns and cities, and as we have indicated elsewhere, this general pattern reflects the underlying racism that has characterized Nova Scotian society since the abolition of slavery in the nineteenth century.[25] In consequence of the separatist expectations among both blacks and non-blacks and the neglect that accompanied racism, Africville was obliged to develop structures parallel to those found elsewhere in the city. Africville was, traditionally, not merely a rural community but a segregated black settlement. There was a parallel between governmental policy towards Africville, reinforced by everyday expectations, and its relative geographical isolation.

Community Transformation and Functional Autonomy

Especially during the last thirty to forty years of its existence, Africville underwent profound changes. From what was described in 1895 as a "community of intelligent young people, much is expected of them,"[26] it increasingly became identified as "a national blot on the city of Halifax."[27] Sociologists characterizing communities and forms of social life have often used the term gemeinschaft [28] to denote a system of social relationships that can be described as communal, familistic, informal, primary, isolated, and sacred.[29] Gemeinschaft can be applied to the traditional Africville social structure that we have described, but in the several decades preceding relocation, the social structure began to assume a different character. New forms of social differentiation emerged, a mobile heterogeneous population was grafted on to the indigenous group, the encompassing character of the kinship system was attenuated, and there was a significant decline in the leadership role of the church "elders," and in the status of the church as a focal point for community solidarity. There appear to have been three important causes of this transformation; namely, the poverty of Africville, the racism of Nova Scotian society, and the economic and population growth of Halifax.[30]

In discussing the plight of the poor in American society, one sociologist has observed that "they learn that in their communites they can expect only poor and inferior services and protection from such institutions as the police, the courts, the schools, the sanitation department, the landlords, and the merchants."[31] Africville residents were always poor. They had been petitioning the city for services available to other residents of Halifax since the middle of the nineteenth century, but successes were few. Although many community delegations met with city officials about water and sewerage, Africville was never linked to the city mains. Residents had to do with makeshift wells that ran dry in the summer months and were a constant threat to health. In addition fire was a particularly serious hazard in Africville because of its isolation, the poor housing, and absence of water facilities.

Lack of facilities and of standard public services extended beyond matters of water, sewerage, and fire protection. For instance, Africville lacked recreational facilities although the Halifax Recreation and Playgrounds Commission did provide facilities to other areas of the city. Discrimination by neglect grew increasingly serious as land in and around Africville was gradually utilized by government and industry. An editorial in the local newspaper noted that Africville residents "can but contrast public tennis courts in Halifax South, and swimming pools in Halifax Centre with the complete lack of facilities for recreation and play in their own section of the city."[32] Inadequate police protection was also a matter of long-term complaint of Africville residents.[33] In discussing welfare and other services, most of the inhabitants indicated that their claims were neglected. Local officials and middle-class professionals reiterated their conviction that, at least in the years immediately preceding relocation, a number of Africville people who should have received welfare assistance were not given it. An outside expert in social welfare summed up the situation in asserting that "the delivery system of social service was obviously punitive."

Being poor means not only less likelihood of obtaining necessary facilities and services; it also involves the strong likelihood of receiving negative consideration. For Africville, it meant that the city was less than rigorous in enforcing housing standards and, by declining to issue building permits,[34] in encouraging the orderly residential development of the area. The ultimate negative consideration in Africville's case occurred during the 1950s when the city moved its open dump from within walking distance of Africville to the very doorstep of the community. This action was a "finishing touch" that established Africville as a place to visit if one were interested in observing slum conditions. A prominent city official noted that, when she was a teenager:

> A sort of high-school prank was to drive out to Africville on the weekends and turn out your lights and sit on the main road for a few minutes and turn them on and watch the rats run.

Africville residents were oppressed by poverty and neglect, but their plight was not unnoticed. The minutes of the Halifax City Council show that, since the turn of the century, council repeatedly received petitions and considered taking action about conditions in Africville. In 1945, for example, the Halifax Civic Planning Commission reported that "the residents [of Africville] must, as soon as reasonably possible, be provided with decent minimum standard housing elsewhere."[35] In this and other instances, the matter was shelved and nothing was done. One local black leader complained that Africville people were "objects of pity, not justice." The Chief Justice of the Supreme Court of Nova Scotia was reported in 1966 as describing Africville as a social problem "created by whites, because time after time, year after year, municipal councils had ignored the problem."[36] A city official, familiar with the Africville situation since 1945, observed:

> I believe that given a little incentive the people of Africville would have had lovely homes and would have made a real effort to come up to a level but, being neglected, forgotten, no sewerage, no water, they did become, they did take on, the attitude of not caring: 'What's the use, the city will do nothing!' I think the people of Africville could have risen very highly.

In accounting for the fact that little was done about the acknowledged plight of Africville, most of its residents and many other concerned Haligonians emphasized that racism, as well as poverty, was responsible.

One prominent white businessman described the relationship between Africville and city officials as follows:

> I think perhaps the first thing, [Africville] wasn't regarded as part of the city of Halifax...and [the city] didn't regard, I suppose, the people as people, certainly not as citizens; and apathy, prejudice, fear, discrimination [existed].

An Africville woman put the matter more explicitly:

> The city didn't do anything to improve Africville. All the city did was to try and get it, and they did, in the end. They just did it, too, because we were coloured. If they had been white people down there, the city would have been in there assisting them to build new homes, putting in water and sewers and building the place up.... There were places around Halifax worse than Africville was, and the city didn't do to them what they did to Africville.

Such judgments are consistent with the general pattern of race relations that has existed in Nova Scotia for the past 150 years. Blacks were not, in general, so much subject to direct economic exploitation as to a "definition of the situation" wherein they were regarded as marginals and outsiders and their deprivation was seen as the ordinary, although perhaps unfortunate, state of affairs.[37]

Generally associated with poverty and racism is a certain "functional autonomy," which, in Africville, meant that the inhabitants had certain "freedoms" unavailable elsewhere in the city. Building codes could be ignored. People could loiter and make excessive noise. A "deviance service centre" could be established in this off-the-beaten-path and poorly policed area. In the thirty to forty years before relocation, Africville became increasingly identified as a place to go for bootleg booze and fun.[38] One social scientist observed, in 1948:

> Africville has also been the setting for some low level associations; due to its proximity to Halifax they are probably quite frequent. But as one man expressed it, 'Whenever whites want to go on a bat they come to Africville.'[39]

Important social structural changes developed in Africville as a consequence of the poverty and racism that its residents experienced. During the several decades preceding relocation, residents became apathetic, lost confidence in the capacity of indigenous leaders to effect desirable change, and lost hope in the viability of the community itself. Pursuit of redress through standard and legitimate avenues had yielded little fruit, and militant collective action by Africville residents who have been hampered by the prevailing political consciousness. The church elders were unable to translate their ties with city officials and outside voluntary groups into substantial gains for the community, and their status in the community declined. Concomitant with this trend was the diminishing role of the church as a focal point of community consciousness and as a generator of solidarity sentiments. By the time that relocation became imminent, the church was a divisive as well as an integrative presence in Africville.

During the last thirty to forty years of its existence, Africville lost much of its close-knit and *gemeinschaft* quality. A mobile, heterogeneous population of blacks and some whites began drifting into Africville, primarily because of the housing shortage elsewhere in Halifax and the exploitative freedom possible in Africville because city policy and practice towards the community had led to a decline in morale. A Halifax alderman, who had grown up near Africville and knew many Africville residents, described the situation as follows:

> As a boy, I knew Africville as a very nice community. It was in the days of the old railway station in the North End, and all the homes in Africville were well-kept, whitewashed or painted white; they had gardens, flowers. From the end of the War on, there seemed to be a general deterioration of the whole area...the class that got in there sort of ruined the area...they weren't people who had steady incomes and they couldn't rent in the city of Halifax.

In-migration and Social Differentiation

The immigration of this new population complicated and "loosened" Africville's social structure. Africville became socially differentiated in a manner characteristic of slums elsewhere in North America, accommodating temporary and permanent dwellers as well as opportunists.[40] For the most part, the new migrants were not absorbed into the community through kinship ties or church affiliation; rather, new roles and patterns of interaction were grafted on to the crumbling traditional social structure. Important distinctions developed concerning the area in Africville where one lived (there were, in this period, three areas which were socially differentiated by many Africville residents); one's housing status (whether one had a deed, or rented, or was a squatter); and whether one was involved in church life (through either worship, services, or church organizations).

There were chiefly four groupings that differentiated residents in the immediate pre-relocation period. One grouping, the marginals/transients consisted of all the white residents plus blacks without kinship ties or land and housing claims in the community; these people typically rented and were uninvolved in Africville church activities. The whites were mostly (about a dozen) middle-aged and elderly transients, unattached, hard-drinking, and without regular employment. Although before the turn of the century it was not unusual for a few white families to settle temporarily in Africville while trying to secure housing elsewhere, the number had increased considerably. In addition, there was a handful of racially mixed families in which the fathers were white "outsiders." Whites were clearly marginal, living in Africville at the goodwill of the residents. In most of the mixed families the women were referred to by their maiden names by other residents, and the homes were regarded as "belonging" to the women. The marginals/transients, both black and white, found toleration and inexpensive accommodation in the community. Many of them lived in the part of Africville referred to in the community as "around the bend." Here the poorest quality Africville homes and many of the frequenters of Africville's deviance service centre were to be found.

A second group of people, the mainliners, consisted of blacks who had married into the community and were, comparatively speaking, the socio-economic elite; typically these persons had lived in Africville for a significant period of time, had regular employment, and had property claims in the community. Some participated prominently in church-related activities and were community leaders. For the most part, mainliners lived in that section of Africville referred to as the "main settlement," an area co-terminous with the original Africville boundaries and featuring the highest-quality Africville housing.

Thirdly, there were the oldliners, people with kinship ties in Africville dating back to the 1840s. Some of the older people in this group were heavily involved in church affairs and, in their younger days, had been leaders in the community. Many oldliners lived in the "main settlement" area but a few lived "around the bend." Usually oldliners owned their homes and land, but sometimes the house was on land adjacent to ancestral property for which they did not possess legal title.

The fourth grouping, the residuals, refers to blacks who were not able to claim ancestral ties in Africville beyond the last quarter of the nineteenth century, were less well-off than the mainliners, and, typically, were uninvolved in church activities. Many residuals did not have legal land claims and some had squatted there as late as the early 1940s.

This fourfold social differentiation was related to residential location. In the 1950s and early 1960s there were three separate areas of Africville as identified by residents. The westernmost set of homes was referred to as "around the bend;" land and dwellings in this area were owned by the oldline residents, but the inhabitants were mostly marginals/transients; there were found the poorest-quality Africville homes and many of the frequenters of Africville's deviance service centre[41] (See map—Africville Area, 1964). A second residential area was the main settlement divided by railway tracks into the "basinside" and "the hill;" it was generally coterminous with the original Africville boundaries, featured the highest-quality housing in the community, and was peopled chiefly by the mainliners and the oldliners. Finally the southeastern corner of Africville was often referred to as "Big Hill" or "Big Town;" it housed, chiefly, persons in the residual grouping. It, too, was a centre for much of the bootlegging-conviviality that went on in Africville. There were approximately ten households in the "Big Town."

Much of the increase in squatting that occurred in Africville in the two decades before relocation took place in "Big Town." Mainliners and respectable oldliners, frustrated by the decline of the community and the lack of public understanding of their oppression, as reflected in the stigma that outsiders associated with the name Africville, often vehemently denounced the "Big Town" residents and drew a distinct line between that area and the rest of Africville. An elderly oldliner, formerly a leader in the community, observed of some "Big Town" residents:

> They were cast-offs from other places who came to Africville because no other place would have them. They would come with some cock-and-bull story and maybe someone would take them in; then they would build little shacks.

Africville Area, 1964

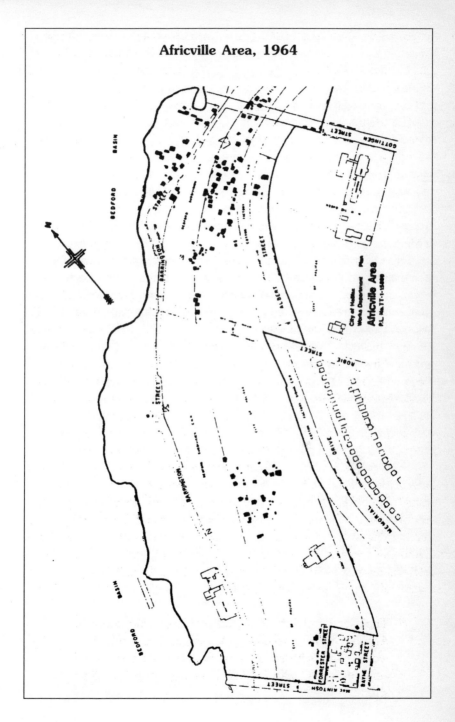

One young, regularly employed, oldliner noted:

> That ["Big Town"] was the baddest part of Africville. People
> there were always in trouble with the law and gave
> everybody else a bad name. I remember when someone
> got killed in "Big Town." The police came down and herded
> everyone up like a bunch of cattle. This is how Africville
> would get a bad name.

Many white city officials did appear more knowledgeable about "Big Town" residents, and their observations of Africville life were extrapolations based on their contacts with these people. Then, too, ordinary Haligonians visiting the community for booze would interact primarily with some of the "Big Town" residents. Several of the latter were open, resourceful, and hard-living people readily acknowledging their squatter status and candid about their lifestyle; unlike the mainliners and respectable oldliners, and unlike the more retreatist-oriented marginals/transients, they were rebels, although rebels without politics.

This distinction between the four major social groups is important since there was significant variation by group in terms of orientation to community, attitude towards relocation, relocation negotiation style, and post-relocation adjustment. Pre-relocation data[42] revealed that the minority of Africville residents who disliked Africville and were willing to move were chiefly the mainliners, the better-off people, among whom were found the more vocal community leaders. Among the majority of residents who enjoyed living in Africville and were unwilling to move were the oldliners, who were most rooted in the community, the resourceless marginals/ transients, and persons of the residual group who had found a haven there. Particularly among elderly oldliners involved in the church, there was an idealization of the "old Africville," a sense of pride in the community's survival, and an anguish over the seemingly vanished possibilities of the community. Many of these elderly oldliners showed a strong sense of pride in their independence, but they also recognized that they had lost control over the destiny of their community. They therefore withdrew into their memories, and the church became a critical point of reference for them. Over the years the church activities, and especially the "spectaculars" such as baptismal and sunrise services that attracted outsiders, had been the chief means by which they temporarily overcame feelings of oppression and deprivation and shouted, "Look here, we have something valuable and we're trying our best!"

While it is important to appreciate the social differentiation that existed in Africville, it has to be remembered that it was a small, stable community. Intermarriage linked people in the diverse social groupings. Some of the "Big Town" residents had roots in Africville going back to early in the century, and some of the Second World War squatters had married into the oldline families. Awareness of differences did not lead to a constant challenge of the rights of some people to call themselves residents of Africville, and even the marginals/transients had generally lived there for more than five years.

Emigration From Africville

Emigration from Africville also appears to have had important social structural implications. Many of the Africville residents who were relatively high achievers, especially the young single adults and those possessing special work skills, began to move out of Africville in the decades immediately before relocation. The young adults, like their black and white peers throughout the Maritimes, moved to large urban centres such as Montreal, Toronto, and Winnipeg in search of a new and better life. Another group of Africville residents, who had ancestral ties in the community, moved away in the decade before relocation. These young married men, who had regular employment and whose wives were socially active, acquired Halifax properties just beyond the Africville settlement. They moved primarily to obtain the benefit of urban facilities and to escape the stigma of living in Africville. One of these migrants observed:

> No sense building a nice home in Africville when you have
> no service — had to get out of the area to get that.

The son of one of these migrants accounted for his father's leaving the community in 1946 as follows:

> Well, some of the men from Africville used to go into the
> city to work. My Dad, _____, [and] _____ were among
> them. They used to talk to the men they worked with, who
> told them how easy it was to own a home in the city. These
> men were homeowners in the same wage bracket. Still,
> the men waited until _____ set the example. _____
> bought a piece of land which was in the city but not too far

from Africville. They didn't dare move too far into the city, yet they wanted homes with modern facilities. When _____ was all set up, I remember Dad got us all together and told us what he was going to do. He told us he was going to build a home next to _____ on _____ Street. 'This is going to be your home and I want you to respect it — something for you when you grow up. You will have a place to come back to, so that you can say I left you something.' And I'm back here now.

This emigration sapped the morale of the remaining Africville residents. Potential leaders were lost, and the community as a collectivity was transformed and began to drift. Their successors were, as we have noted, people with different social ties and patterns of behaviour. The very existence of a small group of former Africville residents living beyond the community, employed steadily, and enjoying standard city services, cast an unfavourable reflection upon Africville itself. It tended to create an oversimplified impression that the plight of Africville derived from the personality of its residents rather than from the social context in which they had had to function. The migrants were often seen by the people remaining in Africville as a "better" class of people, the so-called "four hundreds,"[43] who were better off financially and deemed respectable by the white-dominated society.

Pre-Relocation Population Characteristics

In 1959 the Institute of Public Affairs, Dalhousie University, conducted a survey in Africville; it revealed that the population was approximately 400. As Table 2.1 reveals, almost half the residents were under fifteen years of age. This finding reflected the existence of large families in Africville. About one-third of the population was between the ages of fifteen and forty-four. There was a slight excess of males in the forty-five-plus age category, evidence of the pattern of transients often finding a home in this relatively hidden corner of Halifax.

Since the turn of the century it was not unusual for a few white families to live in Africville. Older relocatees could list a large number of white families who had lived in Africville at one time or another; school registers confirm that the pattern was for the white families to remain in the settlement for only a year or two, while they were trying to secure housing

Table 2.1
Population of Africville, 1959*

Age	Male		Female		Total	
	No.	%	No.	%	No.	%
0-14	96	48	95	50	191	49
15-29	34	17	36	19	70	18
30-44	30	15	31	16	61	15
45-59	29	14	22	11	51	13
60 and over	12	6	9	5	21	5
Total	201	100	193	101	394	100

* Data from the 1959 survey conducted by the Institute of Public Affairs, Dalhousie University

elsewhere. In 1959 there was one large, poor, white family living in Africville; the family remained for three years. In the decade preceding relocation, the whites who lived in Africville were mostly middle-aged and elderly transients who found toleration and inexpensive accommodation in the community. In 1959 there were nine such persons, most of whom had been living there for several years and previously had been regular visitors to Africville. For the most part they were unattached, hard-drinking, and without regular employment. In addition, there were six racially mixed families; half of them were common-law relationships of doubtful stability and five of the six fathers were white "outsiders."

Most residents of Africville had been born and raised in the community and had inter-connected ties dating back to the middle of the nineteenth century. As Table 2.2 indicates, in 1959 seventy-five percent of the population were life-long inhabitants and over seventy percent of the household heads either had been born in Africville or had lived there for more than twenty years. Virtually all the white residents had been living in the community for less than ten years. Table 2.3 shows the previous place of residence for those persons not born and raised in Africville. The vast majority of these persons were blacks who had come from other black settlements. Most of the household heads emigrating to Africville from "other Halifax County" and "other Nova Scotia" either married into the commuity or had relatives there; a handful of men from the West Indies

Table 2.2
Length of Residence in Africville, 1959*

Length of Residence	All persons		Household Heads	
	No.	%	No.	%
Life	293	75	39	49
20 years or more	31	8	18	22
10-19 years	15	4	7	9
5-9 years	12	3	6	8
0-5 years	25	6	7	9
No data	18†	4	3	3
Total	394	100	80	100

* Data as in Table 2.1.
† Ten of the eighteen were boarders, and several were children.

Table 2.3
Previous Place of Residence of In-Migrants, Africville, 1959*

Length of Residence	All persons		Household Heads	
	No.	%	No.	%
Halifax	22	22	7	17
Other Halifax County	22	22	12	29
Other Nova Scotia	27	27	9	22
Other†	13	13	10	24
No data	17	17	3	8
Total	101	101	41	100

* Data as in Table 2.1.
† Five of the thirteen persons came from other provinces in Canada, and five from the West Indies.

also married into the community. One white man who had married an Africville woman gave as his reason for residing in the settlement the discrimination he found in Halifax and the heckling he anticipated receiving had he lived in navy married quarters.

The rootedness of the Africville population at the time of relocation was evidenced not only by length of residence but also by migration

Table 2.4
Household Structure, Africville, 1959*

Type of Family		No.	%
Nuclear Family†		35	44
Basic	29		
Variant	6		
Childless Couples†		9	11
Basic	6		
Variant	3		
Extended Family††		16	20
Basic	8		
Variant	8		
Single Parent†††		8	10
Basic	5		
Variant	3		
Single Person†††		8	10
Basic	6		
Variant	2		
No data		4	5
Total		80	100

*   Data as in Table 2.1.
†   The variant cases refer to marital relationships that are common-law or to households where boarders are present.
††   In seven of the variant cases the household structure consists of an older couple plus a grandchild or nephew.
†††   In the variant cases boarders are present.

patterns. Only a handful of those adults with a life-long residence in Africville reported ever having left the community for a significant period of time. Fully eighty-five percent of the relocatees born and raised in Africville had never lived elsewhere.[44] The data indicate that Africville was a relatively stable community although it had an overlay of transiency which resulted from persons who "drifted in and out" especially on weekends and in the summer.

Table 2.4 shows that close kinship ties among the relatively stable Africville population were manifested in household structure. Less than forty percent of the households had "nuclear" families. Approximately one-fifth of the households were extended families. As already noted it was common for an older couple to "take in" a grandchild or nephew; this made sense in terms of available household space and provided, as well, pleasure and "labour supply" for older couples. It appears, also, that this pattern developed, in many instances, from mutual affection between the older persons and the children. The remaining one-third of the households was divided evenly among childless couples, older single persons, and single-parent families. Table 2.4 also indicates that there were eight single-parent households. Twelve additional single-parent families were integral subunits of other households. All but one of the twenty single-parent families were headed by a female. The large proportion of such families indicates both instability of the marital relationship — a pattern related to high under-employment and low earned income and the supportive function of a tolerant extended-family system.[45]

Africville's Pre-Relocation Social Structure

When Africville relocation began in 1964, residents were economically hard-pressed and poorly organized. The social structure was complex, diffuse, and dynamic. It was as if two radically different structures had been placed in a melting pot, but without a recipe for guiding or forecasting the outcome. The schizoid character of the social structure (a deviance service centre co-existed with the major community institution, the church, and the sixth generation residents rubbed shoulders with white transients) makes the use of terms like "community" and "social structure" problematic. These terms seem to imply greater system, stability, and homogeneity than Africville possessed. Africville was characterized by many anomalies; by diverse patterns of behavioural expectations among residents and of interactions not tightly interlocked, and by radically different social types and role models. Africville was still predominantly a small, black community, most of whose population was interrelated through kinship ties and possessed an exceptional sense of historical continuity. Africville was, however, much more than this. Through poverty and racism, its people had virtually been fated to eventual relocation. There were still a number of vigorous and proud people living in Africville, but the community lacked structural unity, all-encompassing sentiments of solidarity, and other resources. It was hard to organize residents and it was hard for outsiders, black and white alike, to see Africville as viable or its continued existence as desirable.

Notes

1   Brookbank, op. cit., p. 30.

2   A clear example of this process can be seen in the settlement of the Alexandra Park area, in Toronto. Albert Rose ("The Individual, the Family and the Community in the Process of Urban Renewal," *Urban Renewal* [Toronto: Centre for Urban and Community Studies, University of Toronto, 1968], p. 324) describes it as "an area of 'first settlement' for newcomers to the city from abroad." The pre-First World War British and Jewish immigrants were eventually succeeded by Eastern European and Portuguese immigrants. In both Canada and the United States, the traditional "ports of entry," from the point of view of housing, have been the oldest and least desirable sections of the cities; that is, in and around the central business districts.

3   See, for example, William Morrison, *A Study of Some of the Social Aspects of Urban Renewal* (Winnipeg, Manitoba: Community Welfare Planning Council, 1967). A majority of the family adults in the redevelopment areas were not born in Winnipeg and the modal number of years of residence in the city was five to fourteen years for family heads. For the four samples into which the population was divided, the average length of stay in the old slum core area was 5.9, 7.6, 5.1, and 5.4 years. Moreover, respondents in all four groups indicated a considerable movement, typical of contemporary North American urban dwellers. For a report of the urban movement generally, see Peter Henry Rossi, *Why Families Move* (Glencoe, Ill.: The Free Press, 1955).

In the Alexandra Park area, only forty-three percent of the residents (1961) were born in Canada and thirty-six percent were immigrants to Canada during the years 1946-61 (Rose, op. cit., p. 325). For large American cities, see Paul L. Niebanck, *The Elderly in Older Urban Areas* (Philadelphia: University of Pennsylvania, Institute for Environmental Studies, 1965), p. 56.

In Topeka, Kansas, the urban renewal relocatees had lived in their homes for an average of 11.7 years, although the group with the most apparent subculture, the Mexicans, accounted for much of this high average residence (Key, op. cit.). Because of racism and lack of economic opportunity, some predominantly black areas in American cities have also tended to exhibit high residential stability; for example, in redeveloped southwest Washington, D.C., some sixty-five percent of the relocatees interviewed had lived in the neighbourhood for more than ten years prior to relocation (Thursz, op. cit.).

The North End redevelopment area of Hamilton, Ontario, which was similar to Africville in some important respects (a strong sense of identification by the residents and a reputation as a deviance service centre), was also characterized by residential stability. One study revealed that fifty percent of the respondents had lived in the North End for more than twelve years. However, only fifty-three percent of the respondents were born in Canada. See Social Planning Council of Hamilton District. *The Social Costs of Urban Renewal,* (Hamilton, Ont., 1963).

4   In general, the pattern of invasion and succession does not operate independently of the racial traits of the groups involved. Historically in North America, blacks, Puerto Ricans, and Chinese have succeeded poor and immigrant whites, but the reverse has not occurred so frequently. With the extensive restructuring of cities through urban renewal programs, impoverished minority groups are more likely to be succeeded, nowadays, by an upper-middle class dwelling in luxury apartments. See Thursz, op. cit.; Charles Silberman, *Crisis in Black and White* (New York: Vintage, 1964); and *Commission Report on Relocation* (Washington, D.C.: United States Department of Health, Education and Welfare, 1965).

5   Frank Doyle, "Dwellings at Dump Not Very Historic," *The Mail-Star*, Halifax, N.S., January 18, 1963.

6   The population of Halifax increased from 20,749 (1851 census) to 46,619 in 1911 and 92,511 in 1961. The Halifax city limits were unchanged between 1851 and 1961.

7   Since 1915 it has been illegal to keep swine within city limits. *Minutes of the Halifax City Council,* 1915.

8   Frank Doyle, "Africville's Shackdom Shows Lack of Action," *The Mail-Star,* Halifax, N.S., February 10, 1965.

9   Interview, July 1969. It is important not to interpret this statement literally but as being indicative of the marginality felt by Africville residents vis-à-vis the rest of Halifax. Even prior to the turn of the century, they had petitioned city officials for needed services. Their lack of success, and consequent sense of powerlessness and isolation, created a profound feeling of estrangement. Additional factors, of course, such as racial origin, affected their relationship with other Haligonians.

10   As we have already noted in the discussion of myths of settlement, a sense of historical continuity does not necessarily reflect an accurate knowledge of historical fact.

11   See P.A.N.S., R.G. 1, Vol. 451, *Census, City of Halifax,* 1851; and *The Condition of the Negroes of Halifax City, Nova Scotia.* Erich Fromm has suggested that about 400 is the optimum population of a community geared to meeting individual needs and capable of providing healthy social relationships. See Erich Fromm, *The Sane Society* (New York: Rinehart, 1955).

[12] The population doubled during this period. See Frank Doyle, "Dwellings at Dump Not Very Historic," *The Mail-Star,* Halifax, N.S., January 18, 1963.

[13] See Africville Genealogical Charts, Donald H. Clairmont and Dennis W. Magill, *Africville Relocation Report* , p. 69. The names used in the charts are pseudonyms.

[14] For this concept of fluid social structure, we are indebted to Frank G. Vallee, *Kabloona and Eskimo in the Central Keewatin* (Ottawa: Northern Co-ordination and Research Centre, Department of Indian Affairs and Northern Development, 1962), pp. 61-97.

[15] In 1959 there were eight single-parent households. Twelve additional single-parent families were integral subunits of other households. All but one of the twenty single-parent families were headed by a female. The frequency of single-parent families in the immediate pre-relocation period was in sharp contrast to their rarity in previous generations, which is, perhaps, an indication of the decline of community viability.

[16] This fact posed difficulties for the researchers trying to discern the basis of social differentiation in Africville and to draw appropriate inferences from anecdotes.

[17] This statement is based on interviews with outsiders during the summer and fall of 1969, and on the minutes of the Halifax Human Rights Advisory Committee and the minutes of city council's Africville subcommittee.

[18] The above-quoted respondent noted also that, as a result of church activities in Africville, "You get people from all over the place, and when I say people from all over the place—not just Negro people, not just black people; white people, too. People came from the First Baptist [white church], the Second Baptist [white church]...."

[19] Specific examples will be given in the following chapters. General documentation of this role behaviour can be found in *Minutes of the Halifax City Council,* 1860-1960.

[20] P.A.N.S., Africville File, Assembly Petitions (Education, 1860).

[21] *Report of the Halifax School Commissioners,* City of Halifax, 1883, p. 11.

[22] In most instances, the store was simply part, or an extension of a residence, and the sales volume was such that one can only conclude that the store contributed marginally to family income.

[23] One midwife and "therapist" recalled proudly that a doctor had offered her a licence as a first-aid attendant. Her usual remedy, she reported, was "one-half aspirin, hot bath, and castor oil." Interview, September 1969.

[24] A knowledgeable local politician who had examined the voting record of Africville pointed out that, typically, the vote was heavily in favour of one

party, although not the same party in every election. He ascribed this bandwagon effect to a common practice, not exclusive to Africville, of buying votes.

25 Clairmont and Magill, *Nova Scotian Blacks.*

26 MacKerrow, op. cit., p. 65.

27 Interview with city official, December, 1969.

28 The term was applied first by Ferdinand Tönnies, *Community and Society (Gemeinschaft und Gesellschaft),* Charles P. Loomis, trans. and ed. (New York: Harper and Row, 1963).

29 For these components and others, see Charles P. Loomis and Zona K. Loomis, *Modern Social Theories* (Princeton, N.J.: Van Nostrand, 1961), pp. 69, 269, and 484.

30 The poverty of Africville residents and the presence of racism were clearly related, for racism meant that occupationally, educationally, and socially, blacks had much less opportunity than whites.

31 Lee Rainwater, "Poverty and Deprivation in the Crisis of the American City," Occasional Paper No. 9, mimeographed (St. Louis, Missouri: Washington University, 1966).

32 "Africville, Too, Needs a Playground," *The Mail-Star,* Halifax, N.S., July 15, 1961. In pre-Second World War days there were many good ball teams and hockey teams composed of Africville players competing regularly against other teams in the Halifax area.

33 Africville residents were petitioning for police services as long ago as 1919. See *Minutes of the Halifax City Council,* 1919.

34 It was an expression of this policy that caused Africville residents to organize a ratepayers association in 1961.

35 *The Master Plan for the City of Halifax as Prepared by the Civic Planning Commission,* Ira P. MacNab, Chairman, Halifax, N.S., November 16, 1945.

36 *The Free Press,* Dartmouth, N.S., December 8, 1966.

37 See, for example, references in Clairmont and Magill, *Nova Scotian Blacks.*

38 Prostitution was not a salient feature of social deviance in Africville.

39 Brookbank, op. cit., p. 76.

40 See John R. Seeley, "The Slum: Its Nature, Use, and Users," *Journal of the American Institute of Planners* 25 (1959): 7-14.

41 Some middle-aged respondents indicated that as early as the 1920s the area "around the bend" was a locale for boot-legging and conviviality; accordingly, it was differentiated from the basinside area, and parents in the latter area advised their children not to go there.

42 For a more elaborate discussion of these data, see the authors' *Africville Relocation Report.*

43 Throughout the black community in Nova Scotia, the term "four hundreds" is used to designate high-status persons. For discussion of this term, see Clairmont and Magill, *Nova Scotian Blacks*, p. 120, footnote 2. Within Africville itself, several persons were considered by the majority of residents to be "four hundreds."

44 Data from the 1969 survey by the authors.

45 "Tolerant" does not mean that this situation was preferred. Female heads of single-parent families often were embarrassed and their parents disapproved of their marital status.

The Major Institution: The Seaview African United Baptist Church

We had beautiful services, and people used to come from all around — coloured people and white people — to our services. People called it a spiritual church.
—Interview, Africville Relocatee, July, 1969.

Most of the major themes in terms of which we have been discussing the social structure of Africville can be readily discerned in its religious life. Here, too, we find anomalies: a very rigid code of conduct and a progressive identification of the community as a deviance service centre; a widespread, heartfelt grief over the loss of the church and the fact that not many of the Africville residents went to the church when it did exist; an expressive style of life and the slow erosion of leadership and structure. One would expect that the ethos typifying a social structure would permeate all its institutions.[1] In this instance, the consistency is especially marked: the church signalled the coming into existence of Africville, and it is through the trust fund,[2] established with monies obtained from selling church property to the city, that Africville continues to exist in any official and formal sense.

The African Baptist Movement

Like the vast majority of blacks in Nova Scotia, Africville blacks were, with few exceptions, Baptist. The Loyalist black settlers in Nova Scotia apparently had not been church-affiliated prior to their immigration.[3] Their mass conversion to the Baptist faith was partly the work of an escaped

Virginian slave, David George, who reached the province at the time of the Loyalist exodus from the rebellious American colonies. George's evangelism was part of the "Great Awakening," centred largely in the Baptist and Methodist churches, that swept the North American colonies during the latter part of the eighteenth century. A substantial effort was made among both blacks and whites to win converts. Few blacks became affiliated with the Church of England or with the Roman Catholic Church, a circumstance due perhaps as much to discrimination and unfriendliness on the part of these churches as it was to the attractiveness of the evangelists' appeals.[4] Some of these early congregations were racially mixed and, in fact, a number of whites joined George's church. The seeds for segregated churches were sown, however, by the pattern of establishing separate congregations. This pattern was reinforced by the Shelburne race riot that forced George to leave the settlement.[5]

After initial efforts at Shelburne, George preached among the blacks of Nova Scotia and New Brunswick for a decade before accompanying his people to Sierra Leone in 1792. Mobilization for emigration was in terms of congregational or community units, and a large number of the Baptists participated. The depleted ranks of black Baptists were replenished twenty years later through the conversion of most of the 2000 black refugees by the English evangelist John Burton. Initially Burton's church was racially mixed, but as his evangelism met with great enthusiasm among Halifax-area blacks, "in time his church was made up mostly of Negroes and was much despised."[6] As soon as another minister arrived from the United States, the whites established their own Baptist congregation, while Burton continued his work among the blacks. During the influx of refugees from 1813 to 1816, he became the prinicpal liaison in the government's efforts to settle the refugees. Soon afterwards, he began organizing other black Baptist congregations in the Halifax area.

Burton and his hand-picked successor, Richard Preston, a former Virginian slave, were primarily responsible for the actual organization of the African Baptist movement.[7] With Richard Preston elected as pastor (April 14, 1832), the African Baptist Church was organized in Halifax, and branches were established at Dartmouth, Preston, Hammonds Plains, and Beech Hill (now Beechville). During the 1840s the local mission churches were formally organized as autonomous congregations. Preston supervised the establishment of the Baptist church in Africville (known then as Campbell Road) in 1849, and became its visiting pastor, as he was for the other congregations in the Halifax area. In 1854 representatives of all the black Baptist churches, meeting in convention, formed the African Baptist Association of Nova Scotia.

When Richard Preston died, a total of thirteen churches had been organized into the African Baptist Association. By 1905 the number of affiliated black churches had reached twenty.[8] In the 1880s a movement developed to merge the African Baptist Association with its predominantly white counterpart, the Maritime Baptist Convention. The black organization was in financial need, for at this time its relatively impoverished constituency was being depleted by heavy emigration to the United States. Within the association, however, a strong opposition succeeded in retaining the independence of the black Baptist movement.[9]

During the last quarter of the nineteenth century and until the Second World War, a chronic shortage of ministers was compounded by the great poverty of the black communities. This situation resulted in the fact that three of the nine successive pastors of the Cornwallis Street Baptist Church, Halifax (the mother church) were brought from the United States; by this means, Nova Scotian blacks were linked with developments in America. Despite many problems, the African Baptist association continued to grow and, by 1953, in its one-hundredth year, the Association encompassed twenty-two congregations, plus its "preaching stations," and some thousand members and adherents.

The churches provided, throughout the history of black settlements in Nova Scotia, the basis for whatever genuine black subculture developed. Black leaders and spokesmen vis-à-vis the wider society were usually the religious leaders,[10] and the association was the base for unity and contact among the isolated black communities. Within the black communities, the church provided a variety of services and organizations, and social status was closely associated with participation in church activities. The association was active on a number of fronts. For instance, around the turn of the century the temperance movement found enthusiastic promoters among the African Baptist Association. In Mrs. Oliver's opinion:

> It was an intemperate age and liquor flowed freely. To an
> illiterate, poverty-stricken people,…over-indulgence in this
> evil would have proven disastrous. Had not this Association
> taken such a fierce stand on this question our people might
> have sunk to the lowest levels.[11]

Since the last quarter of the nineteenth century, the association has been active in education, seeking to maintain adequate conditions in the rural schools and often struggling merely to keep the schools open. In 1921, with government assistance, the association founded the Nova Scotia Home for Coloured Children. The social-work function of the association was considerably restricted, however, by lack of funds. Even to fund the travelling pastors or circuit preachers was difficult. The economic depression which began its fifteen-year course in Nova Scotia in 1923 virtually paralysed the association's cultural and economic efforts. After the Second World War, the association continued to provide the structures for leadership. Church leaders organized the Nova Scotian Association for the Advancement of Coloured People (NSAACP) in 1945 and, in 1949, the association formed an Urban and Rural Life Committee to stimulate cooperative efforts at the community level.

The Africville Church

We have noted that almost as soon as the original black settlers had reached what was to become Africville, Richard Preston called them together and, at their request, organized a church. The offices of elder, deacon, and licentiate were instituted and Preston himself became the non-resident pastor. All the families but one were recorded as Baptist in the 1851 census. At the organizational meeting of the African Baptist Association in 1854, the Campbell Road congregation reported thirteen adult baptized members.[12] In these early years, Africville was neither sufficiently large nor wealthy enough to have its own resident minister, and the chronic shortage of pastors throughout the association often prevented the Halifax ministers from allocating time to the tiny church at Campbell Road.[13] As in recent years, however, the Campbell Road church functioned by utilizing the offices of licentiate and deacon, supplemented by occasional pastoral assistance. By 1895, the small church appears to have achieved a favourable reputation:

> This little Zion of late has been the subject of much
> comment, being in such close proximity to the city, with a
> fine day school in which nearly all the children of schoolable
> age takes advantage of [sic]. A community of intelligent
> young people, much is expected of them. In former years
> the pastor of the Halifax church divided his time with them,

but in the lapse of time things change, and so has that. The District Committee [which included persons from the white congregations] has now taken them under their care, so they are zealously looked after. A brother from each church in the city, of which there are five Baptist, goes out consecutively on Sundays, and exhorts to the brethren, and a very precious time is often realised....

Deacon Brown can always be found with the keys in his hand to open or close the church, hence I think the right man is in the right place. A few hundred yards from the church is the placid waters of Bedford Basin, beneath whose surface Fathers Burton, Preston, Thomas, Bailey, Carvery, Dixon and Boone has buried in the likeness of Christ many willing converts in the ordinance of baptism, whose pilgrimage here was of short duration, and by their lives and actions are to-day shouting with the redeemed in glory, whose sins have been forgiven, whose robes have been washed in the Blood of the Lamb.[14]

The fact that Africville was set away from the city proper on a slope by the harbour gave it a scenic beauty and made it, in the pre-war era and prior to the city's establishment of the disposal dump on its border, an especially attractive gathering place. Bedford Basin was an ideal baptismal font and, throughout the years, numerous believers were led into the waters at Africville. The first baptism was conducted in 1849 by Reverend Richard Preston; the last took place in 1963, shortly before the relocation. In 1874 the Reverend James Thomas conducted at Africville one of the largest baptisms on record in the Halifax area, with forty-six candidates; the ceremony, it was reported, "attracted a large concourse of persons from the city."[15] Africville frequently catered to picnic festivities for the Cornwallis Street Baptist Church, Halifax, and the Nova Scotia Home for Coloured Children. Many long-time residents of Africville remember still, with pleasure and pride, the occasion when Africville hosted the quadrennial provincial convention of the African Baptist Association.

We have noted earlier that until the First World War Africville was *in* the city but not *of* the city. It was relatively isolated, both physically and socially. With the coming of the war, Halifax reassumed its historic role as a strategic wartime port. Facilities were expanded and railway connections to the port were further developed. The "little brown church" at Africville was a casualty of this development. When the CNR put in a double line on the east side of the cotton factory track quite close to the old church, the building deteriorated and had to be torn down. Later, the Africville congregation requested and received permission from city officials to build a new church on city-owned property in the Africville area.[16] This church stood for some fifty years, until it was levelled during the relocation period. Soon after the construction of the new church, the name was changed from Africville African United Baptist Church to Seaview African United Baptist Church. Apparently some members of the church congregation disliked the word "Africville." Not everyone, however, shared their objection. One elderly Africville resident reported: "Some people came in, in recent years, who weren't satisfied with the name Africville and changed it to Seaview. Meddlers, I call them."[17]

The Expressive Style

Over the years, the Seaview church participated in an exchange network that encompassed most of the black Baptist congregations in the area and occasionally the West End Baptist Church. Members of these congregations circulated frequently among the communities in order to attend a variety of church services, shared visiting preachers as well as their own pastors, and exchanged local lay preachers. The Africville congregation was a particular favourite in this network because it was considered to be the most "spiritual" — an expression which connotes, among other things, heightened emotional involvement and congregational participation. As Brookbank discovered in his study of Afro-Canadian communities in Halifax County in 1948-49, "the most emotional services are held in Africville and the least emotional at Cornwallis Street, with the rural settlements falling in between."[18]

It has been suggested by Brookbank and others that the deep emotional participation which characterized the Africville Baptist congregation, at least during the last thirty years of its existence, points to Africville as being a "main area of social unrest and disorganization." This interpretation is fallacious, as it fails to take adequate account of the historical development of the community and its traditional style of expression. The service certainly was not conducted in a sedate, middle-class fashion. A former deacon of the Seaview church recalled that, "at the old church in Africville people would get together and sing and clap and have a great time and when the church would really get emotional the whole congregation would get up and lock hands together and dance around." Another church member observed that "the people of Africville used to have so much spirit that [they] would get on the floor and shake." Several elderly church members have spoken of the mysterious cures which occasionally resulted from intense "spirituality."

It appears from the testimony of long-time Africville residents that intense congregational participation had always characterized the church and was unrelated either to the changes occurring in the community population after 1930 or to the more recent labelling of Africville as a slum or "deviant" area. At church meetings in Africville the members rose and "testified," specifically citing difficult times they may have had that week. In this emotional testimony, the member referred to the spiritual fulfilment experienced through prayer. Other members of the congregation joined in and gave support to the speaker's enthusiasm with shouts of "Amen," "Praise to God," and so on. The profound meaning of such services would probably escape the uninitiated. One black who took up residence in Africville in the early 1930s described his reaction in these words: "I'm supposed to be a Baptist, but the hootin' and hollerin' they did in that church, that's not for me." Thus it appears that, as far back as 1930, Africville had an atypical mode of church service.

It is easy to understand how this kind of tradition could be maintained in a "close community," with its deep and strong kinship ties. The Seaview church resembled, in its style of worship, a popular image of the American black Baptist church. One minister, who served Africville as well as other black churches in the Halifax area for over thirty years, made the following observation:

> There certainly was a big difference between worshipping
> in Cornwallis [Street Baptist Church] and in Africville. [The
> Africville people] were a free people. The only way I could
> describe their worship would be to…if you know anything
> about soul music today they had it in Africville. I often tell
> some of them: When the sophisticated people in town were
> laughing at you and your prayer services — clapping your
> hands and singing and enjoying yourself — they didn't
> realize that Sammy Davis Jr., and other celebrities would
> come along and make millions for the same thing that you
> had right here and they didn't recognize it…. I always made
> a point, when I really wanted to put some life in my church,

I brought them in. Whenever I announced that the Africville group would be there, the church would be filled.

The application of the term "soul," with its contemporary connotations of genuine black culture, to the religious style of the Africville church, appears apt. Not only did the religious services exhibit a deep expressive style, but the church was also a means of community and communion among the black people in Africville. An observer at the last Sunrise Service in Africville noted:

> The thing that got to me was the third song called, "What He Done For Me," and all of a sudden people started to come out of their pews...they were primarily older folks but they were standing and they were clapping their hands and bringing on the others...the total church community in the congregation joined hands around the church along the edge, pushed the chairs out of the way and they sang this song. I found that it was a 'shout' and the 'shout' is simply a joyful gospel kind of song.

When the Africville relocatees were questioned about the importance of the church in community life, they particularly emphasized two functions; namely, "bearing one another's burden" and "visiting after church." With respect to the former, one respondent observed: "On Sunday morning, we all came together; if someone had a problem we would all listen." Another respondent noted: "You could get up in church and stand and talk. You felt free to do this, but now people have lost their freedom to move. They can't get up in the churches and talk." The church provided a focal point for intense interaction, and the buoyancy fostered by the style of service made the visiting after church especially conducive to a sense of group consciousness.[19] As one respondent put it: "After church was over, that was when people would have a strong community spirit. Their homes would be opened up and people would go from one house to another, visiting and talking with each other." Given the social patterns that constituted church behaviour and the concomitant emotional intensity, the implications for group cohesiveness are obvious. It becomes possible to understand equally well the remarks of a white transient who knew Africville people for most of his life and eventually came to live in Africville for several years prior to the relocation: "Seaview was essentially a coloured church. There was no place for a white man in that church. Of course, anyone was welcome to attend, but only the coloured really belonged."[20]

Church Structure

Throughout the approximately 120 years of Africville's existence, the church elders were in effect the governing body of the community although their authority declined in the years immediately preceding relocation. A detailed examination of the minutes of the Halifax City Council shows that it was church members, usually deacons, who dealt with the white power structure and who petitioned the city for various kinds of services.[21] They were, so to speak, the "official" representatives of Africville. One local black authority on life in black communities in the Halifax area observed: "You could say the church leaders were the community leaders. The people looked to the deacons particularly, the indigenous workers in the church." Most of the religious activities were conducted by the deacons, who were elected by the church members. Respectability and popularity were as important as religious involvement in determining who was elected. One man was not elected deacon because he smoked regularly and occasionally drank heavily. Another was not elected because his religious fervour was deemed excessive and created social embarrassment; reportedly, he was a favourite among the so-called "respectable" people in Africville.

Thus the leaders of the church tended to be regularly employed, relatively puritanical in behaviour, and to have stable families. The strict Baptist code apparently was seriously applied to differentiate between members and non-members and among various status ranks within the membership. The internalization of such expectations is indicated in the following remarks of one church elder. "I was a trustee of the Seaview Church for years. They wanted me to be a deacon, but I refused. You had to be an uprighteous person; I used to be, but my wife died and I got 'nature' — you know — I didn't want to put myself in that responsible a position as a decon."

Membership in the Africville church was never large. The theological position of the Baptist Church made baptism a condition of membership, and only adults (persons at least twelve years of age) were eligible for baptism. One church elder explained, "You have to be old enough to know, before you can become a Christian, belong to God. Don't you think so?"

More important than age was the criterion of having a "vision" whereby one deemed oneself to have been "saved." Most church members who were interviewed about "visions" indicated that they had had their own particular vision while sleeping. It is not surprising, in view of the Bedford Basin location of Africville, that the reported visions usually had a "sea" context. Some Africville residents participated regularly in church activities but failed to experience an "adequate" vision; consequently, they never became members of the church.

The above-mentioned requirements of the Africville church also characterized the other black Baptist churches in the Halifax area. Church membership in the black communities at Hammonds Plains, Lucasville, and North Preston, as well as at the mother church in Halifax proper, was quite small in relation to the respective black Baptist populations.[22] Moreover, in Africville as well as in other communities, there was a pattern of small attendance at regular church services. Ministers serving the Africville church reported that, even prior to 1950, an attendance of thirty at the regular Sunday service would have been considered good.

Although church membership in Africville was restricted, and regular attendance was small, traditionally the church was the fundamental community organization. Not only did church elders represent the community to the external world, but community meetings were held in the church. The first school in Africville was held in the old church, and church-sponsored special activities traditionally brought together both the church-going and the non-church-going members of the community. The baptismal ceremonies held on the shores of the basin attracted most community residents, and entailed much pomp, singing, and the wearing of impressive white robes by candidates. The Sunrise Service held on Easter Sunday was another colourful religious occasion that signalled community festivities and, like the baptismal ceremonies, helped to lessen social and physical isolation. One church member described the Sunrise Service as follows:

> They [church members led by the deacons] went into the church, singing spirituals, around four or five o'clock in the morning when the sun came up, and did not come out until three p.m. When the people came, they would just flop with the spirit. People, including whites, used to come for miles around to the Sunrise Service, sometimes from Truro and New Glasgow and usually from Preston and Hammonds Plains.[23]

Weddings and funerals held in the Africville church were also special occasions which brought the people together and fostered a sense of community.[24]

The church thus traditionally provided ceremonies and festivities which gave Africville a sense of community. It reached beyond the relatively small number of regular church members and adherents, developing a solidarity among most residents. One church elder recalled: "We had revival meetings all the time. Everybody would come to renew their souls. In olden days we used to go from house to house to gain souls, just like all country places." Moreover, the church was supported by the community at large. One deacon, after discussing the pattern of small church attendance, observed that "the people were good to support their church. We never had any trouble making ends meet." Another resident, who did not participate in regular church services, mentioned the widespread practice of making contributions to the church in "the little brown envelopes." He recalled that he had always sent his children to the fund-raising dinners because "that was the thing to do in Africville."[25] Traditionally, too, the church provided the leadership and the structures that effected relationships between the people and outside groups and communities. A survey of Africville households conducted five years before the relocation, in 1959, indicated that personal involvement in organizations was limited almost exclusively to church organizations. The few community services that existed were provided through such church groups as the women's auxiliary, youth groups, and the missionary society, which also structured interaction with the broader society.

Erosion of Leadership and Structure

Starting with the First World War, Halifax underwent a major expansion which resulted in a decline of Africville's rural character and its social and physical isolation. Africville as a community underwent profound change, and the place of the church in the community was altered. By the time residents faced relocation as an imminent actuality, the church had ceased to be the focus of the community and church elders were no longer the effective community leaders. The population increased during this period as Africville came to house some of the people, black and white, suffering from the lack of adequate housing for the poor in Halifax proper. The new migrants had neither kinship ties with Africville families nor did they participate in church affairs. The 1959 survey cited above indicated that,

PLATE 3.1 THE SEAVIEW AFRICAN BAPTIST CHURCH. This church was to some extent a focal point of community activities; its loss was considered a major psychological cost of relocation by many older residents.

in the twenty-seven households where the household head or spouse reported participation in church groups or clubs, either the household head or the spouse was a native of Africville.

As Africville became socially and physically encompassed in Halifax's accelerating urban growth, and as expectations concerning facilities and lifestyle generally began to rise among the younger people in Africville, there appears to have been a concomitant decline in the status of church elders. One thirty-five-year-old Africville resident who was not a participant in church activities observed:

> The Baptist Church began to die out in the last generation because the young people were not accepted by and did not accept the ways of the older people. There was no compromise. The older people demanded respect due to their age and the younger ones saw no reason to respect them—thought they were old fools.

A complex set of factors on both the societal and local levels appears to account for the change. Very few baptisms took place during the last thirty years of Africville's existence. The practice of seeking visions and the Baptist code of conduct came to seem incongruent with improved education and greater urbanization. Moreover, the functional importance of the church for individuals and for the community as a whole diminished. The presence of the city's refuse dump on the border of the community and the unsavoury implications of Africville's label as a slum led to outside black church groups finding Africville less attractive as a locale for church-related festivities. In the religious exchange network referred to earlier, Africville people apparently visited more often than they were visited. The church's function of providing opportunities for structured interaction with the outside world became less important. This tendency was accelerated by the increasing incorporation of Africville residents into the social life of Halifax proper and the development of Africville as a deviance service centre, a place to go for fun, parties, and bootleg booze.

The loss of status by church members and officials also appears to have been related to an increasing awareness among community residents that the former's power to effect change and to obtain an acceptable lifestyle was very limited. This new and different perspective of the church and the elders was deepened by the decline, both physical and social, of the "close community." The many delegations to Halifax City Hall for fire, police, water, electric, and snow-removal services had yielded little fruit. A local black authority on Africville observed:

> There seemed to be in the community the feeling that nothing could happen anyway, sort of a pessimistic, not cynical, but a lack of confidence and a feeling that nothing is going to happen and, if it does, so what? There is nothing we can do about it. They tried in so many ways to get little improvements. They tried for the ordinary services…and they had failed. The threat of relocation had been over their heads for years. There were always rumours that the land was valuable industrial land, and they would eventually be allowed to stay there only until the powers-that-be wanted to remove them; so by this time, you see, the community had reached a stage where it became a sort of a haven, a refuge for people who couldn't keep their heads above the water in the city, not the stable and solid families that settled the community initially. This brought about a change in the community and in the community spirit.[26]

Added to the discovery of their political vulnerability was a general disparagement of the "respectable elders" because of their poverty and their blackness.[27] Given the lack of regard shown Africville residents by both the larger black community and the whites of Halifax, and given the loosening of the close community, it became difficult for the elders to provide leadership or to retain status within the community. In other words, a climate was being established wherein status and leadership could not effectively augment each other. Moreover, the general poverty of Africville limited the possibility of a ramifying community exchange system.[28]

By the decade preceding the relocation, the 1950s, these patterns had effected such a change in Africville that it appeared to be a black ghetto in the typical American sense. The decline in community significance of the church and the elders was apparent. One transient who moved into Africville several years prior to relocation observed that "there wasn't very many used to go to church, mostly a few older ones because the older ones didn't have any place else to go." One church deacon at Africville noted the decline in the number of church services offered: "Services used to be 10:00 a.m., 3:00 p.m., and 7:00 p.m. a few years ago, but at the end of [Africville], only once each Sunday…youth didn't attend. Most people didn't attend." The service, however, consisting of prayer, singing, sermon, and testimonial, remained essentially unchanged. Deacons held the service, while the sisters sang. There were no female deacons, but every Tuesday evening there was a sisters' meeting, a prayer meeting held by women.

By the time of relocation the church had become an inadequate base for community action, and the church elders were not accepted leaders. To a large extent, the "church people" became a small clique, unable either to perpetuate itself as only a few of the approximately forty baptized Africville residents were under forty years of age, or to exercise much direct influence on the rest of the community. One deacon, pointing out that he had not had much to do with others at the time of relocation, observed: "I am a deacon and I don't visit people that much. You see, I don't approve of drinking and the other people drink. I must observe a high standard of virtue in my life; therefore, I keep pretty much to myself." Discussing community organization at the time of relocation, another resident noted that "the people who belonged to the church were a big-feeling bunch of hypocrites who stuck pretty much together." One non-church-going resident described as follows the relationship between his circle of friends and the church group:

> Yes, there was a bit of a gap. They were a little bit uppity about us, and frowned on us when we did certain things. But there was no proselytizing, much less conflict. The only thing was the time the church people had the community hall [dance hall] demolished because of the behaviour of the young people. I guess it wouldn't have mattered so much, if it hadn't been right next to the church.

For the most part, the relationship between those who went to church regularly and those who did not attend at all became one of tolerance and avoidance. This polarization with respect to church participation had, however, only developed in the years preceding relocation. Since the bulk of the Africville population was related by kinship ties to the church clique, there was little manifest derision or conflict. There was, however, open strain between the church group and the group of people who had migrated to Africville, especially during the thirties and after the Second World War, and who were mainly involved in the deviance service centre aspect of Africville. The invective exchanged between these two groups, and the bandying of terms such as "hypocrite" and "bad people," arose as much from the fact that one group had roots in Africville and the other did not as from differences in belief and practice concerning morals. Despite the tensions, by the time of relocation the church-going residents had come to accept this "other Africville" and their own limited sphere of influence. This accommodation is illustrated in the following statement from an interview with a church member:

> Somehow Mrs. X got on the subject of whites who came down to Africville. In almost so many words, she said they came for women and alcohol. They were always all over the place, often falling asleep, drunk, on the railway tracks — which caused Mrs. X great worry. Very frequently, strangers arrived at her door, drunk or wandering. She treated them to tea and sober conversation. They got to know her after awhile. As she was walking by, they would call out:
> "Are you going to church, Mrs. X?"
> "Yes, to church."
> "Pray for me."
> "I will, but you have to pray for yourself, too!"

Despite the reduced influence of the church and its members, until and during the relocation they continued to have a preferred status in relation to the "official" societal power structure and to voluntary organizations representative of the "official" morality. It was through them that do-gooders entered the community[29] and that the Sunday school, recreational programs, and the like were established for the "poor Africville residents." Official city communiqués were usually transmitted through the church leaders.[30] But by the time that relocation had begun it was clear to everyone in Africville, churchgoers and non-churchgoers alike, that this "external status" was insufficient to make the broader society adequately responsive to the needs and aspirations of Africville's residents. Similarly, it was apparent to Haligonians seeking booze in Africville, and to politicians seeking votes there,[31] that the church elders no longer constituted the community's governing body.

Since the relocation, the church has become an entity around which considerable "relocation grief" has crystallized. The church was the only formal organization in Africville and, consequently, it represents a concreteness to which people can readily refer when asked about the costs of relocation. Common sense or folk knowledge holds that in relocation programs the people most aggrieved are the elderly.[32] They are said to be the group for whom relocation would most likely constitute a personal crisis. Whatever the validity of this assumption, such a definition of the situation applies to Africville. The elderly have often indicated that what they miss most is the church life in Africville. Others, unable to articulate their reasons for grief, have emphasized the supposed crisis of the elderly; given the relationship between the elderly and the church, and given the concreteness of the church, it follows that the loss of church has come to symbolize the loss of community. The post-relocation survey and the initial interviewing of Africville residents reveal an exaggerated assessment of the focal relevance of the church for the community and of the degree of church attendance. For instance, some thirty percent of the respondents[33] indicated that, while in Africville, they regularly attended church services; this figure is too high and is not congruent with other data. First interviews often brought forth strong positive remarks about the community significance of the church, but further interviewing and increased rapport yielded more reliable statements.

The phenomenon of idealization with respect to the church has been encouraged by the symbolic relevance that the Africville relocation has assumed in the emerging black consciousness in Nova Scotia. Africville is often mentioned as an example of how black people can be uprooted unless strong community-based organizations are developed. Uprooting would not be undesirable if there were nothing intrinsically valuable about the community. Seen as being valuable in this context are Africville's inherent possibilities as a genuine black subculture. The indicators of the latter include Africville's long history and its church life, especially the "soul" that has been attributed to the style of church services. As a symbol, the Seaview African United Baptist Church may be more important now, as a focal point for Africville residents' dissatisfaction with the relocation and as a stimulus in the development of a black consciousness in Nova Scotia, than it was during the years immediately preceding the relocation.

Notes

[1]   The concept of an ethos and its being mirrored in social structure was developed philosophically by the German historicists. In sociology and anthropology the two best-known applications of the concept were made by G. Sumner, *Selected Essays* (New Haven: Yale University Press, 1924), and R. Benedict, *Patterns of Culture* (London: Mentor Books, 1934).

2   For a discussion of this trust fund, see Chapter Six.

3   Interview with James A. Walker, a doctoral candidate at Dalhousie University specializing in black history, August 2, 1969.

4   The hostility with which blacks were greeted by both Protestants and Catholics in Guysborough County is described in Clairmont, et al., op. cit.

5   For a discussion of this race riot, as a consequence of which white settlers obtained lands on which blacks had settled, see Greaves, op. cit.

6   Pearleen Oliver, *A Brief History of the Coloured Baptists of Nova Scotia, 1782-1953* (Halifax, N.S.: 1953), p. 21. Burton became a Baptist during a year's stay in the United States. When he returned to Nova Scotia in 1794, he won converts among dissenters from St. Paul's Anglican congregation, Halifax.

7   Several legends have developed around Richard Preston. Burton trained Preston as a successor and sent him to England for study and ordination in 1831-32.

8   The association faced a brief crisis after the death of Preston in 1861. Preston had designated as his successor James Thomas, a white Welsh immigrant married to a black woman at Preston. Thomas became moderator of the association and pastor of the mother church in Halifax, as well as minister for neighbouring member congregations such as the Africville congregation. As a consequence of Thomas' leadership, a schism developed and a number of congregations withdrew from the association.

9   It would be interesting to determine the source of the opposition. It may be that the opposition was strongest among the black leaders whose interests would be threatened. Alternatively, it might also have stemmed from the grass roots and have signified the need and desire to maintain cultural autonomy — of which the African Baptist Association was the only institutionalized expression and safeguard.

10   See W. P. Oliver, *The Advancement of Negroes in Nova Scotia* (Halifax, Nova Scotia: Nova Scotia Department of Education, 1949). Oliver also notes that "eighty per cent of the teachers who have taken advantage of Normal School training were children of ministers of the African Baptist churches." (p. 9) It is apparent that the link between school and church in the black community was substantial.

11   Pearleen Oliver, op. cit., p. 34.

12   Ibid., p. 26.

13   Campbell Road itself produced an ordained minister, the Reverend E. Dixon (1848-1908). After 1886, Dixon gave most of his time to the larger congregation at Hammonds Plains and Preston and drove his horse and wagon around the district as a travelling preacher.

14 MacKerrow, op. cit., p. 65. In 1895, the church at Africville reported twenty-one adult baptized members.

15 Ibid., p. 33.

16 *Minutes of the Halifax City Council*, April 27, 1916.

17 Interview, August 1969. The title Seaview African United Baptist Church, applied until the 1940s; subsequently, the title was Seaview United Baptist Church.

18 Brookbank, op. cit. p. 92.

19 The relationship among ritual, intense emotional experience, social interaction, and group consciousness and solidarity was analysed brilliantly by E. Durkheim in *The Elementary Forms of the Religious Life* (Galt, Ontario: Collier Books, Collier-Macmillan, 1961).

20 Interview, July 1969. An Africville relocatee to whom this chapter was shown took exception to this comment of the white transient. The black relocatee noted: "This is not wholly true. Some years ago—in the thirties—Dr. Fader [white] and his group of white people were regular visitors and participants in Africville church activities and were totally welcomed in the community. The white person who lived in Africville and made this remark had to be a 'sinner,' a person of no Christian character. To be considered a 'sinner' in Africville meant ostracism and rejection by the Christian community." The relocatee has missed the point; the point is not that whites were unwelcome, but that the church was an embodiment of the community.

21 See petitions for wells (1909), police protection (1919), and sewerage, in *Minutes of the Halifax City Council*. Numerous delegations of Africville people, mostly male and female church members, visited city hall during the past hundred years.

22 See, for example, Brookbank, op. cit.

23 Interview, September 1969. The last Sunrise Service in Africville was held in 1966. Preston and Hammonds Plains are black communities approximately ten to fifteen miles from Africville. Truro and New Glasgow, each more than sixty miles from Africville, contain large black populations.

24 There are no graves in Africville. The dead were buried in cemeteries outside the community.

25 Interview, September 1969. In a later chapter, we shall discuss the pattern of grief expressed over the loss of the church. Grief was expressed by many relocatees who had not participated regularly in church services, but felt that the church had, nonetheless, been their church.

26 Tape-recorded interview, December, 1969. The authority quoted spent approximately twenty-five years endeavouring to develop community

organizations among the Africville residents, as well as among other black communities in the area.

27   See discussion of this theme in Chapter 2. Rainwater's remarks, made with reference to the American experience, are applicable to Africville in the period that we are discussing: "To those living in the heart of a ghetto, black comes to mean not just 'stay back,' but also membership in a community of persons who think poorly of each other, who attack and manipulate each other, who give each other small comfort in a desperate world." Lee Rainwater, "Crucible of Identity: The Negro Lower-Class Family," *Daedalus* 95, No. 1 (1966): 205.

28   Clark has suggested that three factors limit the range and complexity of exchange systems. One of these factors is the absolute quantity of resources present in the system. He remarks that the poor "cannot become involved because they do not have the necessary quantity of resources either to maintain themselves over a certain minimal period of time before they are reimbursed or to support the infrastructure devoted to the mechanics of organizing and coordinating exchange." Terry N. Clark, *Community Structure and Decision-Making: Comparative Analyses* (San Francisco: Chandler, 1968), p. 53.

29   For example, whites directed a summer Bible school in Africville in the years preceding relocation. See Alexa Shaw, "Two-Week Project A Big Success at Africville Church," *The Mail-Star*, Halifax, N.S., July 18, 1963.

30   See, for instance, Chapter Five, which deals with the decision to relocate Africville.

31   Politicians selected as captains for their respective parties in Africville; people who could deliver the vote. The captains in the years preceding relocation were not usually regular church attendants. In the last provincial election prior to Africville's relocation, the captains were comparatively young and fairly recent arrivals in Africville.

32   See, for example, W. F. Smith, *Preparing the Elderly for Relocation* (Philadelphia: University of Pennsylvania, 1966).

33   Respondents included every Africville resident who was given any kind of relocation compensation. Thirty percent indicated that they were regular church participants, fifty percent indicated that they occasionally attended services, and fifteen percent said that they rarely participated.

C H A P T E R   4

Africville as a Social Problem

It was lovely, lovely. They talk about Peggy's Cove but I am going to tell you, it was the most beautiful sight you would want to see — Africville. You get on the hill, and look over the Bedford Basin in the fall of the year, say from October to around December, and that was a sight to see, especially at twilight when the sun is sinking over the hills at Bedford.... And another thing, during the war...when the convoys were in the basin, there was another beautiful sight. It was one of the most beautiful spots I've been in, in Nova Scotia. *And the city didn't develop it.* Africville should have been developed years ago when labour was cheap. Africville would have been a pretty sight. *Why didn't they do it? There is only one meaning I can put to it. Because black people was living out there.* (Italics added).
    —Tape-recorded interview with an Africville relocatee,
October 1969.

In the last quarter of the nineteenth century, Africville was referred to as a "community of intelligent young people, much is expected of them."[1] In 1957 a field representative of a national human rights group visited Nova Scotia's black communities: she referred to Africville as "the worst and most degenerate area I have ever seen." This chapter attempts to explain how such a dramatic change, discounting some overstatement in the 1957 characterization, took place with the result that Africville became "a social problem" and, consequently, "ripe for relocation." Basically, two processes account for the peculiar development of encroachment by the various levels of government and by private economic interests which aborted Africville's possibilities as a potentially fine residential area. Railways, city disposal yards, and fertilizer plants were situated in and around the Africville community. One relocatee, reacting angrily to the mistaken but widely held idea that Africville residents were mostly squatters, pointed to these developments and observed: "They said the people in Africville encroached on the government, but I would say the government encroached on the people."

The other important process was an internal one that ate away at Africville's potential from the inside. Winks, while perhaps misleading concerning the origin of the community, aptly refers to this process:

> From the 1870s to the 1930s the condition of the Negro Canadian declined. Nova Scotia Negroes in particular fell into a chronic state of depression, and they were soon trapped in the classic pattern of a vicious cycle: badly educated and often physically ill, they were unable to find steady employment and, unable to find employment, they were in no position to rid themselves of ignorance or disease. Slums developed around Halifax, first in the harbour-hugging self-segregated community of Africville and later in the middle of the city.[2]

The classic cycle to which Winks refers led to a continuing deterioration of the community, a development most apparent in the period after the First World War but rooted in earlier socio-economic conditions and opportunities.[3] Manifestations of this decline of Africville include its reputation in later years as a deviance service centre, its becoming a haven for underachievers as a consequence of migration patterns, both immigration and emigration, and its segmentation into cliques and different lifestyles.

These two processes, external and internal, were not, of course, unrelated. To a significant degree they underline the kind of negative exchange which, from the point of view of Africville residents, characterized their relationship with the broader society. City council did little that was positive for Africville and, on the whole, was unresponsive to petitions and requests from its residents. Africville residents came to recognize their marginality which was shaped by the negative exchange system vis à vis the outside world and reinforced by the social processes through which they "made out" economically and educationally. Given this marginality and the functional autonomy (analysed in Chapter Three), they adjusted their coping behaviour, and reciprocated by not following certain city rules and directions.

Early Beginnings

The Africville settlers, seeking to create a new life away from the hardships and privations of the refugee settlements in Hammonds Plains and Preston, quickly established themselves on Bedford Basin. They began by clearing lots and building shelters, at least some of which were log shacks. The 1851 census shows that several Africville settlers had improved acreage and acquired a few farm animals. The approximately eighty residents were concurrently laying the basis for a church and school in the community. A Baptist congregation was formed in 1849 and, although few adults could both read and write, residents' recognition of the value of education was evident in a petition that they addressed to the legislative assembly in 1860, requesting funds to obtain the services of a schoolmaster.

The Africville petitioners of 1860 apparently did not receive any governmental assistance for their school as it was not until 1883 that the Halifax Board of School Commissioners granted school privileges to Africville. Despite this, as early as 1872 a black resident from Hammonds Plains who had married into the Africville community had undertaken the instruction of Africville children, first in the old church building and later in a private residence.

In the last quarter of the nineteenth century, residents opened two small penny stores. In later years, a post office and a social club were added to the community's organizations. Social life during the first fifty years revolved around the church. Very old relocatees reminisced happily about picnics and ceremonies associated with the church. They related stories of their parents riding on horseback through the "woods" around Africville; they talked of skating on Bedford Basin and of riding the trains into the North Street Station. In general, the older relocatees referred to these early years as good years; they recalled the greater independence of residents and the greater well-being of the community, in contrast to their experience in the later pre-relocation period. One woman, who had been a teenager in the last quarter of the nineteenth century, observed, "I didn't see no hard life all the time I was comin' up." Another respondent, when pointing out how clean and solid the older Africville homes used to be, emphasized that "they [the Africville settlers] never had no help from the city to keep it clean neither." This latter comment alluded to the governmental and industrial build-up in the area which ruined Africville as a prime residential site.

Plate 4.1 THE VIEW FROM AFRICVILLE. "...I never felt about any other place as I did about Africville. If you know art, or could feel anything about art, and could see the sunset over the basin on a summer evening—it would strike you right in the heart." (Interview with an elderly relocatee, July 30, 1969)

Encroachment

Situated on the basin and along Campbell Road, a secondary and infrequently used route connecting Halifax and the eastern part of Halifax County, Africville in 1850 was in an idyllic rural setting. The scene was soon shattered by the roaring of trains and the buzzing of industries. The population of Halifax grew from 21,000 in 1851 to 47,000 in 1911. In the late nineteenth century, the expanding Africville community was being confronted by an industrial complex that gravitated towards Bedford Basin and reduced Africville's potential as a superior residential area. The forward thrust of this industrial development consisted of a large oil plant/storage complex,[4] a bone-mill plant manufacturing fertilizer[5] on the shoreline several hundred yards to the west of the settlement, a cotton factory and a rolling mill/nail factory back on the hill overlooking Africville,[6] and, along the eastern shoreline, a slaughterhouse and a port facility handling coal. Encircling these operations in turn were a tar factory, a shoe plant where leather was tanned, another slaughterhouse, several stone-crushing industries, and a foundry. Most of this economic activity developed in the area surrounding Africville long after the black refugees had settled along Campbell Road.

Intermixed with the industries and businesses encircling the community was a considerable amount of vacant land owned primarily by the city and the railroads. Trains passing through Africville on several tracks enjoyed a significant increase in passenger and freight traffic in the late nineteenth century.[7] City service facilities were also prominent in the area; in 1853 Rockhead Prison was established approximately one hundred yards away on the hill above Africville, and the "night-soil" disposal pits for the city were located on the eastern edge of the settlement in 1858. In the 1870s the city's infectious diseases hospital was built on the hill and about one and one-half miles beyond it was the northernmost reach of the sprawling, open, city dump. In 1905 a trachoma hospital was built to the west of the prison. The noise of trains and industry, the smell of the city's disposal pits, irritated the residents, signalled the future development of the area, and set in motion the cycle of deterioration that led to Africville's being labelled as a slum.

The relative isolation of Africville from the rest of the city was reduced with the development of railway systems in Nova Scotia[8] around the middle of the nineteenth century. In 1853 the Nova Scotia Railway Company was incorporated,[9] and within two years the Bedford Basin track, which ran parallel to Campbell Road and passed through Africville, was constructed.

This construction required the acquisition of some Africville land and the removal of some buildings; it resulted in the first of a series of relocations to which the blacks were subjected. This first experience of Africville residents with forced relocation was not pleasant; in 1855 the Board of Railway Commissioners reported:

> Difficulties have arisen during the past year, in adjusting the damages due to parties whose land has been taken by the Commissioners. None of the parties have been paid...cases of hardship have already occurred.[10]

Some Africville claimants did not receive compensation until five years later and then only after petitioning the legislative assembly.[11] By 1912 two additional railway tracks passed through Africville: one, to freight goods to and from the cotton factory located above Africville; the other, to combine existing rail lines into a consolidated system.[12] For the latter, acquisition of Africville land and the removal of buildings were once again required.[13] At least five Africville properties were expropriated and the residents compensated.

Subsequent to 1912 a new railway line was built bordering the western side of the Halifax peninsula, and the railway tracks through Africville declined in importance as passenger lines. Even with this decline in importance, however, the Africville tracks were still valuable for potential industrial development. At the outset of the Second World War, as Halifax was a major wartime port, Canadian National Railways (originally the Intercolonial Railway) constructed the Basin Yard, which once more necessitated moving a number of Africville residents.[14]

There is little doubt that the presence of railway tracks in close proximity to waterfront property increased the importance of the Africville land as an industrial site. Certainly the railway development through and around Africville affected the community's aesthetic image. The more obvious consequences — noise from passing trains, layers of soot before the change to diesel engines in the 1950s, and the inconvenience and danger of traversing railway tracks in order to visit a neighbour or to attend school — do not require special comment, although it may be noted that at least two Africville residents were killed by trains passing through the community.

By the turn of the twentieth century, the city of Halifax acquired property to the south, east, and west of the black community, and was in

Plate 4.2 ALMOST LIKE A RURAL COMMUNITY. Africville, though within the boundaries of the city of Halifax, had many rural features. The house, the goat, and the isolation paint a rural image. The picture was taken fifty years ago (1948).

a favourable position to bargain with industries seeking land. Minutes of the Halifax City Council show that, in addition to using the area around Africville as a location for city facilities not tolerated in other neighbourhoods, the eventual industrial use of the Africville land was a matter of long-standing implicit intent. This policy is clearly illustrated by the following reply the city gave to a company interested in expanding its operation in the area in 1915:

> The Africville portion of Campbell Road will always be an industrial district and it is desirable that industrial operations should be assisted in any way that is not prejudicial to the interests of the public; in fact, we may be obliged in the future to consider the interest of the industry first.[15]

Despite considerable negotiation, no major industrial development forced the relocation of Africville people in war years. This was not due to lack of effort by city officials, nor to special concern for Africville residents; throughout the negotiations there is no mention in the minutes of city council concerning what might have happened to Africville residents had the land they occupied been expropriated, nor what their wishes may have been.

An explosion in Halifax Harbour, in December 1917, almost obliterated the north end of the city, and created an occasion for rebuilding much of the area around Africville. But the fundamental pattern of industrial and governmental encroachment referred to earlier continued unabated. Many small industries and businesses collapsed in the years following the First World War as Nova Scotia became a satellite of "metropolitan" economic interests based in central Canada and the United States. The tar factory, the shoe factory, the oil plant complex, the nail factory/rolling mill, and several slaughterhouses disappeared from the Africville neighbourhood. The bone-mill and the O'Leary Coal Company, which flanked the Africville shoreline on the west and the east respectively and provided much of the occasional wage labour of its residents, were also phased out between the wars. But other industries took their place; prior to the relocation a co-operative abattoir was established on the site of the old bone-mill and, in the 1930s, a Canadian Industries Limited plant was constructed near the O'Leary Coal Company. Another stone-crushing plant opened, in 1931, southeast of Africville. A huge tower of the Nova Scotia Light and Power Company became subsequently a background feature of the easternmost Africville homes. Small industries and businesses, warehouses, and oil tanks were scattered throughout the surrounding area.

After the "happy days" of the First World War, Halifax, and Nova Scotia generally, experienced decline in an economic depression that began in the 1920s. The Second World War, like the First World War, was a major population and economic stimulant. By the end of the war, Africville had passed from being a neighbourhood on the outskirts of the city, and suburbia itself had shifted beyond the peninsula and outside the city limits. By 1956, the population of Halifax had reached 93,000, a more than fourfold increase since 1856, but the city boundaries remained the same. The metropolitan area was also growing rapidly; between 1945 and 1956 metropolitan Halifax gained an additional 60,000 people. It was in the context of increased population and economic growth that an ever-present threat to Africville was finally translated into action.

The city and other levels of government continued to be prominent in the Africville area in the period after the First World War. Additional railway tracks were laid through the community, and on the far western side of the Africville shoreline the Nova Scotia Department of Highways expanded its work plant and supply depot in the direction of Africville. The city-owned hospital[16] and prison facilities on the hill overlooking the community remained operational. Between the wars the night soil disposal grounds and the infectious diseases hospital were phased out but in the early fifties the city moved its large open dump into Africville, a mere 350 feet from the front door of the westernmost group of houses; two years later, the city opened an incinerator some fifty yards beyond the south boundary of Africville.

The city still possessed for economic development a large amount of vacant land in the Africville area, but despite the development indicated above, the area did not emerge as a major industrial site. This fact had more to do with the nature of the Nova Scotian economy and its metropolitan-satellite relationship to central Canada and the United States than to the policies and wishes of the city leaders. City council records show that there was considerable talk about attracting new industries. However, the principal push for economic development was coming from the waterfront side of the settlement. Port facilities in the south end of Halifax were being used to capacity, and it was becoming apparent to city council that Halifax's economic growth would spring more from its harbour facilities than from industry.

Plate 4.3. TRAINS AND AFRICVILLE. Trains rolled through the centre of Africville, cutting the community in half and causing numerous problems; layers of soot, noise, and the inconvenience and danger of crossing the track to visit a neighbour or attend school. In an interview completed in 1969 one elderly relocatee reported that at least two adults had been killed by locomotives in Africville.

In 1945 a civic planning commission submitted to city council a plan calling for the removal of the Africville settlement. Again no reference was made to the wishes of the Africville people and, again, nothing happened to the proposal, but in 1947 Halifax was rezoned and council approved the designation of Africville as industrial land.

That same year a major fire occurred in Africville and seven homes were destroyed. This crisis resurrected the question of extending water and sewerage services to the black settlement. The issue became enmeshed with the larger question of relocation, and still another alderman pointed out that the "property could be cleared in case some industry might want to go there."[17] This time Africville residents were consulted. They expressed a strong desire to remain in the area and to work with the city in developing it as a residential area. City council authorized the borrowing of funds to provide water and sewerage service, but the services were never installed.

As the 1950s unfolded, discussions in city council concerning the industrial potential of the Africville site increased in quantity; qualitatively an observer could detect a new sense of imminent relocation. The city's placement of an open dump and incinerator in the Africville area was clear evidence of its unwillingness to see the site as residential. A former mayor of Halifax during the 1950s reported that the "official" thinking on Africville during the period preceding relocation was that "unless there were very strong, clear advantages to the community as a whole by going on the side, shall we say, of the industrial developers, you would be very cautious about removing these people unless they themselves wanted to go." Since most of the industrial and port plans advanced in the pre-relocation period were vague and long-term, and since Africville residents wanted improvements but were on the whole opposed to relocation, concrete discussion of relocation did not emerge until 1961 despite a plethora of earlier plans.

Making Out Economically

The work activity of Africville residents over the past 125 years has reflected two general factors: the ecological context of the community, and black-white social relations. The latter channelled blacks into specific occupations such as labourers, domestics, and porters; the former provided the context for their "making out," in that they found employment in the area immediately surrounding their settlement, which they supplemented through gardening, fishing in the basin, and salvaging from the nearby dump.

Between the founding of the community and First World War, most Africville male adults were listed on official documents of the period, such as the census rolls and deeds, as either yeomen or labourers.[18] There were several craftsmen — mainly coopers and masons, both of which were occupational specializations of blacks in Halifax County — and several small contractors and truckmen. The latter occupation was presumably the horse-and-wagon forerunner of autotrucking. The truckmen carted earth, lumber, baggage, and, in particular, night-soil disposal. An elderly relocatee who did such "truck work" explained:

> A lot of Halifax didn't have no sewers; they used out-door water-closets before they had water-closets in the houses. The men who had horses and carts went during the night to clean them. The carts were made of a special kind of wood, you know. The rule was that it could only be done after midnight, when everybody was off the streets. You couldn't haul along North Street until after midnight. They dumped it in pits [near Africville] at the rockhead.

Given the rocky, non-arable land at Africville, it is not surprising that few residents engaged in farming. In the 1871 census only one very elderly man gave his occupation as farmer. Since several Africville men were engaged in carting operations, there were a few horses and barn-like structures in the settlement. During this period cows, geese, chickens, and pigs, while not plentiful, were part of Africville's ruralism. The only market production consisted of several modest-scale piggeries, another specialization of blacks in Halifax County, although many people in Africville attempted to grow garden produce for home consumption. Subsequent to the First World War, the truckmen became obsolete, virtually all farm animals disappeared from Africville, and the combination of land scarcity, rocky soil, and hopelessness brought gardening attempts to an end.

Located on Bedford Basin, Africville residents were well situated for fishing and port-related employment. Elderly relocatees were unanimous in referring to the abundance of fish in the basin prior to the First World War. No one in the history of the community ever listed his occupation as fisherman nor was fish marketed, but occasional fishing was part of the traditional Africville lifestyle. Over the years, a number of Africville men worked on ships, mostly on an intermittent basis. This line of employment, although never engaging a large number of Africville men, continued beyond the Second World War.

Africville residents were able to obtain employment in several of the industrial and governmental operations functioning in their neighbourhood. Most of the work available to them was of the unskilled labour type, paying low wages. One elderly relocatee, asked about jobs at the various plants in the area consistently replied, "Oh yes, Africville men worked there, but only as ordinary labourers, not tradesmen."

In line with black-white social relationships and expectations, a significant number of Africville people worked as domestics, cleaners, and porters. The 1871 census of Halifax listed an "African" female work force of approximately seventy-five, all but a handful being employed as servants and washerwomen. Government institutions in the Africville area and throughout the city hired Africville women to clean and to cook; and in the nearby industries and businesses it was not uncommon to find blacks involved only in the cleaning of the buildings. Employment as railway porters began well before the First World War, but became more numerous in later years; through this work Africville blacks discovered the Canadian cities to which they began to migrate in significant numbers after the First World War.

In the years following the First World War and up to the time of relocation, socio-economic conditions in Africville worsened. Economically the gap between its residents and other Haligonians widened. Unemployment and underemployment became part of the Africville lifestyle. The skilled trades of cooper, mason, butcher, and shoemaker, although never widespread, disappeared entirely. The entrepreneurial small contractors also vanished. The bone-mill, an economic mainstay of the community into the Depression, with its seasonal low-paying work (sewing and carrying fertilizer bags from December to May) was subsequently phased out. For Africville women, work outside the community became exclusively domestic/cleaning labour; for the men, intermittent work on the coal and salt boats was the basic work activity and the job of porter, when full-time and regular, marked the upper limits of occupational achievement. These three chief employment lines had been established prior to the First World War, but subsequently they became more extensive. A few men found employment at the Canadian Industries Limited plant which opened a few hundred yards from Africville in the late 1930s and, after the Second World War, a few men obtained regular, average-paying jobs at the government-operated dockyards. Such limited employment opportunities did not obscure the underlying fact that as society became more industrialized, the occupational sector more skilled, and white-collar and second- and third-generation Canadians elsewhere occupationally more mobile, the Africville workforce became increasingly typified, to use a Marxian concept, as "lumpenproletariat."

The increasingly poor economic conditions of Africville residents after the First World War relate to more than employment opportunities. The possibilities of "making out" by supplementing wage work with limited farming, garden produce, and fishing also lessened. A city ordinance in 1915 forbade the keeping of swine within city limits; thus while the city continued to pour its night-soil on Africville's doorstep, the residents had to forgo the piggeries of their ancestors. The chickens, geese, and other fowl also disappeared, and for a variety of reasons, garden produce could not be grown. The pollution of Bedford Basin reduced the quality, quantity, and variety of available fish and made fishing for food less productive as the years went by, although some persons continued to fish as late as the relocation. "Making out" to supplement wage work focussed on collecting, and occasionally pilfering[19] the spillage of trains loaded with coal and other materials and on foraging from the nearby city dump.

In 1959 the Institute of Public Affairs, Dalhousie University, conducted a survey of socio-economic conditions among blacks in Halifax.[20] Data from this survey, recalculated and revised, point out clearly that underemployment and low earnings characterized the work world of Africville residents in the immediate pre-relocation period. Table 4.1 indicates that only about a third of Africville's labour force had regular work (that is, a scheduled work life); less than a third had full-time work. Except for the postmistress and the keepers of the two small stores, all the women who reported significant work during the year preceding the survey had worked as domestics in Halifax. As shown in Table 4.2, employment was more diverse among the male labour force. Most men, employed as stevedores or labourers, worked well under fifty weeks a year even when they were regularly employed.

A handful of males were employed regularly as cleaners and a similar number had secure, semi-skilled dockyard jobs; people in this latter activity were referred to as "civil servants" by many of the other residents. A few males were tradesmen — all mechanics — and two whites living temporarily in the community were members of the armed forces.

Table 4.1
Africville Workforce 1958*

	Male		Female†	
	No.	%	No.	%
Regular Work	29	35	15	40
Irregular Work	24	29	10	26
Unemployed	20	24	10	26
No Data††	9	12	3	8
TOTAL	82	100	38	100

*   Data from 1959 survey by the Institute of Public Affairs, Dalhousie University.
†   Data refer to women defining themselves as being in the labour force.
† † Additional information suggests that the persons for whom there are no data would be
     distributed evenly among the other categories.

Table 4.2
Occupational Distribution of Employed
Africville Residents 1958*

	Regular Work		Irregular Work	
	Male	Female	Male	Female
Porter	4	–	5	–
Domestic/Cleaner	6	12	–	10
Stevedore/Labourer	8	–	17	–
Clerical	–	3	–	–
Tradesman	3	–	2	–
Dockyards	6	–	–	–
Armed Forces	2	–	–	–

*   Data as in Table 4.1. This table excludes the unemployed and the "no data" group.

The considerable dependence on stevedoring and general labouring meant that most of the available occupational opportunities revolved around casual employment. The report of the Institute of Public Affairs in 1962 noted that "many jobs relating to stevedoring and cartage during Halifax's winter shipping season may provide some work during a week and yet not a full week's work." For example, one Africville man reported in 1959 that while he received $1.65 an hour from working the coal boats, he usually handled one boat per week, a twelve-hour job. Much of this casual labour was seasonal; the coal, salt, and grain boats had to be worked when the St. Lawrence River was frozen. While at least ten Africville males were union members, even this group did not obtain steady seasonal employment; Africville males were not on the top of the list when work became available. A few Africville males charged discrimination concerning union membership. The other factor which contributed to the casualness of this line of work was the pattern (not restricted to Africville men) of working a few days, then drawing one's pay and "living it up."

Africville residents had a reputation for shrewd salvaging off the dump; for them, this was really a subsistence, survival activity. Only two persons in 1959 had access to a small truck for carting junk obtained from the dump; others had to collect materials, pile it in one spot, and then rent a truck to pick up their collection and take it to the junkyards. The economic significance of the dump was much exaggerated both by some residents and some city officials. It provided a convenient, even sanguine, popular explanation of how Africville residents "made out," given their considerable unemployment and underemployment.

Table 4.3 indicates that over forty percent of the workforce earned less than $1000 in 1958. The severity of poverty in Africville is brought into sharp relief when we compare Africville data with the larger Halifax situation. Approximately seven percent of males and thirteen percent of females in the 1951 Halifax labour force reported an earned income in 1950 of less than $1000; nearly a decade later, thirty-two percent of males and sixty percent of females in Africville's labour force were earning less than $1000 a year. One Africville male who had a macabre sense of humour noted, "When I filed my income tax report for $125, they [tax officials] were amazed. The large households and boarders that some Africville residents took in were, at least from one point of view, a way of adjusting to this situation. Nevertheless, about one-third of the households (Table 4.4) reported a total earned income in 1958 of less than $1000; in half the sixteen households where the total earned income was $3000 or more there were multiple wage earners.

In addition to earned income, transfer payments were crucial to the survival of Africville residents. In 1959 some fifteen persons lived on pensions, and several households depended to a considerable extent on the meagre family allowance payments. Unemployment insurance was helpful, but a major problem was to continue in employment long enough to establish eligibility. Even so, surprisingly few Africville residents received welfare assistance.[21] Economic prospects for Africville youth were not

Table 4.3
Earned Income, Africville Workforce, 1958*

	Male		Female†	
	No.	%	No.	%
Under $1,000	26	32	23	61
$1,000–$1,999	16	20	8	21
$2,000–$2,999	21	26	–	–
$3,000–$3,999	9	10	–	–
$4,000 and over	1	1	–	–
No Data	9	10	7†	18
TOTAL	82	99	38	100

* Data as in Table 4.1.
† Four of the seven were unemployed and likely to have earned less than $1,000 in 1958.

Table 4.4
Earned Income, Africville Households, 1958*

	No.	%
Under $1,000	27	34
$1,000–$1,999	14	18
$2,000–$2,999	14	18
$3,000–$3,999	10	12
$4,000 and over	6	8
No Data	9†	10
TOTAL	80	100

* Data as in Table 4.1.
† Auxiliary information indicates that the nine cases would be distributed evenly among the income groupings.

promising as indicated by the fact that half the unemployed in Africville in 1959 were in the fifteen to twenty-nine age category, and few of the employed worked a full fifty weeks. One older resident emphasized this problem, observing that, "I know there are some here who are no good and they make it bad for the rest, but there are several around who are fine young men who want work."

Despite such a depressing employment and income situation in Africville, the 1959 survey indicated that most respondents were optimistic about the future for the children and reported the belief that things would be easier for new additions to the labour force. This belief may have reflected an underlying sentiment that things could hardly get worse. Several respondents pointed to a decline in racial discrimination as a major factor in their optimism; one male observed that "everything has changed," and a female noted that "you see coloured girls working downtown…if we'd only had that break." The majority of respondents did not refer to discrimination but, rather, they emphasized educational improvements as the reason for their optimism concerning the future.

Making Out Educationally

It was noted above that early Africville residents, even without significant government assistance until 1883 made an effort to provide their children with educational opportunity. Subsequent to 1883 Africville had its own one-room schoolhouse and outside teachers of varying degrees of training and ability. The Africville school was almost entirely segregated and, like the pupils, the teachers over the years were predominantly black although several whites taught at the Africville school for short periods. Until 1933 none of the teachers had obtained formal teacher training, although the schoolmaster during the period 1902-33 was considered to have been "dedicated to the education of his people."[22] After 1933 the quality of teaching would appear to have been average, if one judges by the rank of licences held by teachers and their formal training.[23]

Inadequate data make it difficult to assess the segregated Africville school in the early years. Discipline was considered a problem by several teachers[24] and attendance was generally much less than the enrolment; until 1920 the average attendance never exceeded two-thirds of the enrolment, and not until 1945-50 did the average attendance rise to approximately four-fifths. In the pre-First World War period several Africville children went beyond the elementary level and attended the nearby Richmond School. According to some relocatees, such children received a less than cordial welcome from the white pupils and Africville children stopped attempting to attend the school.

Judging by the educational attainment of the older Africville residents at the time of relocation, it would appear that the quality of education in subsequent years was poor and that Africville, relative to other parts of the city, declined educationally. It appears from migration data that the slightly better-educated children would have left the community upon, or shortly after, leaving school. Virtually all of the generation that graduated from Africville to other schools in the 1920s did not remain in Africville. A number of parents during these years migrated to places such as Montreal and Toronto, partly to see that their children received better educational and occupational opportunities.

Recalculated and revised data from the 1959 survey by the Institute of Public Affairs reveal that males and females who were out of school had similar educational attainment. For both categories, slightly more than forty percent obtained Grade 6 or less. Only four males and one female had reached Grade 10.[25] Perhaps what is more significant is evidence that out-of-school youth living at home had not obtained an education appreciably better than that of their parents. None of the former obtained more than a Grade 9 schooling and virtually all reached only Grade 7 or 8; fully sixty percent reached Grade 7 or less. This pattern of stagnation and relative decline in contrast with developments in the broader society was common among blacks throughout Nova Scotia.[26]

The situation in 1959 for those Africville children still in school did not appear much more promising than that for their parents and older siblings. After 1953 Africville schoolchildren were transported by bus to schools outside the community. Due to geographical factors the children attended schools in more prosperous working and lower-middle-class neighbourhoods. Given their poor educational background, the Africville pupils were obviously at a relative disadvantage. The data revealed that over sixty percent of the Africville children were behind in educational achievement; that is, they were older than they should have been for the grade level that they were in.[27] Commenting on this situation, a former Africville resident observed in 1969 that, when bused to outside schools, many Africville children never entered a normal educational situation; they were moved into auxiliary classes set up for slow learners and the children who went into auxiliary never graduated from these classes; "today there are many Africville young adults walking the streets, the end result of this system."

While the out-of-school population in 1959 did not have significant educational achievement and while the prospects for the children still in school were dim, most respondents were optimistic about the future for their children. The authors of the institute report did not share this optimism. They concluded their analysis of the 1959 educational data by observing that "the probability of Negro receptitvity to increased education is very slim."

While the institute report contended, reasonably under the circumstances, that education was not the answer to "Africville problems," respondents did not take this position. Being relatively powerless, lacking in resources, and often politically unaware as a result of historical neglect and deprivation, what solution other than education could they suggest? Education had to be the key to improvement — it was part of society's official morality to emphasize education; it was something that they, themselves, might perhaps be able to do something about, even if it were no more than telling children to "get it." Respondents did not think that their children were inherently inadequate and they knew facilities were available; small wonder that they experienced frustration and confusion. They still clung stubbornly to education as the key to a better life, but it was a hope, not a fact.

Relationship with the City

Africville's residents observed that, as long as they could remember, the city had been threatening to relocate their community. The cloud of relocation appeared eventually to have sapped the vitality of the community; certainly in later years it deterred people from investing in the construction and upkeep of their homes.

A contemporary American sociologist has defined powerlessness as "the expectancy or probability held by the individual that his own behaviour cannot determine the occurrence of the outcomes, or reinforcements, he seeks."[28] Such powerlessness was prevalent among Africville residents in the immediate pre-relocation period. One very old but still sprightly Africville relocatee conveyed this feeling in her remark that:

> We had our land. We paid our taxes. And Jee-zus Kuh-rist, they got bothering us, and they finally got the place. Well, you come into this world with nothing and you go out with nothing…. We never had no peace anyway, so maybe it [the relocation] is all for the best. The city [was] tormenting us. And now they've got it [the Africville land]…. Look, if they hadn't got it, I'd still be there livin' and jumpin'…dammit! Still, what can you do…getting yourself all messed up with insults.

Powerlessness may also be understood as a community characteristic, a mood or atmosphere that hangs over the community and vitiates grassroot organization. In this sense, powerlessness is an emergent historical phenomenon, a function of factors that extend over several generations. Furthermore, the later decline and futility can only be seen in contrast to collective memories of earlier and different times when there was little or no feeling of powerlessness. Retrospective idealizations concerning the community's capacity to deal with city authorities were frequently found among older Africville relocatees, especially those born and raised in Africville. Such observations and reports of past conversations are largely idealizations in the sense that, virtually since the founding of Africville, its residents were, in fact, unable significantly to influence city policies towards Africville. The idealizations are understandable; Africville was a stronger, more viable community in times past, and the threat of relocation, though always present, was not translated into action until the 1960s. The idealizations brought into sharper focus the powerlessness felt by residents, particularly the older ones, at the time of relocation. Perhaps, too, these idealizations provided a psychological compensation facilitating the residents' silent, though often grudging, acceptance of the relocation.

Throughout Africville's 125 years of existence, marginal and relatively powerless blacks often had to put up with conditions that residents elsewhere in the city would not tolerate. The night-soil deposit pits in 1858, the trachoma hospital in 1903, and the open city dump in the 1950s are all examples of undesirable institutions that were relocated in Africville.[29] In addition, Africville enjoyed so little in the way of public services, such as police protection, paved roads, or snow-plough services, that the residents felt they did not belong to the city.

It is common for areas facing relocation threats to undergo a cycle of deterioration. Africville residents, especially the oldliners and mainliners, often pointed to the city's lack of concern about Africville. They observed that, by not applying standard city ordinances to Africville, and by allowing some people, especially around the time of the Second World War, to squat on government property, the city allowed Africville to deteriorate into a slum and did nothing to change the impression that everyone in the settlement was a squatter. The city did little to facilitate orderly residential development, and, in fact, its policy attenuated the viability of the community and was a factor in the emigration of many of the more ambitious residents and in the immigration of "opportunists."

Under these circumstances it is understandable that a sense of powerlessness and alienation developed in the Africville community. A brief rejuvenation of protest and petitioning took place in the mid-1930s occasioned by the return of several strong leaders. During this period Africville residents obtained their own post office (prior to the 1930s they had to walk several miles to obtain mail), succeeded in having a few street lights installed in their community, and received street numbers; the latter was psychologically quite important for it enabled people to give an address other than Africville and thereby avoid some of the stigma that outsiders attached to the name Africville. The rejuvenation was of short duration and no fundamental change took place in the orientation of city authorities towards Africville. Subsequently, protests and petitions faded[30] and the seemingly irreversible historical decline continued. Residents lacked trust in city officials because, as one relocatee put it, "they had been stung so many times; the older people had a real memory for these things." Some residents struck back by not paying taxes, but this action appears not to have disturbed city council; in fact it made it easier for city authorities to remain impervious to the history of negativism on the part of the city and perhaps, from the perspective of some officials, justified that policy. The relationship between the city and Africville can be stated in terms of three considerations — water and sewerage facilities, Africville's deviance service centre, and the dump. It is these components of the city's negative exchange system with Africville which contributed to the public definition of the community as a "social problem."

Water and Sewerage

One of the more blatant examples of city neglect towards Africville is the fact that the area never obtained water and sewerage services. In 1852 city council agreed to assist in constructing a common well in the Africville area[31] and, in 1909, in response to a petition from Africville residents, city council approved a motion calling for repair of the well.[32] By 1909 many areas of the city had indoor plumbing, as did the hospital and prison on the hill overlooking Africville. The question of extending these services to Africville arose often over the years, but nothing was done.

During the mid-1930s, as part of an effort to rebuild their community, a delegation of Africville residents petitioned the mayor for water service. A relocatee who was a member of the petitioning group reported:

We saw the mayor. The promise was that if the people would pay so much the city would build water lines as far as the foundations of the houses and then the people would have to put in the rest of the pipes. The city promised to reconstruct the road and the side roads. But nothing happened.

In 1944 city council discussed at length the extension of services to Africville; specific proposals and motions were advanced,[33] but the issue was referred to committee and was subsequently lost somewhere in the administration. In 1947 city council's Public Health and Welfare Committee reopened the matter and recommended the extension of water service to Africville.[34] In council, discussion of services became enmeshed with the larger question of whether Africville should be relocated. At a public meeting called to discuss the relocation proposal, Africville residents expressed a desire to remain in Africville and pledged their co-operation "to any move made by the city to improve conditions there."[35] Following this meeting, detailed feasibility studies were conducted, and in 1948 council passed a motion authorizing the allocation of $20,000 to bring both fire and domestic water service into the settlement.[36] Once again the matter became lost in the city bureaucracy and Africville residents, when they were relocated in the 1960s, were still without the water and sewerage services made obligatory by city ordinance.

The issue of water and sewerage facilities clearly shows the historical relationships between the city authorities and Africville. In the period after the Second World War, particularly in the 1940s and the 1950s, community morale seemed to be sapped; the people clung to their chief resource, their land, but apparently they lacked the leadership and community viability to petition effectively and to contest the negative consideration received from the city. The water and sewerage issue also points to the problem of understanding how power functions at city hall; no action was taken, despite the council's 1948 resolution, and apparently neither the director of welfare nor the director of health services had knowledge or power to implement the resolution. Even the mayor, in the 1947-48 period, subsequently expressed puzzlement over the lack of follow-through in relation to the council's resolution.[37] Obviously there was little internal or external advocacy at city hall on behalf of the Africville residents.

Lack of water and sewerage facilities had serious implications for the life and health of Africville residents. Contamination of wells was a constant problem and periodically newspaper headlines made the larger Halifax public aware of the fact. It is remarkable, in view of the water and sewerage situation, and also the presence of the nearby dump, that health was not a continuing crisis in Africville. An outbreak of three cases of paratyphoid "B" occurred in 1962[38] but, according to residents as well as the director of health services for Halifax, on the whole health problems were kept in check. In the late 1950s public health nurses reported that, although many Africville children were thin and undernourished, the incidence of disease was as low, if not lower, than the city average.[39] In 1964, after another test had revealed that wells were contaminated, the local newspaper reported:

> That the contamination of wells in Africville is of long standing is shown by the fact that there have been no serious outbreaks of disease in the district. According to health authorities this indicated that, from infancy on, children have been exposed to water-borne disease germs. As a result they have built up a resistance.[40]

Shortly after this newspaper article appeared, the city put water tanks supplied with city water in Africville. By this time the relocation had been announced, and several families had already been relocated.

A related hazard was fire. In 1948, when the extension of sewerage and water service to Africville was being discussed, the fire chief pointed out that fire service was as necessary as domestic services.[41] City firefighters not only had difficulty getting into the unpaved and unploughed Africville area but, once there, they could do little without equipment to draw water from the basin, and the wooden homes burned quickly. Throughout the years, fires ravaged the community. In 1923, 1930, 1937, and 1947 fires destroyed a number of homes. Some relocatees had seen at least two of their Africville homes burn to the ground. The effect of these experiences, needless to say, did not tend to improve the quality of subsequent house construction in Africville.

The Dump

In the mid-1950s city council resolved that the open city dump be moved to the Africville area. This action illustrates well the negative exchange system that characterized the relationship between Africville and

Plate 4.4 AFRICVILLE: A PROBLEM SITUATION. Printing this picture in 1962, *The Mail Star*, Halifax, reported: "Sewage ran through this back yard in Africville when a line broke. Home owner still uses water from an artesian well in the garden. The pond in back, where many children play, is polluted with waste."

Plate 4.5 UNPAVED ROAD TO AFRICVILLE. Describing the community, one elderly relocatee said, "When the pavement ends, that's where Africville begins" (Interview July, 1969).

city authorities. Little consideration, if any, was given to the wishes or opinions of Africville residents. The latter, having learned what to expect from city authorities, did not protest the dump's relocation; they silently "accepted it" and some residents took advantage of the situation by the illegal salvaging of usable and saleable materials.

After the Second World War, the old rubbish heap within walking distance of Africville began to exceed its capacity. Council discussed a number of alternate sites. One alderman contended that a possible site in Fairview (a community then outside city limits) would be unacceptable to residents there;[42] another alderman stated that "the dump should not be there [at its old site]...it is a health menace."[43] Council agreed finally that the open dump should be relocated to Bedford Basin, at a point one-half mile west of Africville and some 350 feet from the front doors of the westernmost group of homes. There is no reference in council minutes to a concern for the health of Africville residents, nor is there mention of protest by residents. In 1957, after the dump had been moved to the Africville area, council discussed the complaints of residents (presumably including some Africville people) concerning "hordes of rats" in the area of the dump; council members were informed by the city manager that the city was doing all it could but the problem was "partially unsolvable" until an incinerator was built to consume combustible materials.[44] Two years later the incinerator was built just beyond the dump area but, for a variety of reasons including occasional breakdowns of the incinerator, rats continued to be attracted to the dump area.

Some Africville residents, like other Haligonians, had salvaged materials from the old open dump. When the dump was placed on their doorstep, Africville residents increased their salvaging activity; this greater usage and the dump's proximity to Africville resulted in strong public identification of Africville with the dump, although at no time did Africville residents constitute a majority of those who exploited the dump. Only a few Africville males regularly "worked the dump," but another handful or so (and some youths) occasionally supplemented their meagre incomes by salvaging metals that could be sold at junkyards two or three miles from the settlement. According to long-time employees at the junkyards and at the city dump, a diligent Africville salvager might earn a maximum of ten dollars a day. One old man filled his yard at Africville with junk and, when necessary, he would cart five or six dollars worth to the junkyards. A younger man who migrated to Africville in 1951 and was without regular employment noted, "I used to collect junk; could make thirty dollars a week.

Just enough to keep from starving. Now and then someone would get nabbed by the cops." The latter statement also points to the fact that it was illegal to salvage without a licence. Occasionally the police would make arrests. In 1956 the chief of police observed that, if his department were to be effective in the matter, police must be given "authority to arrest without warrant."[45] Interviewed in 1969 employees at the dump observed that in general they had never bothered to call the police since the latter were reluctant to do anything about illegal salvaging. An Africville relocatee confirmed this pattern, noting that dump officials would phone the police only "if we were acting up or grabbing stuff off the trucks as they came in."

While few residents engaged in salvaging for commercial profit, many took advantage of the nearby dump to obtain, again illegally, usable household materials such as wood, nails, paint, furniture, and even clothing. Sometimes when the incinerator broke down and foodstuff was deposited at the open dump, a few Africville persons, along with many other Haligonians, scavenged for items such as tins of fruit juice. One Africville resident, referring to smashed tins of canned food, pointed out "you should have seen all the good food that came to the dump. We used to watch for Canada Packers' and Swift's trucks especially. Now they'd rather burn it than give it away." Africville's undeserved reputation for scavenging enraged the majority of its residents, who drew the normative line at the occasional salvaging of personally usable goods. The authorities' winking at the salvaging and scavenging that did occur perhaps assuaged guilt feelings concerning the plight of the residents. Often too, it appeared to justify a city practice of doing nothing positive at the welfare level. The city's department of welfare, noted for its stringency in assisting the needy, applauded the stereotype of the resourceful Africville resident who, rather than seeking welfare, scrounged amidst the squalor of the dump. The director of Halifax's welfare office, familiar with the Africville situation since 1947, expressed a high regard for its residents, "I never found anyone in Africville that I would call a lazy man." He told the following story in illustration of this resourcefulness:

> I can give as an example a woman who told me she was coming in the week following and she came in looking as spiffy as anyone on Fifth Avenue and she said that 'everything I got from inside to out I got on the dump'; and it was a credit, she looked charming and very much in style.

Plate 4.6 FIRE IN AFRICVILLE. "Fire protection adequate? By the time a fire took place out there, by the time the firemen got out there, it was no good; they just watch the place.... No, when a fire started in Africville you just say, give up your home, it's gone, try to get what you can out of it and forget the rest" (Interview with elderly relocatee).

Africville as a Social Problem 117

Most of them [Africville people] did this sort of thing. They could pick up old dresses and things off the dump and wash them and remodel them, the coloured people have a flair for style, and sew them and press them and look like a million dollars.

Dependence upon this kind of resourcefulness entailed, unfortunately, risks to health as well as occasional legal sanction. Families unable or unwilling to obtain welfare assistance sometimes salvaged truck and car batteries for fuel in their stoves; in one such case, a mother and her four children were hospitalized as a result of lead poisoning caused by burning batteries salvaged from the dump. The husband explained, "I got no money for coal and wood; people got to burn something to keep their families warm." The local newspaper headlined the incident "Africville Families Poisoned," and noted further that at least five other families were similarly dependent on discarded batteries for fuel.[46] Scavenging was not widespread, but it was hazardous for the few residents who engaged in it. In one instance, three middle-aged transient residents of Africville (none of whom was born and raised there) died by drinking a home-brew that contained duplicating fluid found at the city dump.[47]

Although Africville residents did not request that the dump be located at their doorstep, in subsequent years the public definition of the situation painted an exaggerated picture of Africville residents as profiteers of, and encroachers upon, the dump. The survival-oriented behaviour of those residents who did scavenge and salvage was ironically reinterpreted as being the *raison d'être* of the community itself. For instance the managing editor of a local newspaper, attending a meeting of the Housing Policy Review Committee, contended in 1961 that "if the city dump was eliminated or policed more efficiently, part of the desire of some of the people living at Africville to stay there would be eliminated as a number of them make their living by scavenging on the dump."[48]

Some residents did believe that, in view of the city's relocating the dump to Africville, a positive exchange might be city assistance in establishing a co-operative salvaging company among unemployed and underemployed Africville males. The welfare director of Halifax believed that it was a good, constructive idea: "I think [with] a fence around the dump and a franchise granted in some businesslike way, these people could have made a living for many years," and noted that he had raised it several

Plate 4.7. THE DUMP. The characterization of Africville as a slum became quite common once the Halifax city dump was moved, in the 1950s, to the site shown above, only a short distance from dwellings and the Seaview African Baptist Church.

Africville as a Social Problem 119

times with city authorities. Nothing ever came of it; such a positive exchange would have been inconsistent with city practice towards Africville.

Deviance Service Centre

Minority group members, if oppressed and discriminated against, often find a mode of adjusting to their situation by performing less desirable and sometimes illegitimate services for the majority group. Moreover, the minority group members often acquire, under these conditions, a certain functional autonomy; that is, not sharing fairly in society's wealth, they are allowed a range of behaviour in their neighbourhoods by the authorities that would not be countenanced elsewhere. Such indulgence by the authorities reflects not liberality but, rather, a view that the minority people are "different" and a reluctance to expend resources adequate to effective control of the undesirable behaviour in these areas. This model applies aptly to Africville and to the reaction of Halifax authorities.

It appears that even prior to the First World War it was known in Halifax that Africville, being away from the rest of the city and public surveillance, was a place to go for bootleg booze and conviviality. One very elderly relocatee observed that his grandfather had kept "quite a bar, well-stocked with kegs of rum and the works. The sailors used to come in and buy from him. After a while he drunk himself to death. Put himself on the bum, you know." The proximity of Africville to the dockyards and general port activity meant that a pattern was soon established whereby Africville became a deviance centre. Such a development was congruent with the fact that occupationally these blacks were employed in the service sector, carting away excrement and cleaning the homes of other Haligonians.

It is problematic how extensive and how accepted by Africville residents such bootlegging was prior to the First World War. The war stimulated this line of service, causing many Africville residents to write Halifax City Council advising it that the community's well-being and reputation was being destroyed and requesting police surveillance. The petition, dated June 1919, read:

We, the undersigned ratepayers, do hereby make application for better police protection at Africville. We base our application on the following ground: that a police officer seldom or never visits this district, except for a warrant or subpoena; the conditions that now prevail here are worse than at any time before; that these lamentable conditions tend to turn the majority away from the good teaching which they have received; that there is now an utter disregard of the Lord's day by many residents; that there are many persons, strangers in our midst, living openly in a state of debauchery, which must corrupt the minds of youth for we are more or less subject to our environment; that there is nightly confusion, carousal and dissipation which disturb the peaceful night; that these carousals have been the centres for spreading infection throughout the village; that we believe, if this disgraceful state of affairs continue there will be some grave crime or crimes committed.

Our earnest desire is that your Honourable Body, in this period of reconstruction, carefully consider our application so that the omission of the past may be rectified and by your assistance the evil influences now at work may be greatly reduced; then shall we be better able to train the young in the way of good citizenship and place the village on a better plane of Social Welfare.[49]

The Africville petitioners were told that "the city department has no spare men to send such a distance."[50] It was recommended that "the residents of the Africville district form their own police department and anyone they appoint to act as a policeman, the mayor would swear in as a special constable.... In the event of any serious trouble being reported the chief is always in a position to send a squad to this district."[51]

The petition, and the response of city authorities to it, may well be taken as signalling the end of a particular phase of Africville's history, that phase in which much was expected of community residents and Africville's potential as a good residential district was still possible of realization. Residents themselves detected a qualitative change, a new emerging equilibrium, in the community. Their reference to "strangers in our midst" foreshadowed the trend of opportunists and "down-and-outers" who moved into Africville in later years. The response of city authorities illustrates well the kind of negative freedom that they granted the residents; nothing positive was done for the community by city council, which was always busy attempting to decide what to do with the land on which Africville residents were located.

As the years went by after the First World War, Africville's reputation as a deviance service centre continued to grow. The predictions of the petitioners of 1919 were borne out as the bootlegging and conviviality gave way to a definition of Africville as a raucous, hazardous place. The process was gradual and incremental, in the wake of the First World War and its aftermath, a new temporary equilibrium was reached inside the community and between the community and the rest of Halifax, an equilibrium characterized by a higher visibility of Africville's peculiar service role. This new phase was described by a former Africville resident who migrated from the community prior to the relocation:

> There were more white people than there were coloured in the community. This is a fact. They came and stayed to eat and sleep. And they had their drinks. Some who came down were very prominent people.... And they had their drinks. Nobody was ever robbed there or anything.... Look, these well-to-do people came down to Africville...they had their drinks, gave us a quarter...a quarter was a lot of money in those days, you know...and moved on. And when they got drunk and tired and fell down on the road and went to sleep, they would be carried into somebody's house and looked after.

Concurrent with worsening economic conditions and continuing city neglect, the deviance aspect of Africville became less tolerable. One black outsider observed that "just before relocation the younger ones [in the Africville community] would rob a man when he drank. But a few years back, Africville used to be a wonderful place to go on a drunk. You could flop your head anywhere." Another black, non-Africville Haligonian in referring to these latter developments noted that "the people of all sorts used to go to Africville. It had a kind of attraction because it was kind of weird; no law enforcement. One went out there at one's own risk. It really was the other side of the tracks." Most Africville residents who complained of these changes identified the turning point, from "acceptable" deviance service centre to potentially dangerous place, as being around the Second World War, when Africville received a complement of migrants displaced from the mid-city area. One man observed:

The war [the Second World War] came along and the scruff from the city, both black and white, descended on Africville to join with the Africville sinners to form an unholy alliance and turn Africville into a no-man's land, while the city administration worked on unmindful.

Another relocatee ascribed Africville's stigma to this in-migration:

The changes were that a lot of people who didn't belong there came and moved in…. Something happened at that time that never used to happen in Africville, because men came from the city and all around the place. They would come out there in the summer time and they would drink and get drunk…. After the strangers started to move in there, people [who] came out there started to get robbed and all that kind of stuff, and the blame would go on Africville. But it was not the people from Africville doing those things…. It gave Africville a bad name, it gave it a real bad name. Knocking out people, robbing people, that never had a stigma, until they came out.

A relocatee who had moved into Africville in the early 1930s echoed this sentiment:

Things were nice in Africville until they started clearing Gerrish and Creighton streets [during the Second World War] and people came down to Africville. Squatters, bootleggers, and thieves came down, got old boards from the dump and built a shack. Those…were the wildest crew you ever seen. Dangerous, drinking and fighting all the time.

White authorities with some intimate contact with Africville occasionally reiterated this observation concerning a drastic decline in Africville lifestyle and also occasionally linked this development with in-migrants during and after the Second World War. One alderman noted that "the class that settled [in Africville] after the war sort of ruined the area."

There is no doubt that the community changed during its last several decades, but it is too simplistic to explain this development in terms of the relatively small number of later in-migrants. It would be more realistic to see these people as opportunists who, having virtually nowhere else to go, gravitated towards a rapidly deteriorating Africville because of its possibilities for cheap housing, relative freedom, and autonomy and because of contacts established previously with its residents. Most of the outsiders who eventually settled in Africville had, for several years previously, been coming to Africville to drink and to party. Obviously they reinforced the drift of Africville towards a more blatant and hazardous deviance service centre.

The pervasiveness of the simplistic model of change proffered by respectable Africville residents and some white authorities is understandable. Participant models usually are more preservative than explanatory. Respectable Africville residents did not wish to be painted with the same brush as those residents who participated most in "unacceptable behaviour" and, consequently, placed the responsibility for such behaviour primarily with "outsiders." City authorities could find comfort perhaps in a model that interpreted "Africville's problem" in terms of the personality of some of its residents rather than in the historical unfolding of the consequences of city policies, racism, and socio-economic depression. The facts point, however, to the 1919 petitioners' correctness of vision. The relatively small number of in-migrants in the early 1940s neither introduced the deviance service centre nor did they constitute its sole Africville membership.

With the aftermath of the Second World War, a final pre-relocation equilibrium phase was reached within the community and between it and the broader society. Africville became regarded by outsiders as harbouring a risky deviance service centre and being a model of social disorganization. Blacks elsewhere in Halifax advised their children not to go near the community; middle-class whites advised their friends that Africville was an interesting but dangerous place to visit. Inside the community, according to outsiders and some Africville residents, there was a decline in morale. As one Halifax city alderman noted:

> The character of the area had gone down and the character
> of some of the people who lived there had changed too.
> Instead of being a good type of citizen as they were prior
> to the thirties, they seemed to deteriorate to an extent
> that they just didn't care; certain activities went on there
> that didn't lend anything to the area.

Yet it would be unwarranted to see the state of affairs in Africville as socially disorganized and to exaggerate the deviance that occurred. The official crime rate over the past forty years was not particularly high, and only a handful of Africville males were sentenced to prison. The director of health services in Halifax reported that, while venereal disease was not uncommon in Africville in the post-Second World War period, usually the same one or two handfuls of persons were the only residents involved. Moreover, outsiders continued, at little risk, to visit Africville for booze and conviviality right up to the time of relocation. One frequent black visitor observed: "Everybody had a good time. More bootleggers than you could shake a stick at. Girls available for a good time." A white visitor reported that he and his colleagues at the dockyard always went on payday to the community for "drinking and carousing" and that "it was rough, but if you weren't looking for trouble, it wasn't bad." Other black and white outsiders frequenting the community underlined this observation, indicating that the risks were no greater than one would expect from drinking and carousing.

Africville residents themselves indicated that they experienced little sense of danger while living in the community. Even those heavily involved in these activities reported that few acts of violence occurred. Africville remained a small community where most residents were related by kinship ties. Adjustment in the community to this higher level of deviance took the form of segmentation of groups and activities. The community did lose its cultural and structural simplicity and homogeneity, but adjustments were made, and Africville was not an unpredictable social jungle.

Housing and Stigma

The historical processes of external encroachment and neglect, and of internal deprivation and decay, resulted in Africville's being defined as a slum and its residents stigmatized. The quality of housing was the most concrete and publicly proclaimed indicator of Africville's slum condition. A related indictment of the community that struck at the chief resource that Africville residents cherished, their land, was the widespread view that even residents' claims to the supposedly worthless Africville property were questionable.

Elderly relocatees always remembered their ancestors' housing as of good quality. One relocatee observed that "some of the oldest homes were quite solidly constructed with heavy beams, thick plaster, wooden spikes and nice cellars." The respondent herself had, at the time of relocation, a relatively large and attractive home that she had built in 1937 after two previous homes had fallen to fire. Due to fires, and previous relocation occasioned by railway construction, few older homes existed by the 1950s; consequently it is difficult to assess progressive changes in quality of housing. It would appear that, throughout the last half of the community's 125-year existence, housing reflected the community's poverty. In 1903 the local newspaper reported that "the style of architecture of the Africville buildings is not such as to give a stranger an exalted idea of the city;"[52] by 1923 a city report noted that most Africville buildings were quite dilapidated and "little if anything, can be done to better conditions."

As the years passed by, the gap increased considerably between the housing in Africville and that of Halifax generally. A key factor was the city's refusal to provide Africville with standard services. Fires were a deterrent, both in destroying the sound houses that did exist and in inhibiting resident investment in improved housing. Insurance was virtually impossible to obtain. Moreover, population growth compounded the major problem of space, a result being in later years a cluttered and haphazard pattern of houses built on almost any free patch of land. It would appear that, in the forty years prior to relocation, some sheds and garages came to be used as homes with minimal renovation. Sometimes salvaged materials were used and community assistance enlisted in a conspicuously inexpert construction of homes. Visually the community was far from attractive; one young relocatee pointed out:

> I was from Toronto. When Mom told us we were going to live in Africville, I was ten years old. I pictured a little village with white houses. Boy, did I get a surprise! We came in the night so I didn't see anything. But in the morning, when I looked out the window, oh, boy; I said 'My God, Mom! What did you bring us down here for?'

The 1959 survey revealed approximately twenty-three household heads in rental accommodation and about fifty-five claiming some form of home ownership (either home, or land, or both). For the most part the renters were marginals/transients; only ten of the twenty-three household heads who were renting in 1959 had been living in Africville for more than ten years. The rental arrangement was usually only a loose understanding between renters and owners, most of whom lived in Africville or were former residents, and few renters made regular monthly payments. The rental accommodations, many of which were in the area described in Chapter Two as "around the bend,"[53] were of very poor quality, being on the average two-room, wooden shacks without foundation or services. In at least five cases the rental dwellings did not have electricity; in these cases kerosene lamps were used, and extension cords provided occasional electricity. A few rental dwellings having shingles or brick siding were fairly adequate.

Of the fifty-five household heads claiming some form of ownership in 1959, only twenty-two indicated that they possessed deeds. Others reported that while they did not have legal title, they did pay taxes, or they were settled on ancestral property, or both. There was considerable uncertainty regarding land ownership and a number of residents were self-acknowledged squatters. Nevertheless, it was inadequate for city officials to contend that "only thirteen deeds could be documented," or that "there were [no] more than two lots as marketable commodity with legal title in Africville." Such opinions, filtered through the public and officialdom, reflected a lack of historical research and insensitivity to the complex and often informal pattern of land conveyance in Africville. This created a situation that stigmatized virtually all residents and in effect legitimated the city's neglect of Africville.

On the average, the owner-occupied dwellings were of better quality than other dwellings. All but one house had electricity, about fifteen had stone and cement foundations, and a few had brick siding or cedar shingles. About a dozen contained seven or eight rooms and two dwellings had inside sanitation. The best owner-occupied dwellings were found in the main settlement area. Yet in terms of city standards the large majority of homes were inadequate; only nineteen properties were assessed for more than $1000 in 1962, and at least a dozen of the owner-occupied dwellings were substandard two-room or three-room wooden shacks.

There was considerable variation in the maintenance and internal quality of Africville dwellings in 1959. Many homes were clean and well furnished, particularly the owner-occupied dwellings in the main settlement area. Most owner-occupied dwellings had refrigerators and telephones. The relocation social worker evaluated fifty-two percent of the homes as "poor" with reference to maintenance and internal quality; thirty-eight percent were considered as "fair to good," and ten percent as "good to excellent."[54] More than half the household heads whose homes were evaluated as "poor" were either marginals/transients or in the residual grouping.

Africville residents, especially the mainliners and oldliners, were often quick to point out that there were good homes in the settlement and that many residents kept their homes in excellent condition under difficult circumstances. Others, long deprived, echoed the alienated hopelessness of one household head who, when asked about his dwelling's state of repair, replied:

> This shack? What's the use of doing anything to it? It's not worth it; besides, if the city takes this land, we won't get anything for our time and money.

It is to be expected that, given the generally poor-quality housing, the absence of regular city services (such as water, sewerage, and paved roads), the presence of an open dump, the existence of a deviance service centre at two corners of the settlement, and the often erroneous and insensitive public definitions of the Africville situation, considerable stigma would be associated with the Africville community. Some Africville residents found that they could not even obtain car insurance because they "lived in an undesirable area." Even among poor blacks and whites elsewhere in Halifax, Africville was stigmatized. In discussing Africville's stigma the director of welfare observed:

> A man who said that he was from Africville had great difficulty in getting work. I think most of our people were afraid of people from Africville. The police had a lot of trouble with some of them because they were aboriginal in their living, sort of.... The other black communities seemed to take on the criticism that was levelled against Africville and they would keep clear of them. This applied especially in Creighton and Maynard Street area, where it always appeared to me that the coloured people of Halifax thought they were a little better than the people of Africville.

Most residents readily acknowledged the stigma associated with Africville. An elderly oldliner observed "Yes, I minded it [the stigma] a lot; the people in the city...oh, they had the worst to say about Africville." A household head of the residual grouping pointed out that "blacks from other communities thought we were a bunch of tramps, but they came here." Some Africville residents reported that in their youth they had reacted to the stigma by using street addresses rather than "Africville" when they had to tell others where they lived; other residents continued this practice until relocation. In the 1959 survey, Africville residents indicated that visits to friends outside Africville were not always reciprocated; they visited more often than friends came to visit them. Some residents (mostly the mainliners) who especially resented the stigma, tended to reject neighbours and to seek self-identification with what they considered to be the greater respectability of outsiders.[55]

While most Haligonians, black and white, rich and poor, circa 1960, appear to have believed that Africville was a slum, there was considerable ambivalence among the Africville people themselves. In post-relocation interviews approximately forty percent indicated that Africville had been a slum and sixty percent disagreed; regardless of response, the majority of relocatees typically qualified their assessment. There was important variation according to social grouping. Mainliners and marginals/transients were the least ambivalent. The large majority of mainliner respondents agreed that Africville was a slum, pointing to the stigma and the lack of facilities and often reflecting the sentiments expressed by one mainliner in 1959 prior to the relocation: "I'm ashamed of this place; the sewer is almost in my mouth." Typically the mainliners qualified their assessments by noting that not all of the community had been a slum. The resourceless marginals/transients virtually all contended that Africville had not been a slum. While acknowledging the existence of poor housing, they were not bothered by the stigma or the presence of the dump; typically they shared the view expressed by one of their number prior to relocation: "Living in Africville is cheaper, you can pick up things such as kindling wood." One of the marginals/transients commented: "Well, I wouldn't say that [that Africville was a slum] because even white people live in old homes. They had good bread and butter. I'll admit it wasn't the classiest place in the world, but the people did the best they could. Lots of them didn't have money to do what they wanted to their places."

The oldliners were the most ambivalent concerning whether or not Africville was a slum: roughly equal numbers responded in affirmative, negative, and undecided categories. Typically the oldliners pointed out that at least the people owned their own land and that the city had been uncooperative. One young oldliner observed:

> A slum? Well, to a certain extent I have to say yes. But it was something you owned. In a way it was hard to bring up

kids down there, but in another way everybody was happy with it.

An elderly oldliner commented:

> I don't think so. If the city gave the people a chance to remodel their homes, put the water through, it would have been okay. Africville was no more a slum than some parts of the area I know of. I travelled twenty–three years all around Nova Scotia, seen all kinds of places worse than Africville. No, it wasn't a slum. Lots of white people visited. Some real up-to-date houses had wells. Lots of people never visited to see these and had wrong impressions.

Respondents of the "residual" grouping also exhibited ambivalence; about fifty percent contended that it was not a slum and the remainder was equally divided into affirmative and undecided categories. Typically these respondents compared Africville favourably with other poor areas of Halifax; one respondent observed: "I think the housing was bad. If it was a slum, I've seen worse places in Halifax."

For reasons mentioned earlier, Africville as the years passed by became more and more a community of "refuge" and less and less viable. Most residents prior to relocation were eager to have improvements made in their community; this was the major alternative regularly proffered by Africville residents whenever city officials suggested relocation. Despite their fragmentation into cliques and distinct social groupings, they did have a sense of "solidarity in oppression," which was especially manifested in their post-relocation assessment of the friendliness and trustworthiness of their fellow residents. Despite the poverty and inadequate resources, the majority of residents prior to relocation indicated that they enjoyed living in Africville. They cited the privacy and freedom, the clean air, the beautiful view, the open spaces, and the "country style of life." It is important to remember that people in their everyday life compare their status most frequently with others who are, broadly speaking, on the same socio-economic level. Africville blacks usually used mid-city blacks as their reference group on matters of housing and general lifestyle. Thus they could say that Africville "was better than in the city, better than some of those slums downtown;" they could quite legitimately point out that many of the Africville homes on the inside were as good or better than those in the downtown area and the costs of accommodation substantially less. Finally the Africville residents could and did say that whatever Africville was, it was theirs.

It is understandable, given living conditions in Africville, that a resident without roots in the community and having lived there only for a short time might respond chiefly to the stigma, the dump, and the inadequate services and be almost totally negative about the community. One such person anticipating the relocation wrote to city officials as follows:

> I'm writing to ask you are you buying houses. I got a three-room house to sell. I live out here in Africville. I would like to get something for it. I don't like out here and I want to get out of here. There is no water, no lights, no wood; the little wood we do get is off the dump and is full of bed bugs. I have a radio, T.V., fridge, and a washer and can't have a bit of comfort out of them. I am not well myself. I am sorry I came out here. All of the people want to get out here. A lot of houses are disgraces. The people is only living off the dump. A wonder half of us is not poison.

On the other hand, to an elderly oldliner with a vivid historical consciousness, a justifiable pride in her own and her ancestors' hard life-struggle and an acute sense of what Africville might have been, Africville was also friends and relatives, ancestral property, and rich memories. One such woman, a former leader in the community whose husband had been a deacon there and whose sons were successful migrants in central Canada, finished up her interview with the comment:

> I never was ashamed of Africville. I always owned it up as my home and the people as my friends.

Notes

1   MacKerrow, op. cit., p. 65.
2   Winks, "The Negro in Canada," op.cit., p. 465.
3   During the period to which Winks refers, the process of urbanization and industrialization and the organization of the Canadian economy in terms of new staples meant that many areas and economic pursuits experienced relative economic decline. Canadian blacks, living mostly outside the

emerging growth centres, suffered a considerable diminution of opportunities. Prejudice and discrimination abetted this relative decline.

4   The oil storage complex was located on the site of an old lime works.

5   An older bone mill used to function further to the west of the settlement.

6   A tannery previously occupied the site of the rolling mill.

7   Clairmont and Magill, *Africville Relocation Report*, p. 134.

8   It was the dream of Nova Scotia's famed Joseph Howe to have an intercolonial railway join the British North American Colonies. Failing to win support from Britain, in 1852 he embarked on a policy of supporting the construction of local lines to be built and operated by the Nova Scotia government.

9   G.R. Stevens, *Canadian National Railways, I: Sixty Years of Trial and Error (1836-1896)* (Toronto: Clarke, Irwin, 1960), pp. 75, 158, 159.

10   N.S.L.A., *Journal and Proceedings*, 1854-1855, Appendix 17, p. 143.

11   Clairmont and Magill, *Africville Relocation Report*, pp. 130-134.

12   Ibid., p. 134.

13   Ibid., p. 135.

14   Registry of Deeds, Book 820, pp. 732-34.

15   *Minutes of the Halifax City Council*, December 9, 1915, p. 211.

16   The hospital complex was used only intermittently; during the Second World War it was used for military purposes, and after the relocation it became a home for elderly ill people.

17   *Minutes of the Halifax City Council*, January 15, 1948, p. 10.

18   In the 1871 census of Halifax, thirty-six percent of the men of African ethnic origin for whom occupational categories were listed were labourers; surprisingly, twenty-two percent were recorded as seamen; most of the remaining were truckmen, porters, masons, coopers, carpenters, or barbers.

19   Few residents engaged in this activity. One who did observed proudly that before a train passed through the community, it could be thoroughly sacked. The director of welfare, who had a high estimation of the resourcefulness of Africville residents, pointed out that some lived by their wits. This was necessary because, in part, little welfare assistance was given to them.

20   The revised and recalculated data on Africville employment and income differ from those presented in the institute report of 1962 (*The Condition of the Negroes*). In the latter report, Africville boundaries were misread and non-Africville persons were included in the tables; moreover, a significant number of Africville residents, for one reason or the other, were by-passed by the 1959 survey team. The tables reported in the present study depict accurately the pre-relocation, socio-economic conditions.

21. The director of welfare reported that "prior to relocation six to ten families at most would come in occasionally for welfare."

22. Brookbank, op. cit., p. 48.

23. Halifax Board of School Commissioners, Chairman's and Supervisor's Reports.

24. Ibid.

25. Data for 140 persons were available in the "out-of-school" category. A close examination of the cases for which no data existed indicates that the basic patterns remain valid.

26. Clairmont and Magill, *Nova Scotian Blacks*, p. 24.

27. Intelligence tests given to Africville school children in 1959 indicated that almost half scored less than eighty-five, or in the low-normal range or below (see *The Condition of the Negroes of Halifax City, Nova Scotia*, p. 19). Deprived children are usually at a disadvantage in standard intelligence tests.

28. Melvin Seeman, "On the Meaning of Alienation," *American Sociological Review* 24 (December, 1959): 784.

29. *Minutes of the Halifax City Council*, June 29, 1858; ibid., November 5, 1903; ibid., June 16, 1949.

30. In the 1950s, after the Africville school was closed, residents did petition for a bus service for their children.

31. *Minutes of the Halifax City Council*, October 27, 1852.

32. Ibid., September 23, 1909.

33. Ibid., October 12, 1944.

34. Ibid., December 11, 1947.

35. Ibid., February 4, 1948.

36. Ibid., January 6, 1948.

37. "Africville: Ahern Makes Move," *The Mail-Star*, Halifax, N.S., August 2, 1962.

38. Letter from Dr. Allan R. Morton to the mayor of Halifax and members of the city's health committee, August 9, 1962. The letter is in the Africville File, Social Planning Office, City Hall, Halifax, N.S.

39. Draft copy, *The Condition of the Negroes of Halifax City, Nova Scotia*.

40. "Works Department Undecided on Way to Solve Problems," *The Mail-Star*, Halifax, N.S., December 1, 1964.

41. *Minutes of the Halifax City Council*, February 4, 1948.

42. Ibid., June 16, 1949.

43. Ibid., November 16, 1954.

44. Ibid., April 11, 1957.

45. Ibid., November 15, 1956.

46 "Africville Families Poisoned," *The Chronicle-Herald*, Halifax, N.S., January 28, 1958.

47 "Africville Deaths: Fatal Level of Wood Alcohol Discovered," *The Chronicle-Herald*, Halifax, N.S., May 27, 1966.

48 *Minutes of the Housing Policy Review Committee*, City of Halifax, May 19, 1961.

49 *Minutes of the Halifax City Council*, June 17, 1919.

50 Ibid.

51 Ibid., July 7, 1919.

52 *The Novascotian and Weekly Chronicle*, Halifax, N.S., Vol. 69, No. 34, August 21, 1903.

53 An appraisal report of this section of Africville in 1961 noted that "these dwellings are merely shacks built out of second-hand materials with no foundations and no sanitary facilities. They are considered completely worthless." Appraisal Report, June 12, 1961 in Industrial Mile File, Development Department, City Hall, Halifax, N.S.

54 Interview with the relocation social worker, October, 1969.

55 Only thirty percent of the relocatees interviewed in 1969 and 1970 indicated that the stigma had bothered them. It may be that the suprisingly low percentage reflects the presence of post-relocation adjustment problems. If, however, the percentages are considered valid in the pre-relocation situation, perhaps they are a measure of estrangement from the wider society as a whole.

The Relocation Decision and Liberal-Welfare Rhetoric: 1962-1964

The reason for the relocation was because it had been mentioned many times in the press, by other means of communication, and by many people in the community, that this was a disadvantaged area. People were living under very poor conditions and the city fathers were allowing this kind of condition to exist within the city. It was mentioned that this was a social problem and somebody in the city fathers should do something about it, so this actually was the beginning.

The emphasis was on the fact it was a social problem. So, finally, the then city fathers in 1961-62,...attempted to do something for these people who were in the community of Africville and were considered to be disadvantaged people.

—Tape-recorded interview with the relocation social worker, October, 1969.

My reaction [to the relocation]. Well, we moved. We were one of the first ones to move. I thought they needed the property for a road. They said, 'No, purely a social problem we are trying to solve.' Bullshit!

—Interview with an Africville relocatee, July, 1969.

What were the origins of the death of Africville? Why were the people relocated? Were the underlying reasons humanitarian, intended to improve socio-economic conditions among the residents and to end racial segregation; or, primarily, did Halifax politicians and development officials want the land for the industrial economic interests of Halifax? To answer these questions it is necessary to untangle the strands of a complex web. Events surrounding the decision to relocate Africville span the period from July, 1962 to January, 1964. It is impossible now to construct an exact day-to-day chronology of the decision-making process. An overview of the major highlights can be developed, however, through examination of city hall documents, correspondence, tape-recorded interviews, and newspapers and magazines.

In reconstructing a chronology, the underlying perspective focuses on power, exchange, advocacy, and negotiating bargaining strategies. At the heart of this approach is an examination of the possession of and access to resources which determine the structure and distribution of power. The power distribution, in turn, has a dual effect: it permits individual persons to select, to change, and to attain a given set of goals, and it shapes the direction, nature, and strength of exchange relations. During the Africville relocation decision-making, due to historical reasons discussed earlier, the black residents had virtually no financial assets, leadership, or community infrastructure resources; they were in a weak bargaining position with city officials who could draw upon bureaucratic legal, financial, and technical knowledge resources. Thus, city officials in 1962 were able to introduce terms for relocation which were of limited financial benefit to the vast majority of Africville residents. To counterbalance these inequitable exchange terms a small group of Halifax "caretakers" formed a white-black "alliance;" these caretakers became the community's external advocates in negotiations with city officials. The caretakers questioned the wisdom of the city's 1962 relocation plan and its terms; however, their uncertainty diminished when, in 1963, a noted Canadian urban expert legitimized the city's relocation decision and placed the relocation within a liberal-welfare paradigm with modified exchange terms presumably more beneficial to Africville residents.

For analytical purposes, the relocation decision-making can be divided into five phases: (1) the precipitating events (1955-1962); (2) the initial relocation exchange terms; (3) the white-black caretaker alliance; (4) expertise and liberal-welfare rhetoric; and (5) the official adoption of the liberal-welfare model.

Phase One: The Precipitating Events (1955-1962)

For a variety of reasons Africville land was a prime potential site for industrial development: the city of Halifax owned sizable property to the south, east, and west; railway tracks paralleled and criss-crossed the community; and the shoreline was valuable for harbour development. As noted in the previous chapter, the public record in the minutes of Halifax city council warrants the conclusion that the city officials' attitude towards Africville was primarily one of long-standing preoccupation with the eventual industrial development of land.

This industrial-use momentum intensified in the mid-1950s and early 1960s. In mid-1954, the city manager submitted to Halifax city council a report that recommended the shifting of Africville residents to city-owned property southwest of the existing community site.[1] The report noted that the underlying intention of the plan was acquisition of land for industrial purposes.

> The area is not suited for residences but properly developed is ideal for industrial purposes. There is water frontage for piers, the railway for sidings, a road to be developed leading directly downtown and in the other direction to the provincial highway. Therefore, for future industrial expansion the following suggestions are made....[2]

The report recommended the development of thirty-two lots to be sold to Africville residents, and the construction of two-storey houses at a cost, to residents, of $7000 with a mortgage of $6000. The report, approved by council,[3] was not put into effect. However, the potential industrial importance of Africville land did not diminish; in early 1955, council adopted a motion instructing the mayor to invite a number of interested parties to discuss the development of the Bedford Basin shore from Pier 9 to Fairview.[4] The alderman proposing the motion argued, "Everything necessary for the proper development is in the Bedford Basin site. Deep water is there and dredging is not necessary. Access roads lead to and from it...."[5]

The development of the Bedford Basin shoreline was deemed important for both harbour expansion and the economic growth of the city; it was for these reasons that the city wanted to acquire Africville shoreline property. During the period 1954-57 there was considerable discussion among city officials and members of the Port of Halifax Commission and the National Harbours Board concerning the Bedford Basin properties and port expansion.[6] The handwriting was already on the wall and, as events made clear, the relocation of Africville was imminent.

The industrial potential of Africville land was reinforced in 1956 when city council engaged Dr. Gordon Stephenson, then Professor of Town and Regional Planning, University of Toronto, to investigate redevelopment possibilities in Halifax. Dr. Stephenson's report cited the Africville land for industrial and harbour development and as necessary "for the future development of the city."[7] A similar proposal for industrial expansion appeared in 1957 when council adopted a motion to begin land-assembly expropriation procedures for the development of a mile of industrial land along Bedford Basin.[8] Part of the expropriated area included land owned by an Africville resident.

By 1962 the projected development plans for Africville land had reached a new plateau of sophistication. On February 17, 1962, city council's planning board approved engineering and cost studies for the development of the north shore of Bedford Basin. The proposed plan provided for a limited-access expressway of about one and three-quarter miles, the development of industrial sites, and the outward expansion of the Bedford Basin shoreline. In describing the proposal, the local press noted, "The expressway is to be two lanes at first and four lanes later. As it is laid down it will go right through the Africville district which is scheduled for removal starting in spring...."[9] In a 1962 memorandum, the assistant city planner described Africville as the greatest problem in the development of the northern slope:

> Africville stands out as the greatest problem in this study area, and a lengthy legal and administrative problem is likely to stem from establishing ownerships, etc., and forestall an early redevelopment of the 'shanty town.' City council must also clarify its position and policy in relation to the rehousing of the Africville population.[10]

Two months later, the city manager wrote to the mayor and the town planning board explaining that, if the principles of the North Shore Development Plan were accepted, city staff must "examine and recommend a solution to the Africville problem."[11] The Northern Slope Development Plan thus acted as a catalyst initiating a chain reaction of events that led to the eventual relocation. City hall staff proceeded to assemble information about Africville and the city's planning department prepared a map identifying Africville buildings and residences.[12]

Phase Two: The Initial Relocation Exchange Terms

The relocation of Africville became the responsibility of the City's newly-established development department,[13] whose responsibilities included the development and redevelopment of the city, urban renewal, eradication of blight, administration of day-to-day and long-range planning, acquisition and clearance of development property, and management of most city-owned properties.[14] The director of the department, a former employee of Central Mortgage and Housing Corporation, was appointed as development officer in 1961 and undoubtedly became the city's most important senior official in relation to the relocation decision-making and implementation. His concern was with overall city development and economic growth. A former senior and influential member of Halifax city council describes as follows the development director's concern with the economic interest of the city as a whole, and his cost-accounting (systems-oriented) approach to development:

> ...I think that he would tend to opt for what he would see to be the city's interests, keep the costs down, get the thing cleaned up with as little controversy as possible, and therefore not letting too much information out....
> ...it is true that...as a development officer for the city, when looking at any piece of real estate within the city of Halifax, [he] looks at it through the eyes of a developer; that is, a public developer, if you like,...one who sees this land here as being worth dollars today; and five years from now, when certain other things happen, being worth x plus y dollars; and twenty years from now being worth x plus y plus z dollars.... He has this sort of urban economics in his head all the time.

Interviewed in 1969 the development director explained that upon assuming employment in 1961 "his basic function was to start an urban renewal and redevelopment program in Halifax." His three priorities were the central redevelopment area in downtown Halifax, the Uniacke Square

Public Housing Clearance Program and Africville. In reviewing the Africville situation, he had had several discussions with a former resident and perceived the community as an "environmental disaster." He considered that the relocation of the segregated black community was the only solution to the Africville problem:

> It was considered, certainly by us at the staff, that [relocation] was the only possibility. We examined the possibility of co-operative housing. We had looked at the possibility of sewer and water, installing sewer and water, which was a virtual impossibility. We had looked at the question of rehabilitating their homes, which again was a complete impossibility.
> And I personally took the view that I wasn't going to be party to rebuilding a coloured ghetto on the same land. Maybe my reasons were pretty primitive, if you wish. But I had seen the operation in a different context in St. John's, Newfoundland, and I didn't want to be party to it. I could see no way it could go but fail in the long run.

In mid-1962 the development director wrote a report, entitled *Africville*,[15] which described the Africville area, its people, and the ownership of land, outlined alternate courses of action, and noted the reluctance of Africville residents to relocate. The report recommended removal of the blighted housing and dilapidated stuctures in Africville, and the development director estimated that the cost of acquisistion and clearance would range from $40,000 to $70,000. Alternative housing accommodation would be offered in unsegregated, subsidized, rental projects. Residents without legal title would receive a gratuitous payment of $500 for a quitclaim deed and vacant possession of their property. Residents with proof of legal title could claim compensation through the courts or in negotiation with the city. The report recommended that, if these recommendations were adopted, city staff and welfare and church organizations should meet immediately with leading members of the community to explain the city's position and intended course of action.

These initial relocation exchange terms are a good example of the development model outlined in the introduction to this book. Africville residents were not viewed as a specific "interest group" with distinct values and goals; rather, they were considered "disadvantaged citizens" whose community life reinforced their deprivation, a conception which is consistent with the consensus model of society. The ideological premises underlying the relocation were similar to most urban renewal projects: the program was a form of intervention designed to improve imperfections in the social system (remove a black slum) and achieve system development (obtain the land for an expressway important to the city's future development). Policy was formulated by city bureaucrats who had access to legal, financial, and political resources. Africville residents were not consulted in the formation of intial relocation terms, and no attention was given to considering strategies whereby residents could be involved in the planning process. Given the city's power through control of resources, the financial exchange terms had a one-sided advantage in favour of the city. Few Africville residents had registered deeds and would be able to claim compensation through the courts or in negotiation with the city. The vast majority of families would receive a gratuitous payment of $500, hardly an amount sufficient for resettlement in metropolitan Halifax, an area in which the cost of living ranks among the highest in Canada.

The 1962 real estate value of Africville property was, in essence, the criterion that the development department report used for determining settlements. This real estate evaluation, however, neglected the "historical decline" of the community, a decline resulting largely from city neglect. By weighing only real estate values, the suggested settlement formula did not take into account other important factors valued by residents themselves: length of residence, emotional attachment to friends and relatives, distinct values and lifestyle, and the possession of a home that could be maintained without undue financial strain.

Phase Three: The White-Black Caretaker Alliance

When the threat of relocation tightened its grip on Africville, a number of residents concerned themselves about their future. Without a community infrastructure to provide a political power base, they were forced to look to the outside world for assistance and guidance. In 1961 an Africville resident visited the Montreal office of the late Sid Blum, Associate Secretary, National Committee on Human Rights, Canadian Labour Congress. The resident wanted to build a ranch-style bungalow on his Africville land. He complained to Blum that city officials had told him that, because he lived in an area intended for redevelopment, he must wait six months for a building permit and, even then, he might not be given one.[16] Upon his return to Africville, the resident told Mrs. Nancy Edwards of his meeting with Blum. (The name Mrs. Edwards, as are all names of Africville residents used in this chapter, is a pseudonym). Mrs. Edwards, a church leader and a prominent member of an old-line Africville family, wrote to Blum, outlining many of the problems faced by Africville residents.[17] In reply, Blum reviewed the problems[18] and advised as follows:

> Many of the problems you mention are economic or political problems that require leadership from among the residents of Africville and a constant agitation, and delegations to the city council to have your problems recognized and acted upon. In this matter, our committee can't be of much help. You must organize the people of Africville into a group whose voice is recognized by the city council, and continue to press your case until the city takes remedial action.[19]

Following receipt of Blum's advice, a small number of Africville residents banded together to form a ratepayers' association in order to communicate with city hall for the purpose of demanding an adequate water supply, sewerage, and other basic community requirements. The core members were seven residents, five of whom were active members of the Seaview African Baptist Church. After less than one year, the association's activities declined and a group of non-Africville Halifax citizens became the community advocates negotiating with the city officials.

After further correspondence with Blum, it was arranged that Blum or his colleague, A. Alan Borovoy, a lawyer and the Canadian Labour Congress Ontario human rights director, would visit Halifax.[20]

In August 1962 Borovoy arrived and, on his first morning, visited Africville with David Lewis Stein, a Toronto free-lance reporter who was writing an article for *Maclean's Magazine*.[21] Borovoy's first task was to bring together Africville residents and other Halifax citizens; on the evening of August 22, a meeting was held in the Nova Scotian Hotel, where Borovoy was staying (see Plate 5.1).

> The first thing he suggested was that they consider themselves an advisory council. They would come to this council as individuals rather than as delegates from organizations. That way they could decide to do something and act quickly on their decisions. They then could go back to whatever organizations they belonged to to try to enlist

support. The second thing Borovoy suggested was that they immediately collect enough support to make up a delegation to ask the labour minister to spend more money publicizing the fair-employment and fair-accommodation legislation.[22]

The next evening, at the Seaview African Baptist Church, Borovoy spoke to a meeting of Africville residents (see Plate 5.2).

'I have no magic answers,' he explained, 'but last night there was a meeting at the Nova Scotian Hotel. Some representatives of yours were there and so were a lot of other people, both white and Negro. We talked just not about the problems of Africville but of all the Halifax Negroes. At least this much has happened — you're not alone any more.... It's up to you. I can't come back here every week or every month. But if I have at least introduced a few people from Halifax to one another, I can go back to Toronto happy.'

When Borovoy had finished talking, Mrs. Edwards rose in her pew. 'When I got into this,' she said, 'I didn't know it would mean so much work. But now we have friends who want to help us. This is the first time in our history that people from Africville have gone into a meeting like the one Mr. Borovoy called. We've done a lot and with the help of God, we'll keep going.'[23]

Borovoy's Halifax visit and the political strategy he suggested were responsible for changing the direction of Africville relocation politics. Interviewed seven years later,[24] Borovoy explained that he had had little knowledge of Africville before his visit to Halifax in 1962. He recalled that, at that time, he had not conceived a specific solution to Africville's problems. He had emphasized that a black ghetto should not be subsidized and had stressed the importance of racial integration. Perceiving the Africville residents as "squatters and transients" and the community as a slum characterized by lack of facilities and poor housing, he had believed that relocation was inevitable. The residents, therefore, in his words, "had to make a deal," and since they had few resources, their hope lay in organizing with non-Africville Halifax citizens and forming a political alliance that could exert moral pressure on city officials.

Upon his return to Toronto after the two 1962 meetings, Borovoy wrote a memorandum to eleven Halifax citizens, three of whom were Africville residents.[25] He emphasized that the group must organize themselves and continue to meet. Following his advice, four Africville residents and five other Halifax citizens met on September 21, 1962, and organized a white-black political alliance—the Halifax Human Rights Advisory Committee.

Over a six-year period (1962-67), the Halifax Human Rights Advisory Committee met forty times[26] and held, in addition, approximately seven meetings with Africville residents in the Seaview African Baptist Church. A total of seventy-one citizens attended one or more meetings, but attendance at most meetings was low. The core membership consisted of ten members, four whites and six blacks, three of whom, Mr. and Mrs. Peter Edwards and Frank MacPherson, were Africville residents.[27]

The seven non-Africville members of the committee played what Herbert Gans has called "caretaker" roles.[28] They perceived themselves as protecting the interests of Africville residents and, as shown later in this chapter, collected technical information and provided crucial advice.

Interviewed individually at length,[29] six of the caretakers explained that they had become members of the committee through concern for human rights; accepting the "civil rights political climate" of the 1960s, they were against racial segregation and believed in integration. Their political ideology can be characterized as mainstream liberalism: a concern for human rights and the growth and development of individual potentiality, as well as a belief in both rational decision-making to solve problems and an incremental conception of progress. In general, these caretakers possessed what Edward Banfield and James Wilson call a "community — or public — regarding" political ethos.[30] The characteristics of this ethos are a sense of obligation towards the community, a high sense of personal efficacy, a long-sighted perspective, a general familiarity with a confidence in city-wide institutions, a cosmopolitan orientation towards life, and organizational skills and resources.[31] As Wilson observed:

> It is just these attributes, of course, which make such people most likely to participate effectively in organizations whose function — whatever their ostensible purpose — is to create a sense of community and of community confidence and

Plate 5.1. CRUCIAL MEETING: AUGUST 22, 1962. Mobilized by Africville residents' request for assistance, Halifax blacks and whites meet with lawyer A. Alan Borovoy (seated at right) and develop a new human rights organization.

Plate 5.2. MEETING AT THE SEAVIEW AFRICAN BAPTIST CHURCH, AUGUST 23, 1962. Lawyer A. Alan Borovoy suggests to Africville residents the importance of creating ties with other individuals and organizations concerned with human rights.

to win consent for community-wide plans. They are, in short, precisely those attributes which are likely to produce 'citizen participation in urban renewal' that planners and community organizers will consider 'positive and constructive' — that is, participation which will influence some of the general goals of renewal and modify a few of its details, but allow renewal to proceed.[32]

The four white caretakers among the core members of the human rights committee had impressive credentials for their role as "citizens-at-large" advocates in the Africville relocation. Three were university graduates while the fourth was a tradesman. Two had been raised in the Halifax area and the others had resided there for at least ten years. All had been involved, in one way or another, with programs designed to improve socio-economic conditions among blacks in Nova Scotia. Clearly they possessed a community or public-regarding political ethos.

The white caretakers had little or no knowledge of Africville's social structure and, despite their previous involvement in "black social problems," they had minimal contact with Africville and its residents. Although one of them was fairly familiar with the Africville situation through the activities of his church, even he did not know the names of the families with long-standing historical roots in Africville. First-hand knowledge of Africville depended upon the few community residents who were members of the human rights committee.

The three black caretakers had a high degree of "black consciousness" and were deeply concerned about white discrimination against Nova Scotian blacks. One of them described as follows the relationship between the city of Halifax and its black residents:

> I don't think they [city officials] give a damn about black people in Halifax. [We] have never been a group to reckon with. We have never been a political power. We never had a pressure group. We never had money. We were just damn nuisances.
>
> You know, what the hell! 'So we inherited those people from slavery, we've got to do something about them, so give them some land.' In the province, they have been given land that was useless…in the hope that a combination between inclemency of the weather and the infertility of

the soil we would all die. But geez, God must have been
on our side. Man, we have survived, more than survived;
the black population has increased. So I would say, basically,
the city just didn't give a damn.

Only one of the black caretakers was a native-born Nova Scotian, the
second had moved to Halifax from the West Indies, while the third was
raised in the United States. They were all employed in middle-class
occupations. In general, they had only superficial knowledge of Africville's
history and social structure. During the relocation decision-making, they
were the major black "advocates" for the community, and later two of
them became members of an important city hall sub-committee that
reviewed Africville relocation settlements.

Only five Africville residents attended more than two meetings of the
Halifax Human Rights Advisory Committee, and only three residents
attended twenty of the Committee's forty meetings, Mr. and Mrs. Peter
Edwards and Frank MacPherson.

Mr. and Mrs. Edwards were an elderly couple who were the informal
representatives to the world outside Africville. Nancy Edwards was born
and raised in Africville while her husband, Peter, was born in the British
West Indies. Mrs. Edwards' ancestors were among the first settlers, and
she was a member of the largest kinship group. The relocation social worker
described her as follows: "...a leader in the area...she was a midwife to
many of the so-called younger women in the area during their pregnancies
and, for this reason, people came to her for assistance."

The Edwards were articulate spokespersons for Africville. Through
them outside voluntary organizations entered the community. The Edwards
were the core members of the ratepayers' association and it was Mrs.
Edwards who wrote to request help from the Canadian Labour Congress.
The Edwards provided the crucial channel through which the relocation
social worker was able to enter the community and obtain necessary
information about kinship ties and land ownership. As the leading Africville
member of the Halifax Human Rights Advisory Committee, Peter Edwards
was the principal channel of communication between Africville residents
(especially the elderly members of the oldline Africville familes and members
of the Seaview African Baptist Church) and city officials and relocation
caretakers.

Frank MacPherson was a middle-aged black who, although not born
in Africville, moved there after his marriage as it was his wife's home.

She was not, however, from a family whose roots in Africville went back to the 1840s and neither of the MacPhersons was part of the community's church clique. Prior to 1960, Mr. MacPherson played a minor leadership role in Africville. He was interested in world affairs and, in 1961, had been a member of the ratepayers' association and became involved, through the Edwards, in the Halifax Human Rights Advisory Committee. Although not a forceful person nor a widely acknowledged indigenous leader, Mr. MacPherson was regarded by many Africville residents as a "a good guy" who possessed some of the skills necessary for service on the Halifax Human Rights Advisory Committee; in general he was a medium of communication to many of the marginal Africville residents.

It is important to note that MacPherson and the Edwards were neither elected nor appointed to represent Africville residents on the Halifax Human Rights Advisory Committee. They became the unofficial representatives of Africville on the Committee and in the relocation decision-making solely because they had come forward, first in the Africville Ratepayers' Association and, later, in attending meetings of the committee. Africville residents by themselves held no formal meetings to discuss their impending relocation. Thus, while MacPherson, and especially the Edwards, had a legitimacy as indigenous leaders, the precise nature of the mandate on behalf of Africville was always undefined.

While the white-black caretaker alliance was being established, the rumour of relocation preoccupied many community residents. The development department report outlining the initial relocation financial terms appeared in the Halifax press on August 1, 1962.[33] On the evening of August 8, in response to this announcement and upon the calling of a public meeting, nearly one hundred black people crowded into the Seaview African Baptist Church. The local Halifax newspaper reported that the desire to remain in the community was unanimous.[34] "'I wouldn't want to leave here and move into the city,' said [one resident, and] the audience clapped its approval. 'We want to be able to buy land out here and build on it according to city specifications.'"[35]

Two months later, however, Africville residents had resigned themselves to the relocation. Responding to the relocation announcement, one prominent black leader attempted to organize an Africville branch of the Nova Scotia Association for the Advancement of Coloured People. On October 15, a meeting held at the Seaview African Baptist Church was attended by about twenty-five or thirty residents, most of whom were members of oldline Africville familes. Many of these residents had fought

Halifax city hall officials for basic community facilities, but, without a power base from which to act, they had failed. Their attitude was one of pessimism and resignation. After a discussion at the October meeting, they accepted the fact of relocation. The next day, October 16, the local Halifax newspaper reported: [The black leader] said he had talked to many residents of the community and had reached four conclusions:

> (1) **The residents have resigned themselves to the fact that they must relocate.** (2) It is no problem for those who have a deed as long as they can get enough for their property, because they can look after their own relocation. (3) Many people don't want to live in public housing, but prefer single family dwellings. (4) The residents do not want segregated public housing. (Emphasis added).[36]

While the shock of relocation vibrated through the community, both city officials and the caretakers were preoccupied with the political realities of the relocation decision. City hall bureaucracy moved forward at a rapid pace: shortly after the public release of the initial relocation exchange terms reports on Africville were written by the commissioner of health and welfare and the commissioner of works and city assessor.[37] Also, a Dalhousie University study outlining the socio-economic conditions of Africville residents was released to the press.[38] Armed with these reports, the committee of the whole [city] council met on October 24, 1962, and discussed the department's report.[39] After considerable discussion the committee adopted, as policy, the relocation of Africville residents. Members of the white-black caretaker alliance attended this meeting. They were in a weak position to resist council's policy decision as their only bargaining strategy was to put "moral pressure" on council members and city officials. The chairman of the alliance addressed the aldermen:

> The impression the Africville people have of you is of a big white brother pushing the black children around, and they resent it. If they were a majority group, you would have heard their impressions first.[40]

He contended that the aldermen should have consulted with the Halifax Human Rights Advisory Committee and Africville residents before adopting a policy of relocation. The mayor explained "that the committee of the whole had attempted only to set the machinery in motion to procure the views and wishes of the residents before a final decision is made by council."[41] During the meeting, one of the white caretakers expressed dismay that a large portion of the Africville area had been expropriated for the Industrial Mile and that most of the residents, some of whom were still paying taxes on their properties, were unaware of this action. He requested that discussion be held with Africville residents, and the mayor assured him that a final decision would not be made before the discussions took place.

Accepting the mayor's promise at face value, the caretakers were somewhat assured that Africville residents would now become involved in the relocation dialogue before city council made its final decision. But the real world of city politics often operates on the basis of expediency rather than the fulfilment of vague promises that are not legally binding. City council met on the following day, October 25, 1962, and unanimously adopted a report containing the following recommendations:

1. That the blighted housing and dilapidated structures in the Africville area should be removed;
2. That the full legal authority of the city should be used to accomplish this removal;
3. That the use of legal authority should be tempered with understanding and natural justice on matters of housing and matters of compensation for the apparent owners of land and buildings within the Africville areas; and
4. That this policy be implemented with the utmost dispatch after its implications are fully conveyed to the residents affected and/or their representatives in consultation with church and welfare organizations.[42]

The caretakers were now in a quandary. As their involvement was part-time and voluntary, they had few resources and no direct avenues of political power to influence or modify council's policy. How, then, could they respond to the relocation decision? The minutes of the first twelve meetings of their committee reveal that they were initially concerned with achieving clarification of the city's policy towards Africville and with examining alternatives to relocation. During their negotiations, the caretakers' principal channel of communication to city hall was the development director.

In attempting to achieve clarification of the city's policy, the caretakers prepared a list of eleven questions, and in November, 1962, a written reply to these questions was received from the development director.[43] The initial relocation exchange terms were reasserted. Africville residents with "paper" or "possessory" title would receive full market value for their property. Residents with no "apparent legal claim title" could receive a gratuitous payment of $500 in return for vacant possession of their property. The Africville land, he wrote, would be used for a limited-access expressway and for industrial location. He further argued that industries required cheap land and industrial development would contribute to the Halifax economic situation by creating employment.

On Wednesday evening, November 26, 1962, the development director's answers to the eleven questions were read and interpreted by several caretakers to approximately fifty Africville residents assembled at the Seaview African Baptist Church. During discussion, fourteen additional questions emerged. The development director attended the committee's next meeting, December 6, 1962, where these questions were discussed and, in late January, 1963, wrote a letter to the committee secretary answering the questions.[44]

Three months later he attended a meeting with residents and caretakers at the Seaview African Baptist Church in order to clarify city policy towards Africville residents.

During the time the caretakers were attempting to clarify city policy towards Africville, the development director helped steer them towards partial acceptance of a relocation policy. When the caretakers suggested that a special judicial committee be established to examine titles and possession of properties in Africville, the development director replied that the city was developing a formula and that the committee might observe its application to a particular case before formulating plans for further action. When one caretaker suggested the city build new homes on city-owned land and sell them to the relocatees, the development director replied that there was no reasonable basis on which home ownership could be subsidized. When another caretaker asked that the new homes be built "as an act of reparation," the director noted that an undertaking of this kind would require a policy decision beyond the scope of his responsibility. To the caretakers he presented "positive relocation arguments" based on legal and financial considerations: these arguments, in the main, were accepted by the caretakers who understood their complexities. Nevertheless, their attitude towards the relocation was one of ambivalence. They explored alternatives to relocation and various housing schemes.

Interviewed approximately six years later, one of the black caretakers stated that co-operative housing was not possible "because of the lack of the spirit of cooperation within the residents of the community and because of the need for subsidies." The caretakers also explored the possibility of obtaining water facilities and sewerage for Africville.

These alternatives were, however, examined without the active participation of the entire Africville community. The investigation was guided and directed primarily by the black and white caretakers who were familiar with the mechanics and skills required to search for alternatives to the Africville situation. By early September, 1963, the Halifax Human Rights Advisory Committee had held five meetings in Africville; during the consideration of alternatives, however, there was no wide-range citizen participation among Africville residents.

After reviewing various alternatives, the caretakers still remained uncertain about the wisdom of the relocation. Given their liberal belief in rational decision-making to solve problems, they decided they should consult a specialist. One of the caretakers suggested the name of a noted Canadian urban expert, the late Dr. Albert Rose, Professor of Social Work, University of Toronto, and author of *Regent Park: A Study in Slum Clearance.*[45] In mid-1963 several caretakers and aldermen met and decided that the members of the white-black alliance would recommend to city council that an expert such as Dr. Rose be invited to Halifax. A letter was written to council recommending types of housing for Africville residents: a non-profit, limited-dividend housing company, or the construction of high-density housing on the upper slopes of Africville.[46] The caretakers, ambivalent about the relocation and recognizing the housing problems for Africville residents, recommended:

> ...that city council engage a person of outstanding qualifications, in training and experience, to study Africville in depth and for the purpose of formulating specific recommendations of sound ways and means of solving problems in housing.

The committee submitted that, before initiating such a study, a specialist should be consulted:

> The committee advises that, as a first step toward implementing its recommendation, city council bring to

Halifax a specialist who would be requested (after a preliminary survey of Africville, and discussion with city staff, with the Halifax Human Rights Advisory Committee, and with other resources to state whether, in his judgement, a study in depth is indicated.

The letter also contained the following biographical statement about Dr. Rose:

Dr. Albert Rose graduated in 1939 as a gold medalist in the Honours Political Science and Economics course at the University of Toronto, and he received his Ph.D. three years later from the University of Illinois. From 1943 to 1945 he served with the Canadian Army, after which he held the post of Research Director of the Welfare Council of Toronto until, in 1948, he joined the staff of the School of Social Work, University of Toronto, where he is now Professor of Social Work.

Dr. Rose has been associated with the Civic Advisory Council of Toronto, the Canadian Welfare Council, Central Mortgage and Housing Corporation, the Department of Citizenship and Immigration, and the Community Planning Association of Canada.

Dr. Rose has published a number of significant reports on various aspects of housing and metropolitan planning, including *An Experimental Study of Local Housing Conditions and Needs*, submitted to Central Mortgage and Housing Corporation in 1953, and his principal study, *Regent Park: A Study in Slum Clearance*, published in 1958.

On September 12, 1963, the president of the Halifax city council addressed council and requested support of the recommendations set forth in the committee's letter. City council decided unanimously "...that the city manager be directed to: (a) invite Dr. Rose to come to Halifax to make a preliminary survey of Africville; and (b) to report to council the terms and conditions under which the study would be undertaken if the need for same is indicated."[47]

Phase Four: Expertise and Liberal-Welfare Rhetoric

Dr. Rose's Halifax visit had profound implications. Until his visit the structure and exchange terms of the relocation followed the dimensions of the development model; however, his report and its adoption by Halifax city council shifted the emphasis to the liberal-welfare model. Africville residents were recognized as a group of Halifax citizens requiring special attention, and the initial relocation exchange terms were modified. The rhetoric of the new exchange terms was rooted in liberal ideology (end segregation and provide improved opportunities for the disadvantaged) and welfare planning (coordinate employment, educational, and rehabilitative programs with the rehousing of residents).

Dr. Albert Rose visited Halifax on November 24-26, 1963. He had read the city staff reports on Africville, a number of magazine articles about Africville, and the Dalhousie University study, *The Condition of the Negroes of Halifax City, Nova Scotia*. However, as Dr. Rose himself stated, prior to his 1963 visit, he was unfamiliar with Africville.

During a 1970 tape-recorded interview with one of the authors, Dr. Rose noted his tour of Africville was brief:

> [The development director], or the city manager, or both, took me through the community, and we drove through it twice. We got out and we walked around. It is not a very big community in terms of distance. And at that time, this was late November, 1963, the roads were such that you could barely get in and out, so it wasn't something that would take long. I don't suppose I spent more than perhaps two hours in Africville altogether, on two separate visits.

He described his impressions of Africville as follows:

> In a nutshell, my impressions were devastating...my impression was that, in the Canadian context, this was the worst urban appendage I had ever seen. I was overwhelmed by the visual context of the physical surroundings. It seemed to me that the thing was a bottomless pit; that you could pour in fantastic resources and you have no base upon which to rehabilitate; that if you were to build back a viable community you would really have to start from scratch.

You might just as well assume no one was living there. The whole neighbourhood would have to be serviced with water and sewage disposal. The streets would have to be laid out. There was no street lighting, as I remember it. There were no...public transportation facilities. I think the nearest school was outside the boundaries of the area. They had a magnificent view.

I was appalled, frankly, by the feeling that here was a group of Canadians that were as entombed, entrapped, as ever I had even dreamed about.... Even in downtown Toronto, it seemed to me that what we called slums bore no resemblance to the impression that I got of Africville. That was my reaction and it was not a reaction that I certainly wanted to destroy this community. I found it difficult to believe that a community existed. I had no doubt that by the time I left, and that by the time I met with the leaders, there were a great many values here that were worth preserving.

During his two days in Halifax, Dr. Rose interviewed five city officials, two university specialists, and two professional social workers and met informally with others. One City official described his meeting with Dr. Rose:

Interviewer: "What kinds of questions did Albert Rose ask you about the community of Africville?"
City official: "Very little. He seems to have been well-informed but there was a good deal of prejudice injected into what he had been told. I did not feel that he knew the people of Africville."
Interviewer: "Why was this?"
City official: "I think here again the press, [the] news media, had built up an image that here were a group of people living almost in the jungle. There was no way of dealing with them but force them out, force them to do this, that, and the other things, and I think he went along with this."

Dr. Rose described his meetings with Halifax city officials as follows:

The public officials made it perfectly clear to me that they intended to utilize those lands for non-residential purposes. And this is why I warned the mayor, when I had a private audience with him, that if he were to turn this over to developers who might provide high-income residential housing, he would face the same problem of urban removal becoming Negro removals as had been the bone of contention and a very serious problem in many American cities....

But it seems to me that what they told me, and what plans they had in the back of their minds, [may] have been very different. They may have had plans in their minds for various uses that would have been offensive, considering the destruction of the community that was about to occur.

On the evening of November 25, at the Cornwallis Street Baptist Church, Rose met with six of the caretakers, four other members of the Halifax Human Rights Advisory Committee, and four Africville representatives on the committee. During the meeting Rose observed that these residents appeared to be unaware of some of the important possible consequences of relocation:

The reality of [relocation] couldn't have possibly penetrated their consciousness at that point. They would have to move and have to face life in the metropolis...where they would face discrimination in housing. I don't think this impact really penetrated. They seemed to be sort of resigned, and there wasn't any of the militancy that one would expect from black groups say five or six years later.

Rose recalled some details of this meeting at the Cornwallis Street Baptist Church. Unwilling to entertain the idea of a separate black community, he argued strongly against the building of a segregated housing complex on the Africville site. In his words:

I was trying to ascertain from these people what it was they saw as their objective (I'm speaking now of the black people), and what I might do to assist them. They knew that I had some knowledge of housing, perhaps from the introduction and the fact that they had been notified that this person was coming from the University of Toronto.

And so we explored for some time, perhaps an hour or three hours, the whole question of a rehousing program on the site itself. I expressed the view, and I think I was correct, that the chances of their obtaining federal-provincial financial and other support under the then-existing arrangement in the National Housing Act were very slim; in fact, not really worth talking about.

I also tried to explain to them that part of this reluctance might be physical, in terms of the absence of normal municipal servicing. But I think the greater question would have been the reluctance of federal-provincial authorities to rebuild a ghetto or effect what you might call a segregated community. This was the phrase I pounded away at. I said that, as a Canadian, as a human being, [with] a great deal of compassion for their particular circumstances, I don't think I could honestly recommend [that] a segregated community, even a modern one, ought to replace what was there....

They placed a great deal of emphasis on the church, and I thought that their spiritual gatherings could be re-established somewhere else along with other community facilities. They were pretty sceptical of what I was saying, frankly, and admitted only with a great deal of difficulty that the answer to the problem was to tear down Africville and replace it on the site with a public housing project such as the Regent Park in Toronto which they knew I had studied at one point.

I didn't enjoy the evening, particularly, as an experience. It was like making arrangements for a funeral. It was not a pleasant experience at all, and I felt that I was almost in the position of some great authority, say in the field of housing. There was not really a lot of, or a series of, alternatives.

They were desperately clutching at last straws. And yet no one likes to be in a position of saying 'I'm perfectly certain that that's the case and, therefore, you have had it.' And that was, in part, the position I was in that evening.

Two of the caretakers described, in the following terms, the November 25 meeting with Dr. Rose:

> He was quite impatient, in some respects, about the dilly-dallying — studies, briefs, and all that stuff — and said it was studied to death, or words to that effect. And the time was now to get some action on the thing. And he did speak briefly about housing like in Cabbagetown, Toronto.... He was an experienced municipal housing man, worth listening to.... He figured...what the heck, you know the problem, so get cracking.

> The main thing I recall was the viewpoint put forward by the Africville representatives, or people, that they didn't want to move. And they gave him a rough time, it seemed to me. He may have intimated even then what he was going to report. He was a fairly blunt fellow and may have known the answers even before he arrived.

By early December, Dr. Rose had forwarded his report to Halifax city council. (For the complete text of the Rose Report, see Donald H. Clairmont and Dennis W. Magill, *Africville Relocation Report*, pp. A59-A67.) Although he had not had contact with the vast majority of Africville residents, he wrote:

> The residents of Africville appear ready and to some extent eager to negotiate a settlement concerning the ultimate disposition of their community.
> The leaders of the community readily admit that Africville is a slum, that it should be cleared and that it would long since have been cleared if the inhabitants were of a different racial background.

The report incorrectly described Africville as "one of the most intensively studied communities in North America," and recommended against conducting a large-scale research project. During the 1970 interview, Dr. Rose observed that:

> I felt that the city of Halifax and its officials had a tremendous knowledge of the Africville community; at least, in terms

of its physical aspects and its basic demographic data. I knew that they did not have the kind of information that social scientists might gather in personal interviews with the families, with respect to their intra-familial situations, with respect to their attitudes toward the community, with respect to concerns about possible dislocation of the community and the relocation. But my judgment, after a fairly short visit to Africville, was that the real concerns of the city council would not be facilitated by a major social-scientific research program....

They knew the basic demographic situation. They knew the resources of these people. They knew the structures they lived in, whether they had title or they didn't have title. They didn't know all of the sociological aspects of the thing, but my honest view was that perhaps I wasn't competent in that area. I just didn't see the need for refined research in those aspects of the situation, in order to reach a decision. It is very easy for a person who comes in for two or three days to say, 'What you need is a thorough examination of the social interrelationships in this community, the institutions that the people depend upon, their kinship relationships, how they exist from day to day, and what their basic attitudes are.' I could have promoted a major research project involving maybe years of work, at least in the summers, for myself, groups of students, and economically this might have been very advantageous.

The fact that I wasn't promoting some huge gain of a personal nature for myself really made me feel that I was more, rather than less, responsible.

Rose explained that if his report had been written in 1970, rather than in 1963, he might not have recommended against a research project.

I just didn't see the need for refined research...in order to reach a decision. I might make a different decision today, after six years of seeing urban renewal neighbourhoods identified, designated...legally torn apart, uprooted, rebuilt, and then finding that my attitude toward what we were doing was not as clear as I thought it was....

Today I might make an entirely new recommendation about both research and about the nature of the program, and all the rest of it. I don't think I would accept the view that I just swallowed everything the city was saying to me. I must emphasize what I said before, that I was so appalled by what I saw that certainly there was a quick reaction in my mind, in my spirit, as it were. The only solution to this problem was to get the people out of there and into something that more approximated a normal way of life. I hadn't seen in either the United States or Canada, at that time, a segregation as evident as this one.

Viewing the plight of Africville residents as a "social problem" that could be partly solved through the input of financial, housing, and retraining programs, Dr. Rose recommended the following relocation settlement terms:

Housing: The housing solution was viewed as a tripartite undertaking:
1. The families with title to property would receive sufficient financial compensation to make a down-payment on older homes in downtown Halifax.
2. Rental would be provided, if necessary, during a readjustment period, for families that sought admission to public housing.
3. Roughly half the Africville families would arrange their own housing and seek rental accommodation in Halifax or elsewhere in Nova Scotia.

Employment: In this report, Dr. Rose asserted that the employment and livelihood of a large proportion of Africville residents derived from "scavenging on the adjacent city rubbish disposal area." To improve the employment skills of Africville residents, he wrote:

Those persons from Africville who are employable must be assisted to seek and obtain employment suited to their skills and experience, if any, within the city of Halifax or its metropolitan area. This will require not merely the acceptance and enforcement of the Fair Employment Practices Act of the Province of Nova Scotia but more especially, a change in attitude and the sympathetic understanding of the employers, workers, consumers, and general citizenry of the community.

Those persons who do not appear to possess marketable skills or experience must be assisted to obtain vocational guidance, counselling, and, if possible, training or retraining.

Income: In addition to settlement payments and compensation, welfare assistance should be available for relocatees as they create new living patterns in Halifax.

The report recommended that city officials design the relocation program in consultation with Africville representatives and the Halifax Human Rights Advisory Committee, and that:

The development department of the city of Halifax be assigned the responsibility of administering the entire relocation program and that for this purpose a special budget be appropriated to enable:
(a) the employment of a trained social worker or social scientist to visit and document the social and economic situation and requirements of each family unit or single individual, and to recommend the order or priority of relocation; and
(b) the development of a registry of available housing for sale or rent...; and
(c) the creation of a special relocation fund to assist families who require furniture or equipment....

The report also recommended recognition of "the special situation" of residents without a deed to property and that "the compensation for this latter group be varied in accordance with size of family and/or marital status, recognizing the special needs of unmarried mothers with dependent children."

A further recommendation was that "the city of Halifax provide free legal aid through its legal department and the enlistment of volunteers from the legal profession, to assist Africville residents to purchase homes or otherwise relocate themselves...."

Dr. Rose went beyond the two purposes that Halifax city council had designated for his November visit when he made the crucial recommendation that:

The city council of Halifax enunciate a clear policy that the community of Africville will be expropriated and cleared during the period commencing April 1, 1964 (or shortly thereafter) and that this process will be completed not later than December 31, 1966.

Adoption of this recommendation in January, 1964 by the Halifax city council lent an aura of legitimation to council's Africville relocation policy. When asked why he went beyond his terms of reference which were to undertake a preliminary survey and to recommend if a community study was necessary, Dr. Rose explained:

I suppose I should have stopped at that point, and what my report in effect does is make recommendations for treatment of the community. But to me they were really a set of guidelines, or preliminary views on areas of great concern, that I felt they must take into account; such as, the reality of providing people with housing, employment, income, and community facilities if they were to be moved from there into downtown Halifax, and emphasizing the responsibility that city council was taking upon itself if it did this. But I suppose the report could be read as if it were written by a group of urban consultants who might have spent a year there.... I think that I would have to say very frankly that I learned a lot about [what] one might say and what one might not say in a similar situation.

The Rose Report received editorial support from the Halifax press.[48] In a 1968 interview, the development director described the report as:

A document that was clear, brief, well-written and worth every cent of the $500 that the city paid for it.

Interviewed in 1969, the development director recalled that Dr. Rose agreed with the city's premise that Africville should be relocated:

We sent Dr. Rose all of the information that we had, and said we would like him to come down and do a study.... And the only area where there was any real discussion,...was the basis of compensating people on family size, structure, and conditions, as opposed to real estate. We were holding out for the principle of compensation in real estate, and he was holding out for real estate plus all of these other factors.

Now the only reaason we were holding out was from an administrative point of view.... How do you balance apples and oranges? I suppose this was one of the most difficult problems during the whole process. If you give someone $5,000 for this set of circumstances, how does this equate with this other set where you paid $7,000?

In this statement, the development director points to one of the bureaucratic arguments used to justify the initial relocation settlement terms. For homeowners with deeds, the settlement criteria were to be based on real estate market values. City council's acceptance of the Rose Report, however, required city officials to adopt a liberal-welfare relocation model and thereby to enlarge the settlement criteria to include considerations such as family size.

The Rose Report relieved the caretakers' uncertainty and doubt; viewing Dr. Rose as an urban expert, they accepted his judgment and ceased their search for alternatives to relocation. In the words of one of the white caretakers:

I thought that [Rose] was one of the leading men in Canada, and his recommendation was adopted. I had doubts even then, you know, and if his report had been different it would have had tremendous weight with me. But it supported what we were not committed to as a committee. But if the report was different, we could very well have changed that.

The Rose Report performed the critical function of relieving the caretakers of their doubts and uncertainties concerning relocation and of defining the relocation as a special program at city hall. Among all non-Africville people involved in the relocation, the report enacted a common perspective towards the removal of the Africville people. The relocation was deemed desirable and inevitable. The Africville people were designated to be a special group having special problems for which the solution was a liberal-welfare type of relocation. Rational expertise was to be the prime way of solving the "Africville people's problems." Special programs were to be coordinated on behalf of the relocatees. The relocatees themselves were not to be involved directly; they were not to be asked to offer solutions nor allowed to negotiate collectively with the city. The Africville people were regarded essentially as being unable to cope with their problems and as less than competent in knowing what was good for them. They were seen as lacking resources, except perhaps a limited community spirit, and the wherewithal to bargain individually or collectively. This collective perspective was achieved by the caretakers and outside experts accepting the erroneous assumptions about Africville that it was a community of transients and squatters; by the pressure of the then contemporary climate of opinion that integration was desirable and would in itself produce beneficial results; and by the definition of the situation with respect to alternatives as communicated by the development officer.

Phase Five: Official Adoption of Liberal-Welfare Rhetoric

During its January 2, 1964 meeting, Halifax city council considered a motion to approve its finance and executive committee's recommendation that the Rose Report be approved in principle and that the appropriate administrative machinery be prepared for the implementation of the recommendations by April 1, 1964.[49] Eleven members of the Halifax Human Rights Advisory Committee attended the meeting. Addressing council, the committee chairman submitted that committee members had not received copies of the Rose Report until they arrived at the council meeting and that, therefore, they had not had an opportunity to review it. Council subsequently agreed to defer consideration of the Rose Report until its next meeting and, at the same time, instructed the city solicitor to prepare the necessary draft legislation for submission to the Nova Scotia Legislative Assembly.[50]

After council's discussion of the Rose Report, the eleven members of the committee met for almost two hours in an office adjacent to the council chamber. They voted unanimously to accept the recommendations of the Rose Report and to cooperate with the residents of Africville and with the city in implementing the recommendations. The committee further agreed to request two guarantees from the city: assurance that Africville families would not be relocated in areas designated for redevelopment; and payment of monthly rental to relocatees for, if necessary, an indefinite period. The committee also decided to hold a public meeting on January 9, 1964, in the Seaview African Baptist Church to discuss the Rose Report with Africville residents. At this subsequent meeting, which was closed to the press that had assembled to record the historic moment, only forty-one Africville residents met with the committee.[51] One of the caretakers explained that the attendance was small because "the meeting was attended primarily by the older community people, the ones who really cared about the community and went to all our meetings."

When asked if there was opposition to the Rose Report when he read it at the meeting, the chairman of the committee replied:

> There was always resistance to things in the Rose Report. But we on the committee tried at all times to explain that we had explored just about every alternative, every possibility and...to the best of our judgment at the time felt that the Rose Report...was the best thing.

At this meeting thirty-seven voted to accept the report. The next day the chairman and secretary of the human rights advisory committee wrote to the mayor and aldermen explaining that the Rose Report recommendations had been approved unanimously by the committee and by ninety percent of Africville residents present at the meeting on January 9; the letter did not indicate that only thirty-seven residents had voted in favour of the report. The letter to council stressed the need for the city to employ a trained social worker or social scientist who would assist relocatees during the transition period, reiterated the concern about Africville families being relocated in areas designated for redevelopment, and sought assurance that the city would pay monthly rental during a period of readjustment of relocatees unable to pay rent.[52]

On January 16, 1964, council met to consider the Rose Report. The chairman of the Halifax Human Rights Advisory Committee addressed council, explaining that the report was acceptable to Africville residents and requesting council to consider the following additional point: "that those who will be in the process of buying homes shall be protected by a written guarantee in case of lapse of payments due to sickness, unemployment, or minimum pension so that their position will not be jeopardized."[53] The mayor replied:

> All we are doing tonight is establishing broad principles....
> All are prepared to overcome the neglect of many years;

and I can assure you that we are prepared to do everything we can to make this move as painless as possible, and try to look after the people as best we can within our resources, and beyond our resources.[54]

Council then moved that a special committee be appointed, composed of members of council, city staff, and representatives of the Halifax Human Rights Advisory Committee. The special committee was to consider the Rose Report recommendations and report to council with recommendations for the operation of the relocation program. Mr. Edwards, an Africville member of the Halifax Human Rights Advisory Committee, again reiterated the concern of elderly Africville residents with low incomes about buying new properties or paying rent in public housing:

Some [elderly Africville residents] were born there, have lived there all their lives and never gone anywhere else. [They] want to know how they are going to pay for a home. We want to know how we are going to finance these. There is no way for some of us.[55]

The mayor replied:

I think that if this is kept under continuous study, we can overcome the problem by extraordinary action. We cannot discuss individual cases tonight, but we are attempting to start to correct this housing problem; and I have faith in council that they will support the recommendations from the advisory committee to help overcome the problems that arise in making the move.[56]

Council then passed a motion authorizing the relocation of Africville residents over a period of two years and nine months.[57] Nothing was added to specify a legal or moral obligation that the city provide continuing financial assistance to new homeowners or to persons unable to meet rental expenses in the city, or that the city refrain from relocating people in redevelopment areas.

With its 1964 motion, Halifax city council set the stage for the relocation of Africville. By January, 1970, the black community that had existed for over 125 years would be left to the pages of history.

Notes

1   The report described Africville as "a section of land about fifteen acres in extent on the shores of Bedford Basin lying roughly between Gottingen and Robie Streets. There are about ninety buildings used as dwellings by 125 adults and 200 children under the age of 16." City of Halifax, *Report by the City Manager to the Mayor and City Council*, August 19, 1954. For a summary of the report, see Ron M. Slade, "Project to Cost $106,200," *The Mail-Star*, Halifax, N.S., Aug.19, 1954.

2   Report by the city manager, op. cit., p.1

3   *Minutes of the Halifax City Council*, September 17, 1954.

4   Ibid., January 13, 1955, pp. 4-5.

5   Ibid., p. 5.

6   The authors are grateful to the National Harbours Board, Halifax, for permission to examine files. Newspaper reports of these discussions emphasized that it would be necessary to relocate Africville residents and that redevelopment of the basin area would be of advantage to Halifax's industrial growth. See, for instance, "Metropolitan Area Growth Demands Unified Action," *The Mail-Star*, July 17, 1954.

7   Stephenson, op. cit., p. 27.

8   *Minutes of the Halifax City Council*, May 16, 1957, pp. 338-39. Within the industrial mile area, land owned by the Canadian National Railways was not to be expropriated; it was to be acquired by negotiation.

9   "Get Step Closer to Expressway," *The Mail-Star*, Halifax, N.S., February 17, 1962.

10 Memorandum from D.A. Baker, Assistant Planner, to K.M. Munnich, Director of Planning, City of Halifax, January 2, 1962, p. 2.

11 Memorandum from the city manager to the mayor and members of the Town Planning Board, February 20, 1962. This memorandum is in the Industrial Mile File, Development Department, City Hall, Halifax, N.S.

12 *Industrial Mile—Africville Area: Land Ownership and Buildings*, Map P500/46, July 26, 1962, Planning Office, City Hall, Halifax, N.S.

13 The development department was formally established on October 1, 1961.

14 *Curriculum vitae* of the development director, a communication to the authors from his office, April, 1970.

15 For the complete text of this report see Clairmont and Magill, *Africville Relocation Report*, Appendix A, pp. A1-A9.

16 The details of this meeting are outlined in Blum's correspondence. Letter from Sid Blum, National Committee on Human Rights, Canadian Labour Congress, to F.C. Brodie, Human Rights Committee, Halifax-Dartmouth District Labour Council, October 17, 1961.

17 Mrs. Edwards permitted the research staff to Xerox her letters from Mr. Blum. Appreciation is extended to her for permission to quote from this correspondence.

18 Blum listed the problems outlined by Mrs. Edwards, a number of which reflect the existing pattern of discrimination against Africville residents:

"(1) The men of Africville are not able to get employment in the City, either because of racial discrimination or because they come from Africville. (2) The residents of Africville do not have sewerage or running water although there are such facilities available in the districts around Africville. (3) Africville is exposed to the City dump, which is on one side of the district, sewerage water from the old Immigration Hospital runs through the district water supply, the wells are contaminated, and a nearby fish-oil plant pollutes the air of the district." Letter from Sid Blum to Mrs. Edwards, September 6, 1961, p. 1.

19 Ibid., p. 2.

20 Blum repeated his promise in a letter to Mrs. Edwards. Letters from Sid Blum to Mrs. Edwards, April 19, and August 9, 1962.

21 David Lewis Stein, "The Counterattack on Diehard Racism," *Maclean's Magazine*, October 20 1962, *passim*. Bob Brooks, a free-lance photographer, Yarmouth, N.S., took the photographs that accompanied Stein's article. A number of Mr. Brook's photographs are used throughout this book.

22 Ibid., pp. 92-93.

23 *Idem*.

24 Interview, Toronto, Ontario, November 1969. Borovoy is now the General Counsel, Canadian Civil Liberties Association.

25 Memorandum from A. Alan Borovoy, Executive Secretary, Toronto and District Labour Committee for Human Rights, August 1962.

26 The Secretary, Halifax Human Rights Advisory Committee, permitted the authors to Xerox the minutes of the committee's meetings. The first minuted meeting was held on September 21, 1962. The committee's last meeting was held on January 23, 1967.

27 The criteria for defining core membership were: attendance at ten or more of the committee's meetings, and personal involvement with the efforts of the committee. Personal involvement was evaluated subjectively by the authors after a review of the committee's minutes.

28 Gans' definition of this concept is: "The term 'caretaker' can thus be applied broadly to anyone who provides services to people.... Caretakers thus include those people and agencies who offer medical and psychiatric treatment, case work, occupational, social and psychological counselling,

economic assistance, technical aid or information, advice in general, and educational and quasi-educational programs intended to benefit their users." Herbert J. Gans, *The Urban Villagers: Group and Class in the Life of Italian Americans* (New York: The Free Press, 1962), p. 142.

29 These interviews were completed approximately seven years after the inception of the Halifax Human Rights Advisory Committee and two and one-half years after its termination. It was, therefore, difficult for the caretakers to recall precisely some of the events during the relocation decision-making. One of the black caretakers had moved from Halifax and could not be interviewed.

30 Edward C. Banfield and James Q. Wilson, *City Politics* (Cambridge: Harvard University Press, 1963), chap. 16.

31 These characteristics are outlined by James Q. Wilson, "Planning and Politics: Citizen Participation in Urban Renewal," in *Citizen Participation in Urban Development: Vol. 1: Concepts and Issues,* Hans B.C. Spiegel, ed. (Washington, D.C.: Center for Community Studies, National Institute for Applied Behavioural Science, 1968), pp. 49-50.

32 Ibid., p. 50.

33 "Africville District Takeover Being Viewed as Necessary: Halifax Planning Board Considers Report Tuesday," *The Mail-Star,* Halifax, N.S., August 9, 1962.

34 "Residents Want to Keep Homes in Africville," *The Mail-Star*, Halifax, N.S., August 9, 1962.

35 *Idem.*

36 "Africville Ruling: Area Residents Anxious to Have Rights Honoured," *The Mail-Star,* Halifax, N.S., October 16, 1962.

37 Mimeographed report by Dr. A.R. Morton, Commissioner of Health and Welfare, August 28, 1962. Mimeographed report by G.F. West, Commissioner of Works, September 6, 1962. Mimeographed report by J.G. Thompson, City Assessor, September 7, 1962.

38 "Local Negroes Need Help: Far Sighted Policy Needed, Says Dalhousie Report," *The Mail-Star,* Halifax, N.S., October 4, 1962.

39 For the full text of the committee of the whole council's minutes, see Clairmont and Magill, *Africville Relocation Report,* pp. A13-A20.

40 This statement is quoted from: "Africville: Early Action Urged," *The Mail-Star,* Halifax, N.S., October 25, 1962.

41 *Minutes of the Committee of the Whole Council,* October 24, 1962.

42 *Minutes of the Halifax City Council,* October 25, 1962.

43 Letter from the development officer, city of Halifax, to the secretary, Halifax Human Rights Advisory Committee, November 21, 1962. For the complete

text of this correspondence, see Clairmont and Magill, *Africville Relocation Report,* pp. A23-A34.

44   Letter from the development officer, city of Halifax, to the secretary, Halifax Human Rights Advisory Committee, January 23, 1963. For the complete text of the correspondence, see Clairmont and Magill, *Africville Relocation Report,* pp. A37-A48.

45   Albert Rose, *Regent Park: A Study in Slum Clearance* (Toronto: University of Toronto Press, 1958). This is a study of Regent Park, Toronto, one of Canada's first extensive experiments in slum clearance and urban development.

46   Letter from the Halifax Human Rights Advisory Committee to his worship the mayor and aldermen, city of Halifax, N.S., September 6, 1963. For the complete text of this correspondence, see, Clairmont and Magill, *Africville Relocation Report,* pp. A51-A55.

47   *Minutes of Halifax City Council,* September 12, 1963, p. 397.

48   "Africville: Time for Action is Now," *The Mail-Star,* Halifax, N.S., December 23, 1963.

49   *Minutes of the Halifax City Council,* January 2, 1964, p. 2.

50   Ibid., pp. 2-3.

51   "37 Africville Residents Approve of Rose Report," *The Mail-Star,* Halifax, N.S., January 10, 1964.

52   For the complete text of this correspondence see, Clairmont and Magill, *Africville Relocation Report,* pp. A71-72.

53   *Minutes of the Halifax City Council,* January 16, 1964, p. 40.

54   Ibid., p. 41.

55   Ibid.

56   "City to Make Africville Move As Painless As Possible, Mayor Says," *The Mail-Star,* Halifax, N.S., January 17, 1964.

57   Ibid.

Organization and Relocation: Mechanics and Limitations: 1964-1969

Interviewer: "Were there any…strategies that the city used to convince people to move?"

Africville Relocatee: "The only strategy was to move everybody out…you can't buck the government, because they got more than you."

Interviewer: "More, in what way?"

Africville Relocatee: "They got the power. If you have the money, you have the law. You can't do nothing with them in our situation. We are not the educated kind. We don't know how to go around loops and corners. They know what they are doing."

Interviewer: "Did you have a lot of negotiations or discussions with the city before you reached the [settlement] price?"

Africville Relocatee: "Quite a lot, but I got nowhere. As I said, I have no money to fight them, so I lose out in the end."

—Tape-recorded interview with an
Africville relocatee, October, 1969.

Introduction

The establishment of the Halifax Human Rights Advisory Committee and its subsequent involvement in relocation decision making and mechanics was a key factor in making the Africville relocation appear progressive and distinctive in the urban renewal climate of the early 1960s. The committee's participation, along with Halifax city council's acceptance of the Rose Report, stamped the Africville relocation as a liberal-welfare type of planned social change and might have indicated that the relocation would indeed signal new life-opportunities for Africville residents.

During the 1962-64 decision-making phase, the Halifax Human Rights Advisory Committee did attempt to relate information to Africville residents, to obtain their views, and to represent their interests to city officials. Unfortunately the committee did not build a strong community-supported Africville organization; consequently its mandate was always questionable. Only a handful of Africville residents participated in the deliberations of the committee during the mechanics phase of the relocation and these few residents had no delegated authority on behalf of the other Africville residents. Non-Africville members of this black-white alliance continued to play an important caretaker role during the mechanics phase of the relocation; with representatives of city council they formed an advisory subcommittee which examined reports of the relocation social worker and made recommendations to city council. The unorganized Africville residents were collectively excluded from these political-administrative processes and few of them consulted with the Halifax Human Rights Advisory Committee. In effect, the committee had more legitimacy in the eyes of the city administration than in the eyes of Africville residents so that, in a nonpejorative sense, it was co-opted by the city. It was given powers by the city and expected to look after Africville interests; in return, its involvement stamped the relocation program as progressive and humane.

The Rose Report, written in the liberal-welfare tradition of planned social change, was a document marked with the best of intentions. Nevertheless, as a guide to relocation mechanics it left much to be desired. Beyond recommending the appointment of a relocation social worker, the involvement of the Halifax Human Rights Advisory Committee, and the development of educational and occupational rehabilitative programs, the Rose Report did not specify intermediate-level goals or objectives, nor did it indicate how rehabilitative programs might be carried out successfully. The Rose Report was essentially programmatic; beyond recommending that the relocation be administered by the city's development department, the report did not delve into the political-adminstrative realities that any carefully designed program of planned social change must recognize and take into account. For example, given the development department's bureaucratic mandate and its political realities, there was a danger that emphasis in the relocation would shift from rehabilitation and the elimination of inequality to the clearing of the Africville lands and to real estate negotiations. How was this to be checked? In view of the vagueness of the relocation objectives, it would be necessary to ensure the mobilization of advocacy on behalf of Africville residents, especially as they were excluded from the decision-making processes. In the relocation apparatus, the relocation social worker should have played this role, but, since he was employed in the development department, it was difficult to ensure that internal advocacy would be strengthened rather than mitigated. The chief external source of advocacy was the involvement of the Halifax Human Rights Advisory Committee. The relocation apparatus should, therefore, have been organized so that this advocacy function could be optimized. As noted above, the committee's mandate to speak for Africville residents was questionable. Moreover, participation by committee members in the relocation mechanics was on a voluntary basis. It was questionable whether they would be able to handle this time-consuming caretaker function in addition to their regular commitments without getting lost in the myriad of individual relocation cases and becoming increasingly dependent on initiatives from city officials.

Consideration of the advocate role is important since the Rose Report did not go into details or analyse how new life opportunities would be created for Africville residents. Its successful implementation depended considerably more on good will than on detailed legal and organizational recommendations. City council, in adopting the Rose Report, assumed no legal obligation for rehabilitative programs. The lacunae in the Rose Report, though pardonable given Dr. Rose's terms of reference, were serious, for effecting positive social change for the disadvantaged is very difficult. Within the liberal-welfare tradition of change, which was the rhetoric of the Africville relocation, the structural obstacles to equality and full participation in the mainstream of society by the poor, especially the black poor, are underestimated. In view of structural conditions, the realities of bureaucracy, and racism, it would be difficult to alter life conditions radically for Africville residents who were poor, ill-educated, unorganized, and discriminated against. If there was to be any likelihood of success at all, detailed planning and considerable attention had to be given to the mobilization of advocacy and to organizational structure.

The Administrative Framework for the Relocation

The Rose Report recommended: "The employment of a trained social worker or social scientist to visit and document the social and economic situation and requirements of each family unit or single individual, and to recommend the order or priority of relocation."

Shortly after city council adopted the Rose Report, the mayor met with the minister of public welfare and the deputy minister. The provincial welfare officials agreed to "find a person to do the relocation."[1] They suggested a forty-year-old social worker who had been employed with the Nova Scotia Department of Public Welfare since 1948. The deputy minister of public welfare explained why his department had suggested this man as the Africville relocation social worker:

> [He is a person] who can meet and talk to people, and that was what we needed. Someone who could go into Africville and talk to people on their own level. [He] was the person we had with these skills.[2]

The appointment was approved by city council and the social worker took up his duties on June 1, 1964. He spent the first several weeks becoming familiar with the day-to-day routine of Halifax city hall and reviewing information about Africville.

Shortly after the relocation social worker was appointed, the development director prepared a policy statement outlining the operational procedures for the relocation program, and the respective roles of city council's Africville subcommittee and the Halifax Human Rights Advisory Committee.[3] Essentially the former was to concern itself "with the broad issues rather than specific cases," while the latter was to ensure rapport between the city and the relocatees and to see "that the city's commitments to the community are carried out." The development director's report also specified two types of relocation compensation—"for land and buildings and...to assist in the relocation of families." The responsibility of the development department in welfare guidance "for such a period as appears necessary" and the responsibility of the city in employment and educational rehabilitation were also noted. Finally, the report outlined the department's responsibility for finding alternative housing accommodation for the relocatees and moving them to their new homes. These recommendations were adopted and the control of the relocation was totally assumed by the development department. The following recommendation however, was to have particularly grave consequences for the Africville relocatees:

In order to avoid overlapping of responsibil.tes and to avoid the establishment of precedents which co.ld be difficult to deny at a later date, it is suggested t1at the welfare deparment accept responsibility for continued assistance to the Africville community until such time as individual properties are acquired. Immediately upon acquisition of each particular property, responsibilty for all forms of assistance and guidance should become the responsibility of the development department and should remain the responsibility of that department for as long as the commitment to the individual family exists.

Generally speaking, the city appears to have committed itself to a program of assistance and guidance for a minimum period of six months from the date of movement of the family. It is, however, anticipated that the total movement of the community will take place over a period to December 31, 1966 and it seems logical that guidance should be given for such a period as appears necessary. At the end of the guidance period, the responsibility for any assistance would be returned to the welfare department."[4]

As shown later in this chapter, this recommendation operated to the detriment of relocatees. The development department withdrew from the political-administrative arena after completing its mandate of negotiating settlements and moving the vast majority of residents. The responsibility for further welfare and guidance was then transferred to the city's welfare department whose director refused to give special consideration to their financial problems. As responsibility for the relocation was shifted from one department to another, the residents were indeed caught in a bureaucratic maze in which the administrative and political realities were beyond their comprehension.

The Development Department and the Africville Relocation

The control and ultimate success or failure of the early phase of the relocation was chiefly in the hands of two individuals: the development director and the relocation social worker. From a sociological perspective, their actions should not be analysed in terms of individual motivations but in terms of roles within a larger political-administrative framework. The relocation program was drafted by an expert, adopted by Halifax city council politicians, and handed to agency bureaucrats for implementation. These officials were constrained by their mandate, the resources made available to them, and the nature of the surrounding interorganizational relations.

From mid-1964 to late 1967, the relocation social worker was the only city employee directly involved on a day-to-day basis with Africville residents and relocatees. He was responsible to the development director whose formal bureaucratic responsibility included the direction and control of the mechanics of the Africville program. Given the importance of these two men, it is pertinent to consider briefly their respective roles during the relocation.

Undoubtedly the development director was the most important senior city official during the relocation decision-making and the implementation of relocation policy. He had written the 1962 report recommending relocation, he had been the city's liaison with the Halifax Human Rights Advisory Committee, and he had met with Dr. Albert Rose in December 1964. With the social worker, he reviewed the settlement prices offered to Africville residents. In essence, the development director was a city official who regarded his bureaucratic role to be that of supporting, justifying, and implementing city council's Africville policy. In discussing his part in the relocation decision-making and the implementation of policy, the development director explained that he reviewed with the social worker each settlement negotiation and usually approved or amended all reports recommending a specific settlement.

> *Interviewer*: "In terms of the decision-making, what would be your role in the overall relocation?"
> *Development director*: "Well, first of all I developed the general policy statement...which I had to defend before council, and the public at large. Secondly, I was dealing with Albert Rose; or, put it this way, I was his contact point in the city when he was here, as far as the city itself was concerned. And thirdly, I suppose I collaborated with [the relocation social worker] in reaching agreement on recommendations that were made to the committees for acceptance or rejection [of settlement]."
> *Interviewer*: "That must have been a difficult thing, to sort out all the various factors to make a recommendation."

Development director: "It was an exceedingly difficult thing. It was a question of balancing oranges and apples, comparing one case to the other. I am quite prepared to believe that there may have been injustices done to one as compared to another. I might also say that I think if the injustice was done…it was only because somebody else had more than the other.

"I suppose [the relocation social worker] and I met anywhere from half an hour to an hour a day on each individual case. He told me when he had somebody approach him that was interested in settling. We agreed generally on the basis on which he could negotiate with that particular person, both as to compensation and as to alternative accommodation."

Interviewer: "And on the basis of that, reports were written and submitted to the council?"

Development director: "It wasn't all this simple. What you did, once you got some person interested in moving, then the process of talking to the person [started] and this process of negotiation probably went on, on an average of three to four months. It was only when we had come to some conclusion that the report went forward…. It was usually drafted by [the relocation social worker] and approved or amended by me, and from there on I can recall very few cases where [the reports] weren't accepted.

"As a general rule, I didn't participate in the individual negotiations with the individual persons. This was basically wrong, because it would place [the relocation social worker] in the position where everybody felt that he could be bypassed in the discussions."

Interviewer: "Did [the relocation social worker] have trouble in many of the negotiations with the people?"

Development director: "I would say that any negotiation is a difficult thing. It is not a question of adding up 2, 3, 4, 5 on one side and 2, 3, 4, 5 on the other, and balancing everything, and everybody agreeing. It's a process of constant talk. I don't know what you mean by 'trouble.' Put it this way; some person might be coming in and

holding out for a figure of, say, $12,000, which was
completely ridiculous in terms of what they had to offer,
and you think that negotiations would be endless. Then
something would happen on either side, and all of a
sudden things would come together, as is the case with
any type of negotiation."

The relocation social worker was responsible for implementing the Rose
Report recommendations and city council's Africville policy. His role was
multifaceted; he was expected to negotiate settlement prices, to assist
relocatees to find alternative housing accommodation, to arrange for an
occupational and educational retraining program, and to provide guidance
for Africville residents and relocatees. He was the major liaison between
city officials and Africville residents. As an "under-structure personnel,"[5]
he did not determine policy but, to a large extent, the success or failure
of policy execution was in his hands.

If the caretaker members of the Halifax Human Rights Advisory
Committee can be viewed as the external advocates, presumably protecting
the interests of Africville, the relocation social worker can be considered
as the residents' internal community advocate. However, given the
complexity of his relocation tasks and his official position as an employee
of the development department with its real estate mandate, the internal
advocate role was extremely difficult, if not impossible, to perform.

The social worker's knowledge of Africville's social structure contrasted
with that of the caretakers. During his three years in Africville he became
intimately familiar with the day-to-day dynamics of the community's life.
He perceived, more than most outsiders, the intrinsic value of the Africville
community; for instance, the importance of extended family ties. In his
words:

There is one difference that I noticed as far as Africville
was concerned, compared with other areas in which I
worked. The Africville people generally were always able
to make room for one more. By that I am particularly
thinking of the older people, the grandfather, and the
grandmother, and the aunt, and the uncle who were elderly.
These people were looked after. I rarely heard anyone
say, 'I'll have to send my mother, my father, or my aunt,
to...the old people's home.'

When they were thinking of moving out [relocating] and becoming involved in another home, this was one of the factors that they thought about first, that they would have to provide a room for so-and-so.

At a meeting on June 9, 1964, the relocation social worker met Nancy and Peter Edwards and Frank MacPherson, the Africville representatives on the Halifax Human Rights Advisory Committee. Mr. Edwards explained that, several days after the meeting, he and his wife had paved the way for the social worker's entry into the community by introducing him to the oldline families. After meeting the oldline families, the social worker spent four months extending his contacts until he knew all the residents. Interviewed in 1969, he explained that he preferred to interact on an informal basis, "talking to a person in his own home, in the kitchen, or outside in the yard, or in the local store." After the first six months he felt he had gained the trust of the Africville people and he started to negotiate settlement prices. Initially, however, he was perceived as a "city employee" and was viewed with scepticism and suspicion by many residents who expressed to him their intense hostility concerning the city's neglect of their community.

When the relocation social worker was first appointed his office was in Halifax city hall. Approximately three months later, he moved into an office at the Seaview African Baptist Church in Africville, but after a short period he returned to his city hall office because he found that residents did not like being seen coming to his office.

Lack of Citizen Involvement During the Relocation Program

During the relocation there was neither community-wide citizen participation nor an indigenous power base for collective bargaining with city officials; rather, major policy decisions were formulated by decision-makers outside the community, and settlement prices were negotiated on a family or individual basis. In the main, there were three underlying reasons for this lack of collective involvement: powerlessness generated by historical conditions; the structure of decision-making before and after the Rose Report; and the growth of "new" strains in the community resulting from the nature of the settlement negotiations.

Powerlessness

Africville residents, being black and poor, viewed the world with pessimism and resignation. Political bargaining with the "outside world" had been unsuccessful; the dominant attitude within the community was one of powerlessness and political ineffectiveness. The residents had come to expect little consideration from city officials, and the relocation announcement was seen by many as the latest step in a long series of deprivations and outrages to which they had grown accustomed. At the time of the relocation announcement there was no firmly established indigenous power base around which residents could organize either to assure substantial citizen participation or to mobilize against relocation. As noted in the preceding chapter, the Development Department Report, which was published in the local press, was strongly rejected on August 8, 1962, by nearly one hundred black people; only eight weeks later, however, the idea of relocation was "accepted" during a meeting at the Seaview African Baptist Church.

Structure of Decision-Making

Neither before nor after the 1963 Rose Report did the Halifax Human Rights Advisory Committee structure itself in a way conducive to full citizen participation from Africville. As noted in Chapter Five the committee grew out of requests for assistance addressed by a few Africville residents to civil rights leader Alan Borovoy. The committee brought together professional, middle-class people interested in improving race relations and a handful of concerned Africville residents who had formed a ratepayers' association. The latter group was selective, unrepresentative of the community, and without effective organization; little effort was spent in developing a strong community-supported indigenous organization, either by the members of the ratepayers' association or by the volunteer "outsiders" who were the predominant members of the Halifax Human Rights Advisory Committee. With the formation of the committee, the ratepayers' association, as such, ceased to exist.

Although the Africville relocation was the principal concern of the Halifax Human Rights Advisory Committee, there was little meaningful participation by Africville members of the committee. The building of a "citizens-at-large" committee, rather than developing first a strong, less vulnerable, indigenous Africville organization, resulted in there being no authoritative "Africville voice" and in the Halifax Human Rights Advisory Committee having no clear-cut mandate on behalf of Africville residents. Despite their time-consuming involvement, the caretaker members of the committee were seen by community residents as "outsiders."

The committed and hard-working caretakers tended to see the few Africville residents who did meet with them as legitimate indigenous leaders and as spokespersons who represented most individuals and groups in the community. However, the Edwards and MacPherson, the Africville residents who regularly attended meetings of the Halifax Human Rights Advisory Committee, were neither elected nor appointed as members of that committee; they were at best "unofficial representatives" of Africville, solely because they had been involved in the ratepayers' association and, later, in attending meetings of the Halifax Human Rights Advisory Committee. Their mandate on behalf of Africville residents was always uncertain; they were not seen by residents as influential persons in the relocation decision-making. Their role in relocation mechanics became simply to relate, occasionally, information and requests to the caretakers.

Although the decision-making of the Halifax Human Rights Advisory Committee directly involved only a few community members, the caretakers did attempt to communicate with residents through a number of public meetings. Prior to September 1963, while the white and black caretakers were exploring alternatives to relocation, five public meetings were held at the Seaview African Baptist Church, Africville. During these meetings residents frequently expressed verbal hostility towards city officials for failing to supply Africville with basic community requirements. After the Rose Report was submitted to Halifax city council, only forty-two residents attended the sixth public meeting, where thirty-seven voted to accept the report. After city council had adopted the report, the Halifax Human Rights Advisory Committee held six additional public meetings, between August 1964 and November 1965, but attendance by residents declined. After mid-1965, the last four public meetings were predominantly discussions regarding temporary improvement of physical conditions in the community. Understandably there was little apparent interest in these meetings among residents and attendance was low.

Community Strains

The growth of suspicion and jealousy resulting from the nature of the impending settlement negotiations also militated against Africville residents' involvement in the program. The Rose Report had recommended that settlement negotiations be completed on a family-unit or individual basis. Given these terms of reference, there was no concerted attempt by either the caretakers or the relocation social worker to develop an indigenous power base. Without a collective base from which to bargain, strains developed as a number of residents were thought by their neighbours to be "trying to get everything they can out of the city without concern for the rest of the people of Africville." It must be remembered that Africville residents were highly vulnerable in that land claims were often without legal support and there were multiple claims against many pieces of property. Under these circumstances, the terms of reference for the settlement negotiations placed the residents in jeopardy, and created a *sauve-qui-peut* situation. This fact added considerably to strains already in the community and led to increased suspicion and distrust. As one resident observed:

> People just didn't trust each other. A lot of suspicion came along with this [relocation]. One [resident] was getting more than the other. I think it would have been a lot better if they had stuck together.

Settlement Negotiations: Decision Making within the City Council Africville Subcommittee

After mid-1964 the caretakers' attention shifted temporarily from the Africville relocation to the planning of a human rights conference, which was held in late 1964 at Dalhousie University. At their first meeting in 1965, they passed a motion that three black caretakers should be members of the City Council Africville Subcommittee established by city council to review settlements. This motion was accepted by city officials and the City Council Africville Subcommittee (hereafter referred to as the subcommittee) became the decision-making body responsible for adopting or rejecting settlements by the social worker. The subcommittee had eight members: three black caretakers, three aldermen, the relocation social worker, and the development director.[6] From February 16, 1965, to October 5, 1965, the subcommittee held nineteen meetings.

The relocation social worker was the liaison between this subcommittee and Africville residents. Most of his effort, well into the third year of his service, was directed towards physically relocating Africville residents. He tried to encourage them to relocate, acted as the middleman in their real estate negotiations with the city, and arranged new accommodations. Over eighty percent of the relocatees interviewed indicated that virtually all their negotiations were conducted solely with the relocation social worker. He reported that he made it a personal policy not to quote possible purchase prices for their lands and buildings. Rather, he would insist that the residents make an offer and he would then discuss these prices with the development director.

Upon completion of each settlement negotiation, he wrote a staff report which recommended a specific financial settlement and outlined personal information about the individual resident or family unit. Each report was then submitted to the subcommittee for adoption or rejection and usually, as the social worker noted, they were adopted unanimously. Once approved by the subcommittee, the settlement price tended to be ratified automatically by both the city's finance and executive committee and city council.

When interviewed, subcommittee members were asked about the relocation social worker's part in determining settlements. Their answers followed a consistent pattern: the social worker was a "professional;" he was presumed to know the community residents; his staff reports and proposed settlement prices were clearly set forth, and in most cases his proposals were adopted readily. A former alderman member of the subcommittee summarized the decision-making process within the subcommittee:

> Alderman: "There were very few disagreements about these
> reports.... My recollection would be that...if some
> committee members objected...the staff were asked to
> look at it again, and talk with the people again, and
> come back with some possible revision or
> improvement.... I don't know if we ever had any actual
> votes on settlement. I think that normally the committee
> operated by consensus...."
> Interviewer: "Were there many cases then where [the
> relocation social worker] was asked to re-do the staff
> reports?"
> Alderman: "I think it would really be a small proportion,
> [of cases rejected], maybe five or ten percent, something

like that order…. Basically the committee would agree with [his] report."

Interviewer: "What happened once the consensus was reached in the committee? Where would the report go from there?"

Alderman: "The report went into the finance committee of the council, which was made up of the mayor and seven aldermen, normally rubber-stamped there, and then it went to council [where] it was rubber-stamped, and that became the formal decision of the city at that point."

Settlement Criteria and the Cost of the Relocation

There was no set formula for arriving at settlement prices paid to Africville residents for their land or dwellings, or both. As the development director explained when asked how the settlement amounts were reached:

> I suppose it was a combination of factors. There was a certain degree of justification arrived at by taking an artificial land area that presumably could be considered to be owned by a particular person. To that was added the number of buildings that might be of potential value, and to some extent there was allowance made for the age and position of the particular person. There was no formula, believe me. I suppose it was as much by precedent as anything. Once a pattern started to evolve in the first few settlements, then everything else was measured against those. It was certainly an artificial calculation in legal terms, because there was no way in which we could possibly justify any of the amounts we paid, if it were on a strictly legal basis.

The relocation social worker reported that numerous factors entered into his arriving at recommendations for settlement prices: property owned in Africville, age, number of children, and employment stability. Not every settlement was based on objective factors, and, as an alderman member of the subcommittee emphasized, character and reputation were taken into account when the subcommittee reviewed some of the social worker's recommendations:

I hesitate to use the word "character," but I think it had something to do with it. Sometimes a committee member would indicate that a certain fellow had a reputation as being very irresponsible, even though he had a family. If he got a grant of so much money, it would end up back in the provincial coffers via the liquor store, or something like that....

Okay, maybe in these cases we were playing God, I don't know; but in these cases we felt that nothing would be served by giving that person a larger grant. Whereas you had a fellow who had, like I say, a good steady job and was of fairly good character, you would stake him.

City officials indicated that only fourteen residents had legal title to their property.[7] In the vast majority of settlements concerning land, there were no deeds to property. The relocation social worker described how settlement estimates were reached:

First of all, we tried to get a story from the owner, and from there find out something at the records office, both at city hall and the court house, through the registry of deeds office....

Where there were no actual deeds...[we] pretty well went along with the story...the people would give. The property was handed down [from generation to generation], more or less by word of mouth. Older members of the family who had passed away divided their property among their boys and girls.... So there was actually no written document for each particular piece of property saying that one member of the family owned so many square feet and another owned another section or part of the property. So...[we] went along pretty well with the status quo as it was in the community.

In accordance with the Rose Report, settlements were not only paid for land, or dwellings, or both; many included welfare payments, furniture allowances, and the waiving of tax and hospital bills. The specific settlement categories were:

1. **Financial compensation:** money, usually paid by cheque, for ownership of land, or dwelling, or both.
2. **Welfare:** to minimize "bureaucratic red tape" and to expedite the relocation, the social worker was given control of city welfare payments to relocatees.[8]
3. **Hospital bills:** the waiving of unpaid hospital bills.[9]
4. **Tax bills:** the waiving of unpaid city tax bills.[10]
5. **Furniture allowance:** money paid to relocatees to purchase new furniture or household items. The largest payments usually did not exceed $1000.[11]
6. **Sundry costs:** money paid for moving expenses, for compassionate settlements to residents who owned neither land nor dwelling, for repairs to relocatees' new homes, and for land-transfer taxes.

Settlements were concluded with a total of ninety-eight individuals or family units. In some cases, a family-unit settlement was paid to a number of individual people; for instance, parents would receive a property settlement, while elder children were paid a furniture allowance, or given welfare assistance, or both. The settlements paid to relocatees have been classified into five categories:

1. **Propertyless:** residents who owned no property and either rented homes, boarded, or lived without charge with relatives or friends.
2. **Renters with claims:** renters who owned inherited property, or owned a building that they did not occupy, or received part of a relative's settlement.
3. **Home and landowners:** residents who owned a home and land, in some instances without title deed.
4. **Homeowners:** residents who owned a home but not land.
5. **Homeowners with multiple claims:** residents who owned a home, or land, or both, and inherited other buildings or lands.

Table 6.1 shows that a total of $530,687.73 was paid to relocatees, and an additional $18,741.83 was waived for hospital and tax bills. The propertyless residents benefited least; for the most part, they received only furniture allowances or welfare payments. The twenty-eight settlements for the propertyless were not submitted to review by the subcommittee, but were decided by the relocation social worker at his own discretion.

Table 6.1
Settlements with Africville Relocatees

Settlement Category	Property-less N=28	Renters with Claims N=10	Home-owners N=19	Home and Land Owners N=32	Homeowners with Multiple Claims N=9	Total N=98
Financial Compensation	–	$20,825.25	$41,636.66	$269,896.80	$66,758.32	$399,117.03
Welfare Payments	$21,271.04	5984.12	20,377.33	12,452.76	6171.14	66,256.39
Furniture Allowance	18,360.35	5573.95	10,658.54	19,337.01	5471.96	59,401.81
Sundry Costs	4750.00	–	175.00	748.00	239.50	5912.50
Sub-total	44,381.39	32,383.32	72,847.53	302,434.57	78,640.92	530,687.73
Hospital Bills Waived	–	1506.63	2543.83	9395.22	313.95	13,759.63
Tax Bills Waived	–	311.11	183.89	4263.78	223.42	4982.20
TOTAL	$44,381.39	$34,201.06	$75,575.25	$316,093.57	$79,178.29	$549,429.56

These residents could live inexpensively in Africville, but, as they had no resources with which to bargain during the relocation negotiations, they received only limited financial assistance, although they were faced with higher living expenses when they moved into urban Halifax.

In addition to ninety-eight settlements with residents, thirty-eight settlements were reached with non-resident owners of Africville property. Payment of $61,202.47 was made to non-relocatees and waivers of $1864.61 in hospital and tax bills. Also included in the settlement negotiations was the sale of the Seaview African Baptist Church, which was built on leased city land. The community church trustees initially requested a settlement of $30,000, but after three months of negotiations they accepted a settlement of $15,000. The money was deposited as an education trust fund to be used for black children in the Halifax area, with preference to be given to children of Africville relocatees. The church trustees and other Halifax blacks were appointed as directors of the fund.

In total, the monies paid by the city of Halifax to Africville residents and non-residents, and for the Seaview African Baptist Church, amounted to $606,890.20. In addition $20,606.44 in hospital and tax bills was waived.

The City's Strategies During the Relocation

As the Africville relocation was rooted in liberal-welfare rhetoric, it was considered as a program of planned social change that was being carried out in the interests of the people. To some extent, this public definition of the situation did not take into account other goals, such as the real estate pressures to clear the community within a specified period of time. Given this structure and the lack of enthusiasm among some residents to move, city officials had to use certain strategies and tactics during the relocation negotiations.

Undoubtedly the most striking strategy was the employment of a social worker who could relate to residents in their own style and thereby reduce antagonism. Indeed, one of the reasons for selecting the relocation social worker was that government officials considered him to be "someone who could go into Africville and talk to people on their own level."

The relocation social worker himself used certain strategies during the three years he worked in Africville. His first objective was to find the indigenous leaders, but he soon discovered that, although a few people could be considered as spokespeople, there was no clear-cut leadership structure. He therefore had to rely on the Africville representatives on the Halifax Human Rights Advisory Committee to pave his entry into the community. From his initial contacts he was gradually able to build up an informal relationship with most community members before he started negotiations. He soon observed that he could identify a number of distinct community cliques and once negotiations were started with an influential member of the clique, he could approach its other members and start the negotiation process with them. The residents could then, if they wished, compare settlement prices. A related tactic he occasionally used was to bring "third parties" into the relocation negotiations, especially other family members favourably disposed to relocation.

The chief strategy that the relocation social worker followed, with the support of the advisory subcommittee, was to obtain for a number of residents a financial settlement in excess of the market value of the individual properties; these residents then perceived that they were getting a "good deal." For the majority of properties, there were no legal deeds and the resident and social worker had to negotiate the size and value of the property. Thus the negotiations could be arbitrary with considerable room for manoeuvring. The criterion that often guided the settlement negotiations was the amount paid for a similar property. A number of residents were far more inclined to move when they considered that they were receiving more than they would if their property were expropriated. In addition, their settlement was sweetened by other incentives such as welfare payments and furniture allowances. Another strategy to quicken relocation was to find new housing accommodation, particularly for the marginal and most resourceless community members. To expedite the removal of these residents, many were placed in city-owned homes, often in areas scheduled for redevelopment.

Two strategies to expedite relocation were not connected with the relocation social worker. With the approach of the deadline for completing the relocation, four residents refused to accept the city's settlement offers. In response to this resistance, the subcommittee, at its meetings on May 29 and October 5, 1967, adopted a "big-stick" strategy and decided to recommend that expropriation procedures be initiated. This strategy was available as a last resort, in the event that these residents resisted relocation over a prolonged period of time. In the case of the last Africville resident (discussed later in this chapter), expropriation was in fact used as a device for persuading him to move.

The last tactic, although perhaps not consciously used as a tactic by city officials, was "visible demolition." After a resident had moved, his or her dwelling was immediately demolished by bulldozer or burned by the city fire department. City officials contended that such demolition was necessary to prevent fires and possible occupation by squatters. One can well imagine the impact that the demolition of Africville buildings had on community members. As residents surveyed their community, they could watch the destruction of the homes of their neighbours, friends, and relatives. This demolition might also result in the elimination of a nearby water supply as wells were covered over or destroyed by bulldozers. As their community slowly disappeared in front of their eyes, residents were forced into a position where they had to negotiate, accept a settlement, and move.

One case study illustrates the above two tactics. An elderly female resident, who had lived in the community all her life, rejected a settlement price and furniture offer for her property and five-room home. Describing the relocation, she noted, "They [city officials] tried to make the people think they were better off moving. The money the city offered us was a bribe to get us out." She demanded a settlement price $10,000 higher than the city offered, but the relocation social worker noted that her requested amount was "out of line with the amount paid for similar properties in the community." With the breakdown of negotiations, the subcommittee reverted to the "big-stick" strategy and, at its May 29, 1967 meeting, adopted a motion recommending that expropriation proceedings be initiated immediately. Negotiations with her continued after the relocation social worker left Halifax, and she became a victim of the "visible demolition" tactic. Through the destruction of various Africville buildings, her water supply was eliminated; to solve this problem, city staff installed a large water tank which froze solid in the winter. Faced with increasing deprivation, she concluded negotiations by mid-1968, moved from the community, and the city fire department burned down her house as an exercise in its training program.

The Collapse of the Liberal-Welfare Relocation Model

Once the relocation plan became operational, Halifax city officials had an opportunity to carry out a program of planned social change rooted in liberal ideology and welfare policies. The ideology of the Rose Report became rather meaningless, however, when the relocation's manifest goals were translated into action. For five reasons, the relocation slowly shifted from that of a liberal-welfare model to a development model with a real estate emphasis. First, lacking a serious commitment to rehabilitation programs, no serious search was made for an innovative approach and the attempted "traditional" programs failed within a short time. Second, after signing quitclaim deeds, many residents tended no longer to be considered members of a "disadvantaged group" requiring special assistance, and the way they were transported from their homes illustrates city officials' insensitive attitude towards the relocation. Third, after the relocation social worker assumed another job in mid-1967, the city's welfare director questioned the legitimacy of welfare payments to former Africville residents; payments to many relocatees were subsequently discontinued. Fourth, after most relocatees had moved from the community, the caretakers ceased to perform an external-advocacy role and, without the white-black alliance to protect their interests, Africville residents were left in a precarious situation. Finally, the attitude and behaviour of city officials towards the few residents who resisted movement from Africville reflected a real estate emphasis that is an inherent part of the development model.

The Rehabilitation and Retraining Programs

In addition to recommending the clearance and expropriation of Africville land, the Rose Report urged that the city of Halifax initiate an employment and occupation retraining program. Assistance in obtaining employment was to be given, and residents without marketable skills were to be assisted in obtaining vocational guidance, counselling, and, if possible, training or retraining. To implement this recommendation, retraining and employment programs were established. These were to be a vital part of the general plan to alter progressively the conditions of life of Africville residents. Other programs of family counselling and legal advice were also considered. Few Africville relocatees reported that they were aware of family counselling and legal service, let alone that they used them. In general the rehabilitative program fell considerably short of effecting dramatic, or even adequate social change.

A vast majority of Africville residents had meagre formal education and few were eligible to enrol in any of the government-sponsored, trades-training programs. A special one-year, adult-education class therefore, was established in an attempt to enable residents to meet entrance requirements. The class began in September, 1964, with an enrolment of thirteen; at the end of the course, in June, 1965, there were only five in the class, and not enough people were interested in continuing the class in September, 1965, for the program to be continued.

The rhetoric of the relocation program assumed that this educational retraining would eliminate in part the employment difficulties faced by Africville residents. This assumption has been questioned by a noted American sociologist who has observed that vocational rehabilitation tends to have little effect on the poverty cycle:

> In recent years growing awareness that employment is essential if poverty is to be reduced has led to great emphasis on various kinds of educational programs. For example, job training programs have been developed to equip young adults for available employment. *These programs — from the Job Corps to vocational rehabilitation and youth opportunity centers — have had very little effect.* It has proved exceedingly difficult to persuade the trainees to stay in the program, and problems of low motivation and lack of persistence have been characteristic, manifested in high drop-out rates and low levels of achievement. The facts of the labor market have confirmed the suspicion expressed by the trainees; many of the training programs have proved irrelevant to employment opportunities because much of the training has been for non-existent jobs and employers have been reluctant to hire the trainees despite all the high-level exhortation for private industry to 'meet its responsibilities.' [Italics added][12]

The employment program was also a failure. After the relocation social worker was appointed, the Nova Scotia Department of Public Welfare appointed a full-time black employment officer to assist blacks in finding employment in metropolitan Halifax. Most of the social worker's time was required for relocation negotiations, and as he had relatively little time to devote to "employment brokerage," he referred many residents to the department's employment officer. When interviewed in 1969, the employment officer reported that, due to Africville residents' educational disadvantage, he had been able to find employment for only a few of them.

Moving from Africville

The Rose Report recommended the development of a registry of available housing for sale or rent (outside public housing) that might be suitable for families or persons relocated from Africville. The housing shortage in Halifax, especially for low-income families, made it impossible to develop a registry or immediately to find accommodation for some of the residents who had completed settlement negotiations.

Once alternative housing became available, each resident owning land or buildings, or both, signed a quitclaim deed. The way in which many residents were moved from their community clearly illustrates the underlying real estate considerations of the relocation. Interviewed about moving from the community, a number of relocatees complained bitterly about the "big yellow trucks" that moved them. One middle-aged woman expressed her hostility in the following terms:

> Them fucking city people sent a garbage truck to move my furniture. Just think what the neighbours thought when they looked out and saw a garbage truck drive up and unload the furniture.[13]

Asked about the "big yellow trucks," the social worker explained, commercial movers were reluctant to provide the service.

> ...it wasn't easy to always get a moving truck, or a particular moving company, to come in and move a family.
> ...the regular moving companies...trucks...the expenses involved in cleaning the trucks [were] such that they weren't making any money on it. This...was a problem and in some instances fumigation didn't help too much.
> I can't say I was all that happy to see the regular city truck coming in to move the people, but when you can't get...the commercial moving companies, what else can you do?

The Bureaucratic Mazeway

By mid-1967 the relocation social worker's three-year leave of absence from the Nova Scotia Department of Public Welfare had ended, and he moved from Halifax to assume a different job. Most of the settlement negotiations had been concluded, and the development director reported that the relocation social worker:

> had come to a position where he was spending more time disbursing welfare funds than he was really dealing with the [Africville] problem....
> Some of the families had by that time [August 1967] two or three years of guidance and assistance. I know that the last year [the relocation social worker] was spending nearly as much time visiting people who had been relocated.

Many of the Africville relocatees who were receiving welfare funds anticipated that they would continue to receive them; however, as later events revealed, they were mistaken in this belief. Before the relocation social worker left Halifax, he mailed a mimeographed copy of the following letter to each relocatee receiving welfare:

July 28, 1967

Dear

> As of August 1, 1967, would you please contact...[the city welfare office], 5970 University Avenue, instead of my office when you require welfare assistance.
> Thank you for your consideration and cooperation.

After the social worker's departure, relocatees were faced with a Kafkaesque situation; as part of their settlement, a majority had received welfare, but in 1967 responsibility for providing this assistance was assigned to a different agency, the city welfare office. The director of this department would not consider former Africville residents as special welfare cases; unless they could meet the criteria for receipt of regular welfare, assistance was terminated. The welfare director, a critic of the Africville relocation, argued that the transferring of Africville cases was against the policy of the city welfare office.[14] He viewed the payment of welfare money to Africville relocatees as a form of discrimination against other relocated, low-income persons who were not being given welfare assistance as a condition of their relocation. He argued that by paying welfare money to Africville relocatees the city was indirectly subsidizing its acquisition of the Africville land. In his words:

Interviewer: "Why are you against this kind of welfare payment?"

Welfare director: "It wasn't welfare, it was a payment to offset the claim that the coloured people concerned were selling their claim to the property of Africville. The other reason I wouldn't accept it, if we had used our budget in the normal sense in which we were using it with other clients, they would not have qualified in a great many instances."

Interviewer: "An important question connected with this is the fact that on the basis of [the July 28, 1967 letter] apparently many Africville relocatees thought that their welfare assistance payments would be continued. [The relocation social worker] argues that these payments were made for the purpose of rehabilitation, to use his term, and on that basis [welfare payments] should have been continued. What do you think of this argument?"

Welfare director: "Not very effective. What resources could he offer, other than the dollar, for rehabilitation? He was not set up, structured, to provide that type of service. No doubt he used the various agencies when it was feasible. But one worker, with a time limit to remove a whole community wouldn't have too much time to give to rehabilitiation. What he did was in the matter of expediency, the quickest way to get home."

Thus, many Africville residents found themselves confronted by a bureaucratic mazeway, a world of expertise and power which was not, in the main, part of their daily experience. They believed they had a legitimate claim to continuing welfare payments but, upon approaching the appropriate city agency, they were informed that they would no longer be given special consideration or assistance.

The Floundering Period

After mid-1967, Africville relocatees had to rely primarily on their own unaided resources in their new urban environment. The Halifax Human Rights Advisory Committee and the City Council Africville Subcommittee came to an end, and other problems engaged the attention and energy of city council and staff.

After January, 1965, the members of the Halifax Human Rights Advisory Committee maintained only peripheral interest in the overall relocation program; for instance, they pressured city hall to provide Africville with water tanks[15] and petitioned the Halifax Medical Society to inquire why medical aid had not been made available to an Africville resident who subsequently died.[16] In general, however, the caretakers tended to perceive the Africville problem as "solved" and started to broaden the terms of reference of the Halifax Human Rights Advisory Committee and to investigate other issues related to civil rights in Nova Scotia.

In addition, as noted by the secretary of the Halifax Human Rights Advisory Committee, many of the committee's members became involved in a new organization, the Nova Scotia Human Rights Federation. The City Council Africville Subcommittee met five times after the Halifax Human Rights Advisory Committee disbanded in early 1967. At the subcommittee's final meeting, held on October 5, 1967, the relocation social worker submitted a letter, part of which is quoted below:

> Hopefully, the results of the program will have a beneficial effect for both the residents who have been relocated and for the community at large, especially at this time when the brotherhood of man is being advocated by all people of good will. **To guarantee these results, consultant services given by a recognized social agency will assist tremendously to ensure that the efforts of the Africville Relocation Programme will not be frustrated.** [Emphasis added][17]

The letter urged the provision of follow-up "consultant services" but, for a number of reasons, no program was established. Other issues took precedence: city aldermen were divided over the selection of a new city manager; within city hall interdepartmental power struggles continued; and the city was in the process of extending its boundaries through extensive annexation. Within the context of the larger political picture and its preoccupations, the relocatees were overlooked.

The relocatees found themselves in a Kafkaesque web, as responsibility for the relocation was transferred from the development director (whose major concern is the acquisition and development of land and other property) to the city welfare office, where the fact that they were Africville relocatees yielded them no special consideration. While the relocatees became the victims of this bureaucratic buck-passing, the middle-class liberal caretakers assumed that a follow-up program was being developed. Some time after the Halifax Human Rights Advisory Committee had disbanded and a program had not been established, the caretakers, learning of this, expressed surprise and concern.

Left to their own resources and without direct and continuing assistance from any city agency, many of the relocatees experienced a variety of emotional and financial problems with which they struggled for approximately a year with little city aid.

"Pa" Miller: The Last Africville Resident

While the vast majority of residents were facing serious problems in their new environment, a few residents continued to resist relocation. Negotiations with these residents were concluded by the real estate division of the city's development department. When resistance persisted, city officials threatened expropriation. This "big-stick" strategy was shamefully evident in the case of "Pa" Miller who, in 1969, was the only remaining Africville resident. "Pa" Miller was a member of one of Africville's oldest and largest families. He was also one of the most popular people in Africville. In 1941, and again in 1957, part of his Africville property had been expropriated. During the relocation he had rejected city overtures for his remaining property.

"Pa" Miller strongly resisted relocation, ignoring the advancing construction of the nearby A. Murray MacKay Bridge. His home was located in the middle of an intended bridge approach road and the city was being pressured by the Halifax-Dartmouth Bridge Commission and the bridge construction company to obtain control of Miller's land. The delay was costing $20,000 a day.[18] On November 26, 1969, city council approved expropriation, which took place three days later.[19] "Pa" Miller was informed of the expropriation but remained adamant. Officials at Halifax city hall attempted, on December 4, 1969, to persuade him to move by offering him a suitcase containing $14,000 in cash. "Pa" Miller rejected this offer, but several weeks later accepted a settlement of $14,387 and moved into a $13,000 city house rented to him at $20 a month. His account of the incident, as reported in *The Mail-Star*, describes his relationship with city officials and reveals a deep attachment to his Africville home.

Almost 150 years of continuous settlement ended the day Africville's last resident, 72-year old Aaron 'Pa' [Miller] left.

'Pa,' as he is affectionately called by all who know him, relinquished the hold on his Africville home and property December 30, 1969, when the city of Halifax gave him a cheque for $14,387.76.

For city officials, this was the final acquisition of Africville property in a relocation program which saw eighty families and some 400 persons moved off the land between 1964 and 1967.

However, for Pa [Miller] this was not a joyous occasion, rather it was possibly the saddest day of his life. 'The day I left my home a part of me inside died,' he said.

'I didn't want to leave, I was born there, got married and raised my family there,' said Pa. 'I'm getting ready to die so what the hell do I want to leave for — I liked it there.'

Unfortunately for Pa, progress has little sentiment for an old man and his fond memories. His property stood smack in the middle of the approach road to the Narrows Bridge and the city was forced to expropriate the land as it was hindering construction of the bridge.

'If I had been a little younger the city would never have gotten my land.... I would have fought them to the end,' said Pa with a hint of both sadness and bitterness in his voice and in his eyes.

His Africville property consisted of four lots with three houses on them. Up until a few years ago there were four houses and Pa rented them out for $8 a month. 'I also had another lot opposite the Seaview Baptist Church that the city took back in 1967. I haven't received a nickel for it yet,' he said. 'I guess I am going to hire a lawyer to take care of that and another couple of matters for me,' he said.

Relating the circumstances leading up to the city expropriating his property, Pa said, 'It all began in 1966 when a social worker was hired by the city to assist in relocating Africville families, asked me if I would sell my land and move.'

'I told him no, I don't want to sell my land and move, but if you are prepared to give me $35,000 for my land maybe I will consider it. That must have scared them off because nobody bothered me again until 1968,' he chuckled.

'The city in their next approach asked me if I would take $12,000 for my property,' said Pa. 'I told them no. A few months later they offered me $14,000 and I refused that offer as well.'

With time marching on and the Narrows Bridge rapidly approaching Pa's property, city officials continued their pressure in an effort to get the land. 'At one stage they told me that my land was to be expropriated because they had no record of my ever paying taxes,' he said. 'Well I fooled them,' said Pa, boasting that he has kept the receipts of every bill he paid. 'I marched down to city hall and presented them with all my tax receipts,' he said.

Finally, on November 26, 1969, city council moved that Pa be paid a total of $14,387.76 for his land and if he refused the offer the land would be expropriated anyway.

Realizing his time had run out, Pa said he told city officials if they would move his house from its present location to a site next to the incinerator he would accept their offer. 'They agreed to do this only to change their minds later and tell me the house could not be moved,' he said.

After more dickering, Pa finally agreed to move to a six-room city-owned house...where he pays $20 a month rent. He moved from his Africville home January 2 and four days later it was demolished and a new road built over it.

An incident which upset Pa terribly occurred at city hall about two weeks ago. Relating what happened, he said, 'They sent for me and when I got there I was taken into someone's office. There was five or six persons in the room plus a suitcase full of money all tied up neatly in bundles.'

Getting angrier by the minute as he talked, Pa continued, 'The suitcase was open and stuck under my nose so as to tempt me and try and pay me off right there and then,' he said.

'I didn't like that at all...it hurt me,' said Pa. 'I told them "you guys think you're smart...well, you're not smart enough" then I got up and walked out of the office.' Pa added, 'when they finally paid me it was by cheque and they came to my home to do business.'

Pa, commenting on the Africville relocation said, 'The city should never have moved the people from Africville. They should have built homes for them and given them the chance to pay for their homes the same as is being done for people in North Preston and elsewhere.'

'The city gave the Africville people no deal at all,' he said. 'Some were put into places far worse than what they left. Also, when the people lived in Africville, they were not on welfare and in debt because of high rents and the cost of living.'

'I never did like charity, it robs a man of something,' said Pa.

'Most of the people who left Africville, are sorry for it...they don't like the city,' he said. 'They miss the community life and the good times we all had,' he added.

'We even had our own church.'

It's not difficult to understand and appreciate Pa's attachment to Africville since his family ties with the settlement date back to the mid-1800s when his grandfather, escaping bonds of slavery in the southern United States, first came to Preston and then finally settled at Africville.

A Boer War veteran, Pa's grandfather was 125 years old when he died. Pa's father William [Miller], a small contractor, was born at Africville and lived there all his life until he died in 1953 at the age of 95.

Pa, deep voiced, gray haired and with large hands that bear the scars of many years of hard work, says he is in good health and still spry. A coal handler and stevedore on the Halifax waterfront for most of his life, Pa retired in 1965. A widower, he has two sons living, one in Toronto, the other in Halifax.

Reminiscing about the 'good old days,' Pa told of lobster fishing in Bedford Baisin, keeping a garden, a few hens and pigs and of social life in the community.

His favourite story was about the old rum runners who used to unload cases of bootleg booze from their powerful motor launches at the fertilizer wharf where the Nova Scotia Abattoir is located today.

'I remember one Christmas Eve when we unloaded 10,000 cases of every kind of booze imaginable,' he said. 'I never saw so much liquor at one time in my life.... I was given eight cases of whiskey and $100 for helping to unload...man what a Christmas that was.'

'No sir, when you spend a lifetime in one place it's hard to get used to someplace else... I never will,' said Pa.[20]

Newspaper publicity over this bribery incident embarrassed city officials and black organizations demanded a public investigation. City council debated the incident on January 29, 1970. After considerable discussion, aldermen voted to accept motions that acknowledged an error of judgment by city officials and endorsed an apology to Mr. Miller. Council then considered the case closed.[21]

In finally forcing "Pa" Miller from his home, the city closed the Africville relocation on a singularly inept and sour note. If it can be said that the relocation began with a promise of positive change and administrative good will, equally well can it be said that the relocation program ended in overriding attention being given to the city's economic priorities. The manipulation and harassment of "Pa" Miller clearly illustrates both the shift to the development model of relocation and how, in practice, the Africville relocation fell short of its liberal-welfare rhetoric.

Notes

1 Interview with Dr. F.R. MacKinnon, Deputy Minister, Nova Scotia Department of Public Welfare, September 1969.

2 Ibid.

3 Clairmont and Magill, *Africville Relocation Report,* Appendix H, pp. A75-A80.

4 Ibid., p. A78.

5 This concept is borrowed from Floyd Hunter's study of community power. In his analysis of the power structure in Regional City, Hunter argues that "men of independent decision" are a relatively small group while the under-structure personnel who are the executors of policy, "may run into the hundreds." Floyd Hunter, *Community Power Structure: A Study of Decision Makers* (New York: Doubleday and Co., 1963) p. 66.

6 Although not appointed by Halifax City Council as a member of the subcommittee, the development director attended most of the subcommittee's meetings.

7 *Minutes of City Council Africville Subcommittee,* October 5, 1967, p. 6.

8 The development director explained why the relocation social worker was given control of welfare payments to Africville residents: "When [he] came to us...I insisted that he have control over the [welfare] money during the relocation process.... I felt that this was the only way in which we could cut fast enough, and deal with specific problems.... It was always intended that [these welfare payments] would not continue as a separate process, and that...[they] would subsequently be taken...[over] by the welfare department. In fact, this is what happened."

One city official, a critic of the relocation program, observed in an interview (August 25, 1969) that the city indirectly paid for the relocation of Africville with provincial and federal funds. The majority of welfare monies paid to relocatees were paid from social assistance funds related to a cost-sharing program with the provincial and federal governments.

Another city official described the cost-sharing in these terms: "The percentage breakdown between city, province and federal government on social assistance expenditures is twenty-five percent-twenty-five percent-fifty percent respectively. Initially, the welfare expenditures for Africville residents were placed on the standard claim which the city submits to the province for sharing according to the foregoing formula. Although sharing was obtained for the major portion of these expenditures, I am told that the city had to bear the full cost in cases where families received large cash settlements from the city and could not be regarded for social assistance purposes as being in financial 'need'."

(Letter to the authors from Mrs. Alexa McDonough, Special Projects Supervisor, Office of the Social Planner, City of Halifax, May 6, 1970, p. 2.).

9 The hospital bills waived "were actual amounts based on the city collector's records of bills which patients had failed to pay and the city had therefore been held accountable. Since payments for these bills had already been made by the city to the V.G. [Victoria General] Hospital the cheque from the Africville capital account was made payable to the city itself." (Ibid.)

10 "As in the case of hospital bills, unpaid taxes would have been assumed by the collector's department. Therefore, upon receipt of payment from the Africville account, the city collector's office was unable to indicate the debts involved as having been paid." (Ibid.)

11 The social worker described the furniture allowances: "The agreement that the city council passed was to the effect that I could work within a budget of $500 to $1000 for the necessary household items. In some instances, the money was given direct to the individual and, in other instances, the family was told to go to a particular store of their choice, and purchase the furniture required, up to $1000.

"...When the first of the settlements had been made to the people in the rental category, [these allowances were] used to buy things other than furniture and in actuality the money was squandered....

"[Thus] it was felt that it would be better if the money was more or less held at city hall and the bill sent from the store, then the [Halifax] Human Rights [Advisory] Committee were sure that the family received the benefit of furniture."

12 Lee Rainwater, *Behind Ghetto Walls: Black Family Life in a Federal Slum* (Chicago: Aldine Publishing Company, 1970), p. 409.

13 Interview, November, 1969. See also, "People Moved Out in Garbage Trucks," *The Mail-Star,* Halifax, N.S., February 26, 1970.

14 See, "Says City Falling Down on Africville Project: Welfare Director Says Relocation Not Necessary," *The Mail-Star,* Halifax, N.S., April 26, 1965. The welfare director was quoted as saying, "The city has fallen down on its responsibility to Africville. Providing proper waste and sewerage facilities for these people, when needed, would have enabled them to give as good an account of themselves as any other families in the area and would make relocation unnecessary."

15 *Minutes of the Halifax Human Rights Advisory Committee,* March 17, 1965.

16 Ibid., December 10, 1965, January 25, 1966 and February 17, 1966.

17 *Minutes of City Council Africville Subcommittee,* October 5, 1967.

[18] John O'Brien, "Alderman Knew of Difficulties About Property," *The Mail-Star,* Halifax, N.S., January 23, 1970.

[19] "Ward Replies to NSAACP Charge," *The Mail-Star,* Halifax, N.S., January 24, 1970.

[20] Jim Robson, "Last Africville Resident: If I Had Been A Little Younger City Would Never Have Gotten My Land," *The Mail-Star,* Halifax, N.S., January 12, 1970.

[21] *Minutes of the Halifax City Council,* January 29, 1970, pp. 30-31. See also, John O'Brien, "Council Closes [Miller] Case: Error in Judgement Recognized," *The Mail-Star,* Halifax, N.S., January 30, 1970.

Relocation and Relocatees

Interviewer: "Different people had different gains and losses because of the relocation. What do you think are your most important gains?"

Africville relocatee: "Gains, because of the relocation? I haven't gained a thing! The only difference between this home and my home [at Africville] is that this is a little bigger home, and it has water and sewage. Outside of that, I don't see a damn thing that's different. My expenses are overwhelming.... Regardless of our wells going dry in the summertime, and the cold in the wintertime, I still prefer Africville a thousand times to this place I am in now."

—Tape-recorded interview with an Africville relocatee, October, 1969.

Reaction to Relocation Announcement

Many Africville residents really had not believed that relocation would take place. Over seventy-five percent of the relocatees interviewed in 1969-70 reported that, prior to the city's announcement, they had not expected to be moved. The majority of relocatees defined in Chapter Two held such a view, although there was some variation; oldliners, perhaps because of their greater consciousness of previous city encroachment, and mainliners, perhaps because of their greater belief that Africville was a slum, were more likely to have expected relocation than marginals/ transients or the residual grouping. Approximately thirty-five percent of both the oldliners and the mainliners expected relocation, compared to twenty-five percent of the marginals/transients and fifteen percent of the residuals.

Over forty percent of the relocatees reported in 1969-70 that they had been at least to some extent willing to be relocated when they became aware of the city's program. As shown in Table 7.1, there was important group variation concerning residents' unwillingness to move. Age was an important variable; generally, the older the relocatee, the greater the unwillingness to move. However, a significant number of the younger relocatees were also unwilling to be relocated. More so than relocatees in other age categories; those in their twenties and thirties reported that, at the time of the relocation announcement, they had held the view that alternatives such as rehabilitation and installation of facilities should have been pursued further. One young oldliner commented:

> I was mad [upon hearing of the relocation program].... I
> had my own home, cost me $5,500 to build. I liked the
> freedom. They [the city] made it so you had to move.

Among the different social groupings, the relocatees least likely to be unwilling to move were the marginals/transients and mainliners. They were also less likely than oldliners and residuals to report having had any alternatives with which to counter the city's relocation program.[1]

The mainliners who were more or less willing to relocate tended to view the city's program as a challenge or opportunity. Many mainliners believed that they would be able to negotiate a good exchange with the city; one male observed "at [the time of the relocation announcement] since I paid taxes and fixed up the place, I figured I would get a half-decent price." The marginals/transients were somewhat surprisingly the least unwilling to be relocated but did not view the plan as positive city intervention nor did they view Africville as a particularly undesirable place of residence. They responded to relocation typically in a muted, matter-of-fact, unemotional way. Relocation neither created nor destroyed any dreams, though most considered it inconvenient. One marginal transient observed:

> My reaction? Well, we moved. We were one of the first
> ones to move. I thought they needed the property for a

Table 7.1
Relocatees' Unwillingness to Move by Age and Social Grouping*

	% Unwilling
Age	
Between 20 and 39	40
Between 40 and 49	55
50 and over	65
Social Grouping	
Marginals/Transients	35
Mainliners	50
Oldliners	55
Residuals	60

* These are retrospective assessments obtained in 1969-70. The number in each age group was, respectively, 48, 31, and 56. There were six cases where age was unknown. The number in each social grouping was, respectively, 26, 21, 51, and 42.

road. I never went to any meetings because it was none of my business. I was an outsider. I was outside their affairs. I didn't own any property.

Table 7.1 shows that a majority of the oldliners and residuals were unwilling to move at the time of the relocation announcement. This finding is quite predictable since both groupings in the pre-relocation period had indicated a strong sense of belonging in Africville; among the oldliners there was a feeling of historical rootedness in Africville and among the residuals an anxiety due to the absence of legal title to their property in the community. However, what is surprising is that so many respondents in each group were not unwilling to be relocated.[2] Certainly many oldliners, and to a lesser extent some residuals, had given up hope that the city would ever do anything positive in Africville and consequently they were at least fairly willing to be relocated if this meant that they would obtain superior living conditions. Yet the oldliners, even those not unwilling to move, typically expressed grief and sadness when they learned of the relocation, and over seventy percent reported that they would have preferred rehabilitation of Africville and/or co-operative housing.

Anxiety rather than grief typified the initial reaction of residuals to the city's announcement. Many of these were squatters but they had roots extending back to at least before the Second World War; they had an investment in Africville and possessed relatively few resources with which to establish themselves elsewhere. One middle-aged woman observed: "I didn't know what to do. I wondered where I was going to live." A female household head who had a large family commented that: "I felt that we couldn't afford to buy or rent so we didn't know what to do." A young married male pointed out: "I paid no attention to it. I had no plans for moving out."

After the city's announcement, and induced by relocation rhetoric, many of the residuals indulged in a considerable amount of dreaming. Many developed rather high expectations, thinking that the city was really going to provide them with an opportunity to restructure their life conditions; this was particularly true among the young and early-middle-age household heads who had previously, of necessity, muted any middle-class lifestyle aspirations and had enjoyed to the full the freedom and autonomy of Africville life. One female household head commented: "[The relocation social worker] told us that we had to go to a place where we would get plumbing, water, and modern facilities and an up-to-date house. We were so busy trying to figure out what to do, we were really excited."

Although the initial reaction among Africville residents to the relocation program was one of surpise and of preference for alternatives such as rehabilitation and/or co-operative housing, there was considerable variation, and a significant number of people, especially the mainliners and the young household heads, were, in terms of their own retrospective assessments and the judgment of the relocation social worker, well disposed towards a progressive relocation program. Marginals/transients did not see themselves as significant "actors in the relocation drama," while many of the residual grouping were prepared to shed their Africville lifestyles if the relocation rhetoric could be realized.

Relocatees and Settlement Negotiations

It has been noted that there was no organized Africville presence during the mechanics phase of the relocation. The structure of relocation decision-making did not facilitate collective action by the Africville residents. There were no general Africville meetings organized independently of the Halifax Human Rights Advisory Committee, although prior to the formation of the latter, and to the city's announcement of relocation, a few members of the Africville Ratepayers' Association had attempted, with modest success, to collect funds from their fellow residents in order to obtain legal assistance in pressing their grievances against the city.

When the relocation social worker assumed his position and relocation negotiations began in earnest, four or five residents exercised some influence but they disagreed among themselves as to the appropriate response to the city's plan. While not rejecting the alternative of remaining in a more adequate Africville, none appeared to have argued strongly for this alternative; rather, their disagreements centred on whether to bargain for "a home for a home," or for the largest cash settlement possible, or for rebuilding the community in another location. The handful of Africville leaders prominent in the community and in discussions with the caretakers and the city officials were among those who in 1959 had indicated that they disliked Africville and were willing to move. Given this orientation to mobility, their internal disagreements, and their sense of futility in resisting the city, it is not surprising that these leaders were among the first Africville residents to begin individual negotiations with city officials.

Many Africville residents in post-relocation interviews contended that the city's chief strategy was to divide the community and, by offering especially good deals, to buy off the more prominent Africville leaders. One relocatee commented:

> There were community leaders who were going to represent the people of Africville against the city. Of course the people were not well educated and they trusted these leaders to explain why the people didn't want to move.... The first thing you know [these leaders] who were supposed to keep the city from relocating us, are the first ones to move. Well! When we saw them leaving, we all figured that what's the sense of staying if the leaders of the rest of us are gone.

Some city officials in the post-relocation period also contended in private conversation that the city strategy was to buy off one or two leaders in the hope that potential community resistance would thereby be aborted. One official observed that "the city got [two leaders] to move and the rest followed. They [the leaders] got a very good deal. Really [they] were bribed." Another official who had a minor role in the relocation pointed out that "[one leader] was the patriarch of the community. We had to get him to go first and the rest would follow; so we spent a lot of time convincing him about the benefits of the move."

There does appear to be some basis for the above contentions. Not only were the handful of prominent leaders among the first residents to begin negotiations with the city, but they appear to have received a better than average settlement. On the other hand, these leaders did have better than average property claims, and given the necessarily ambiguous settlement criteria it is difficult to establish objectively that they obtained the most favourable exchange. However, using these leaders as scapegoats seems inappropriate since, for the most part, they were explicit in their willingness to be relocated. Certainly these leaders did not particularly intervene on behalf of many residents, but how far they could have done so in any case is questionable given the fragmentation in the community, the strains associated with the uncertainties of land ownership, and the residents' sense of powerlessness in the face of city officials determined on relocation.

There was considerable retrospective feeling among the relocatees that the people would have done better in dealing with the city if they had stuck together and bargained collectively. One female summed up these feelings in her remark: "The people didn't know how to stick together. No organization. Otherwise they'd still be out there." But given the structure of relocation decision-making, there was little place for a collective response. At one point in the relocation a petition was circulated among the residents, arguing for Africville representation on the subcommittee handling relocation settlements, but it was neither strongly supported in the community nor encouraged by city officials (one of the black caretakers did volunteer to remove himself and thereby open a position on the subcommittee for an Africville resident). The few Africville residents who had participated in the Halifax Human Rights Advisory Committee were among the first to open negotiations with the city; thereafter a more collective response was impossible.

In reporting their actions once they knew for certain that Africville was to be destroyed, the relocatees fell into two evenly divided categories: the passive kind who felt resigned, and the active type who set about trying to get the best deal for themselves and their families. Only eight percent of the relocatees interviewed in 1969-70 reported that they had fought hard against relocation; these people also had an active orientation towards settlement negotiations. Table 7.2 indicates that age was an important

Table 7.2
Africville Residents' Orientation to Relocation Negotiations by Age, Housing Status, and Social Grouping*

	Age		
	Between 20 and 39 %	Between 40 and 49 %	50 and over %
Passive	38	45	51
Active	60	50	45
No Data	2	5	4

	Housing Status			
	Homeowners %	Squatters %	Property-less %	Renters with Claims %
Passive	41	27	62	42
Active	55	68	35	50
No Data	4	5	3	8

	Social Grouping			
	Oldliners %	Mainliners %	Residuals %	Marginals Transients %
Passive	30	26	51	74
Active	64	74	47	18
No Data	6	–	2	8

* See text for explanation of active and passive orientation. The data are from the authors' 1969-70 survey.

variable in relocatee orientation to negotiations; typically the older the resident, the greater the passivity and the more likely an attitude of, "I knew I couldn't do anything about relocation and went along with being relocated." On the other hand, the younger residents were less unwilling to be relocated and tended to be active negotiators. In terms of housing status, the propertyless were predictably much more likely to have a passive orientation, whereas the squatters, who did not have legal title to their

Africville property and were therefore more anxious, were clearly the most active.

Marginals/transients, being both propertyless and older, predictably were more passive than members of the other social groupings. Mainliners, having property, resources, and mobility aspirations, were by far the most likely to have had an active orientation towards settlement negotiations. The residuals were about evenly split between passive and active orientations. Most oldliners reported that they had an active orientation; it may be noted that most of the relocatees who indicated that they had fought hard against relocation were oldliners.[3] Several elderly oldliners who did not want to be relocated adopted an orientation of stubborn withdrawal; they did not attend any meetings called by the Halifax Human Rights Advisory Committee, demanded a very high price for their property from the relocation social worker, and for a long period refused to enter into any negotiations.

Few Africville residents consulted with those members of the Halifax Human Rights Advisory Committee who were their advocates on the subcommittee that assessed the recommendations of the relocation social worker. Well over eighty percent of the relocatees reported that they had never met with members of the Halifax Human Rights Advisory Committee. Less than twenty-five percent reported any assistance from local organizations and leaders or from the two or three Africville residents who continued to participate in the deliberations of the human rights advisory committee. Although the city officially made available to the Africville residents legal and real estate services, less than thirty percent of the relocatees indicated any awareness of these services and only fifteen percent used them. Basically, in the relocation negotiations Africville residents, whether they had an active or a passive orientation, depended on their own resources and their relationship with the relocation social worker.

Relocatees and the Relocation Social Worker

In view of the lack of community organization and the inadequate mobilization of external advocacy, the crucial relationship, in terms of both settlement negotiations and relocation benefits, was that between the individual relocatee and the relocation social worker. It has been observed that lower-class relocatees have a tendency to operate at two levels when dealing with government, either overtrusting civic officials or expressing complete cynicism. The latter was evidenced in the remarks of one relocatee when asked why he did not take advantage of the free legal and real estate services offered by the city: "Boy, you can't go against the city. The city provided a lawyer but it was their lawyer."[4] Such a twofold tendency appears to be related to a feeling of powerlessness and that the world of authority and officialdom works in impersonal and random ways. The Africville relocatees depended heavily on the relocation social worker. Many believed that they could influence him, but most were very cynical about his advocacy of their interests, pointing to the fact that he was in the employ of the city and that "one doesn't bite the hand that feeds you." Over seventy percent of the relocatees indicated that one of the main ways that they set about trying to get a good deal for themselves was to depend on their relationship with the relocation social worker, either throwing themselves on his mercy or trying through him to drive a hard bargain with the city. The younger relocatees were more likely to have reported this latter strategy, but a majority of the relocatees fifty years of age or more also reported that they relied on the relocation social worker. The pattern of greater dependency among young adults is consistent with their greater willingness to relocate, their active orientation to the negotiations, and the fact that they were often propertyless or only possessed squatters' rights. Their strategy was obviously born of necessity, but it did dovetail with the relocation social worker's professed goal of trying to assist the young household heads especially. A common tactic used by some young residents was to argue that they should receive a larger settlement because they intended to get married and set up new households. A number of young residents did request and obtain furniture money to help establish themselves elsewhere. In a few instances, the relocation social worker made furniture money contingent upon a young unmarried mother marrying her boyfriend. Generally the liberal-welfare rhetoric of the relocation with its aim of creating new life-opportunities did, in the eyes of most people involved in the relocation program, appear to hold out a special promise and obligation for young people and families.

Table 7.3 compares the four different social groupings in terms of their dependence upon the relocation social worker and their perception of whether or not they were able to influence him in the relocation negotiations. It illustrates a strong inverse correlation between dependency and perceived influence; typically those who possessed fewer bargaining resources and were, therefore, in greater self-professed need of his internal advocacy were the least likely to have perceived themselves as influencing the relocation social worker.[5] This point is most sharply illustrated in the

Table 7.3
Relocatees' Dependence Upon and Perceived Ability to Influence the Relocation Social Worker, by Social Grouping*

	Dependence % yes	Influence % yes
Social Grouping		
Mainliners	50	55
Oldliners	61	51
Residuals	73	36
Marginals/Transients	83	22

* The data are from the authors' 1969-70 survey. The table should be read as follows: sixty-one percent of the oldliners depended on the relocation social worker and fifty-one percent of the oldliners perceived that they could influence him in the relocation negotiations.

case of the marginals/transients, where approximately eighty percent of the respondents indicated dependency but only about twenty percent saw themselves as able to benefit from his advocacy. This finding of an inverse correlation between dependency and perceived influence is consistent with the observation made in Chapter Six that, despite the liberal-welfare rhetoric of the relocation program, time pressure to get the people out and the priority of real estate criteria in the settlement negotiations resulted in the relocation following more closely the development model of relocation. The relocation social worker was hampered by a real estate negotiation mandate and to a significant degree did not successfully perform the internal advocacy function for those Africville residents who needed him the most.

Approximately ninety percent of the relocatees interviewed met with the relocation social worker several times to discuss their position and find what benefits they could get in relocation; in most instances the relocation social worker apparently had to go into the community to get the negotiations started and to bring them to a conclusion. He spent most time with the Africville residents who had initially joined the Halifax Human Rights Advisory Committee and with influential people who were at least fairly willing to relocate. He also frequently visited with some of the "Big Town" area residents who had developed high expectations concerning relocation benefits and whom he, like civic welfare officials before him, admired and sympathized with because of their open, resourceful and rather rebellious or deviant lifestyle. Relatively little time was spent with the young adults, presumably because here the critical relocation aspect was not property settlement but a program to effect new life-opportunities and this aspect of the relocation was in practice accorded low priority. Comparatively little time was also spent with stubborn and resistant oldliners; apparently the city strategy here was to remove as soon as possible those who were willing to relocate and, by demolishing the community bit by bit, increase the costs of resistance. On the whole, the marginals/transients grouping received the least attention from the relocation social worker. They were usually resourceless, usually renting from other residents, and consequently of little importance as far as property settlements were concerned. Moreover, the relocation social worker did not see many of this group as either desirous of, or capable of, rehabilitation; also, to a significant degree, he shared the view held by many residents that the marginals/transients did not really belong to Africville.

Only thirty percent of the relocatees believed that the relocation social worker helped them get a better deal from the city. As might be expected, the relocation social worker's advocacy was assessed favourably by those relocatees with whom he had established good rapport, particularly mainliners, those willing to relocate, and "Big Town" area residents.

The majority of relocatees did not perceive the relocation social worker as an effective internal advocate on their behalf at city hall. Over ninety percent saw him as essentially used by the city to convince the Africville residents to relocate and fifty percent associated him with the city tactics of dividing the people to reduce their resistance to relocation. The basis for their judgment was that he only engaged in individual negotiations and chiefly relied for information on a handful of residents willing to relocate. His task was not without ambiguity and conflict, but the relocation social worker strove to avoid a too-close identification with the city's offers for property and its ultimate weapon of expropriation. At the same time, in order to be effective in inducing people to relocate he had to be identified with the city to make his promises credible and authoritative. To some degree he was successful. A large minority of relocatees viewed him as a buffer between themselves and further city exploitation; in addition a majority of relocatees dissociated him from the expropriation "big stick" which they saw lurking in the background of the relocation program.[6] Nevertheless most relocatees perceived him as more concerned with real estate negotitations and rehousing than with rehabilitation.

Table 7.4
Relocatees' Awareness and Use of City Welfare Assistance, By Selected Groupings

	Aware %	Used %
Age		
Between 20 and 39	60	49
50 and over	70	23
Housing Status		
Homeowners	73	39
Squatters	68	59
Propertyless	71	65
Social Grouping		
Oldliners	70	44
Mainliners	75	35
Residuals	70	60
Marginals/Transients	70	65

* The data are from the authors' 1969-70 survey.

Furniture money, new housing, and welfare assistance were key inducements and rehabilitative tools used by the relocation social worker in his negotiations. The young, the propertyless, and the marginals/transients were especially dependent upon these particular benefits if they were to profit at all by the relocation program. A majority of relocatees indicated that the relocation social worker had made them promises concerning rent and housing as part of his inducement for their relocation. Some respondents referred to promises of "a year's free rent upon relocation." Unfortunately no clear, written commitment was given by the city or by the relocation social worker concerning what some relocatees referred to as the "free-rent deal" and when he left the area, after having moved virtually all residents out of Africville, considerable controversy developed regarding what had been promised them.[7] Table 7.4 indicates that over seventy percent of the relocatees were aware of the fact that the city had promised welfare assistance if necessary and over fifty percent reported that, through the relocation social worker, they did obtain welfare assistance as part of their relocation settlement. All groups and categories of relocatees were roughly equally aware of the welfare policy, but the young, the propertyless, and the marginals/transients were the chief users of this service. It is quite clear that welfare was indispensable in inducing many residents to relocate and in maintaining them in their new environment. Numerous relocatees reported that they had been promised special welfare assistance for an indefinite period of time, but the city disputed such claims.

The overall impression one obtains from examining strategies and orientations during the settlement negotiations is that relocatees related to the city, individually and privately, through the relocation social worker. There were influential people among the Africville residents, but only thirty-five percent of the relocatees indicated that they had discussed their settlements with others within the community.

The privacy and individuality of the settlement is surprising given the extensive kinship ties in the community and overlapping property claims. Only twenty percent of the relocatee respondents reported that they had attempted to get other residents to join them in adopting a tough bargaining position or to work out arrangements concerning property claims with other residents. About the same percentage reported that they assisted relatives in trying to obtain a good deal from the city.[8]

Africville residents were thrust into a situation virtually guaranteed to result in grief and hard feelings. This led to a lack of mutual cooperation. If they were to financially profit from the relocation program they had to obtain some form of property claim. Given the close kinship ties and the lack of legal title in Africville, considerable opportunity for strife and suspicion existed. Such opportunity was heightened by the fact that Africville residents appeared generally to believe that the city had made available a fixed sum for the purchase of Africville property and therefore its distribution was based on a zero-sum principle (that is, for example, if one person got six thousand dollars, then there would be six thousand dollars less to be distributed among other claimants). Underpinning the scrambling, suspicion, and lack of cooperation among Africville residents during the relocation negotiations was the common pattern of the poor and oppressed having a low estimation of one another's value; many residents shared the sentiment expressed by a young female respondent:

I didn't go to the meetings. I didn't deal with some of the people because they were ignorant and had no education.

> I went to a meeting one night, but I didn't stay that long because they were talking ignorant.

Of course a number of relocatees used what they considered "tricks" to get more money out of the relocation social worker, such as pretending that they had lost their rent money, feigning freak accidents with household items which they then sought to have replaced, or temporarily breaking up a household in order that several household members might separately obtain furniture allocations. Within the larger exchange relationship between the relocation social worker or the city and the Africville residents, such actions constituted a *quid pro quo* in relation to the vague and subsequently disclaimed promises concerning rent and welfare assistance in the post-relocation period.

Relocatees and a Fair Deal

The relocation social worker reported that the original settlement terms requested by the Africville residents were generally acceded to, but the latter indicated that they usually obtained less than they asked for. The relocatees who received the least in their settlement exchange were the most likely to have reported that they received the settlement terms they asked for. In fact, over fifty percent of the marginals/transients, for the most part propertyless and admittedly without much investment in Africville, reported that they had obtained what they had requested; this was generally some furniture allocation, although not the maximum allowable, slightly improved housing, and short-term welfare assistance.

Virtually all relocatees reported that the city gained more from the relocation than did the Africville people; similarly, an equal percentage (about ninety-five percent) believed that the Africville people lost most by relocation. The relocatees usually contended that the city had obtained valuable land whereas the Africville people did not receive enough money to maintain themselves adequately in their new environment. Many relocatees shared the sentiment of one young female household head who commented: "I'd say it was a dirty deal. We owned our own places. The city committed highway robbery, got the places and the land."

Among the few relocatees who contended that the city had lost most in the relocation or that neither the city nor the Africville people had gained because of it, a common view was that expressed by a marginal/transient:

"[The] city lost in the long run; now that the people are in Halifax they are on welfare. It's going to cost them [city officials] more than they realize."

Encouraged by the relocation rhetoric and the promises and inducements of the relocation social worker to think that their life-opportunities would be dramatically improved in the post-relocation period, the relocatees undoubtedly became more disenchanted with the relocation deal as time went on. By the time of the 1969-70 survey, many relocatees had reconsidered the exchange with the city; they had spent whatever cash bonus they had received as a property settlement and realized the city had failed to follow up on promises concerning rent and welfare assistance. Such reconsideration undoubtedly accounts for the inconsistency between the data presented above and the reports of the relocation social worker to the effect that most relocatees were satisfied with the relocation settlement.

Most relocatees reported that relocation benefits were not equitably distributed among the Africville residents; eighty percent believed that some groups or individuals obtained a better deal from the relocation exchange with the city than did the other residents. Skill in bargaining and rapport with the relocation social worker were seen as significant in determining the deal one received. Oldliners and mainliners displayed the strongest emotions concerning how relocation benefits were distributed. Many of these relocatees contended that the marginals/transients and the squatters who were not born in Africville profited more than they themselves did in the light of investment criteria such as property holdings, belonging in Africville, and longevity of residence. (Underlying the oldliners' and mainliners' sense of injustice was a zero-sum conception of relocation benefits and an exaggerated estimate of what the marginals/transients and the squatters received in settlement.)

Squatters and those in the residual grouping also held the view that some groups or people had obtained a better deal in the relocation exchange. Typically they contended that the relocatees who received more benefits were those owning greater property in Africville and having legal title to their property. However, squatters and residuals did not appear to be as emotionally upset as oldliners and mainliners over the perception that some people had obtained a better deal.

Relocatees who believed that Africville residents obtained a fair deal, at least vis-à-vis one another, were chiefly the marginals/transients, the people who objectively received the least from the relocation exchange. The apparent irony that a majority of the residents who profited least from relocation would perceive the distribution of benefits to be equitable can be readily explained in terms of the principle of distributive justice; perceiving themselves as having less investment than other types of residents, they did not think it unfair that they should have obtained less in the relocation exchange.

In their own personal exchange with the city approximately eighty percent of the relocatees reported that they did not get a fair deal. Only among the marginals/transients did a majority of the relocatees believe that they were treated fairly, though not necessarily well, by the city. One marginal/transient, who obtained short-term welfare assistance and accommodations for his family in a city-owned redevelopment house, which was condemned a short while after he was placed there, observed: "I got a fair deal. Most of the Africville residents got a pretty fair deal from the city." The generally modest expectations of the marginals/transients was evidenced by the fact that most of those claiming not to have received a fair deal reported that if they had obtained five hundred to a thousand dollars more, then they would have had a fair deal from the city. Among the other social groupings, the unanticipated cost of their new environments was a major problem even for those few who believed that they obtained a fair deal. One oldliner reported: "I suppose I got a fair deal but we'll be in debt for the rest of our lives. I'd sooner be back in Africville. I owned my own home there. I got mortgage payments to meet here." A mainliner referring to unanticipated increases in his cost of living commented: "In Africville I could live adequately on two thousand to three thousand dollars a year. But here I absolutely have to have four hundred dollars a month." A member of the residual grouping, who subsequent to her 1969-70 interview lost her home because of failure to meet mortgage payments, contended that a fair deal would have entailed the city providing homes for the relocatees—"not fancy homes but which had facilities and without mortgage."

Housing

One clear responsibility assumed by Halifax city council in adopting the Rose Report was to provide Africville relocatees with safe, sanitary, and decent housing. The scarcity of land and the population pressure on the Halifax peninsula made it difficult to fulfil this relocation obligation. An alderman member of the Africville Subcommittee observed that housing had been scarce since the Second World War. An additional and specific

Plate 7.1. UNIACKE SQUARE. Most Africville families who were relocated in public housing moved into Uniacke Square.

Plate 7.2. MULGRAVE PARK. A public housing project into which several Africville families moved.

problem in rehousing was the fact that blacks were being dispersed throughout a largely white community where racist attitudes still lingered. Just prior to relocation, some residents of a nearby middle-class neighbourhood protested angrily against a suggestion that the people be relocated there, stating: "We don't want Africville people here." Several instances of discrimination did occur. In one instance, a white person was fined for sending KKK-type threats to a relocatee who had moved into a white neighbourhood.[9]

Nevertheless, Africville relocatees, like relocatees in most urban renewal projects in Canada and the United States, have obtained improved housing facilities in terms of size and condition of dwelling in areas of Halifax adjacent to the Africville site. Between seventy to seventy-five percent of the relocatees were rehoused within walking distance of their former dwellings. Relocatees who moved elsewhere either purchased houses in Halifax County or migrated to the metropolitan centres of Toronto, Montreal, and Winnipeg.

Africville relocatees obtained better housing but at considerable cost; many experienced what they considered to be a loss of freedom and status as they had to become tenants instead of homeowners. Most relocated families owned their dwellings in Africville, whereas less than one-third were homeowners after relocation. To people without adequate and regular income who are unused to paying rent, mortgage, and service and maintenance bills, the expense of improved housing brought new worries, family strains, and indebtedness. The marginals/transients, who were often resourceless renters while in Africville, fared poorly in relocation. Usually considered unacceptable for public housing, they were the least likely to obtain safe, sanitary, and decent housing. None of these circumstances is exceptional but is readily predictable from a review of relocation studies in North America.

By the completion date of the Africville study (1970), many Africville relocatees moved into public housing in an area of Halifax adjacent to Africville, a neighbourhood that Haligonians sometimes refer to as the "coloured," "Negro," or "black" district.[10] As of August 21, 1969, twenty-eight public housing units (seven bachelor units and twenty-one family units) were occupied by Africville relocatees. There is evidence of a clash of lifestyle between some relocatees and the Halifax Housing Authority. Eleven relocatee applications had been rejected (that is, not recommended by the housing authority inspector) on the ground that the applicants were "unsuitable;"[11] in addition, two relocatees had been asked to vacate their public housing units and several others had been warned by the housing authority. Rejection and notices to vacate were usually justified by the housing authority on the grounds that these residents were poor housekeepers, alcoholics, or bootleggers.[12]

From a quite different point of view, there was a further clash of lifestyles. The fluid social structure of Africville was at variance with the cut-and-dried style acceptable to the housing authority. Africville residents had a tradition of extended families, consisting of several generations and quasi-extended family household formation. Such family formations, while tolerated by the housing authority, required special permission and entailed significant costs. One woman who wanted to live in public housing observed: "Well, I wanted to move into Uniacke Square and they told me it would cost ninety-five dollars a month. I wanted one of my grandsons [fifteen years old] to move in with me, but that would have been an extra thirty dollars per month. So that would have been too much money to pay."

Moreover, Africville residents were used to freedom and "elbow room" in their Africville milieu. Prior to relocation, most residents had indicated that what they liked best about Africville was the fresh air, the view, the freedom of the place, and the congenial neighbours. In the 1969 questionnaire survey, relocatees reiterated these as being the prime attractions. Some relocatees abhorred the prospect of entering public housing and, among those who did, there were considerable complaints about housing authority regulations. One elderly oldliner commented: "I kind of thought [Africville] really was a home because I felt so close…the freedom and the home is what got me…I could always sit out on my step and give out with a good morning but can't do that here [in public housing]." Several younger relocatees, oldliners who had been living in public housing for almost two years, complained of a feeling of being trapped; they believed that they did not have any control over their dwelling and referred to inspectors who were always running in and out of their homes and telling them what they could do and what they could not do. As one relocatee put it: "People can't move around as much as they did in Africville."

Despite complaints and the necessity of lifestyle adjustments, on the whole the relocatees in public housing were adapting well to their new environment. Most had neat and attractive apartments and, according to a survey carried out by the city in the post-relocation period, were less debt-laden than other relocatees. Most respondents of course were pleased with the improved facilities and services and, while a few mentioned that they had encountered some prejudice from their white neighbours, a larger number appeared to place some value on the greater integration found in public housing. Among these relocatees public housing was a notch up from Africville, but even they found that relocation to public housing had its costs. For those people who had been homeowners in Africville, the change in housing status was a serious loss; one relocatee observed: "I will die and won't be able to leave my children anything."

Approximately twenty-four relocatee families puchased homes with money received from their relocation settlement. About half the homeowners settled in the North End of Halifax, an area adjacent to the Africville site and considered to be a "respectable working class" area. Seven others settled near metropolitan Halifax. The remaining few went farther afield, two moving out of Nova Scotia. Many of the homeowners in Halifax city and Halifax County, never before faced with substantial monthly bills for mortgage and services and not having found new employment, quickly found themselves in debt. Several took in boarders to defray some of the unexpected expenses. Four or five lost their homes because they were unable to discharge financial obligations. Several others were temporarily rescued from a similar fate by the credit union program initiated by the social planning department.

Since they had owned their own homes in Africville and since the single-family dwelling in an attractive environment was considered the ideal type of housing, a large number of Africville relocatees had wanted to purchase homes upon being relocated. The relocation social worker, recognizing the discrepancy between ideals and actual resources, tried in some cases to advise relocatees against this course of action; he also attempted to secure the cooperation of real estate dealers in advising him of any negotiation initiated by relocatees. However, the relocation rhetoric had often induced high expectations among the residents; this fact, plus their poor comprehension of living costs outside the Africville situation and the unique nest-egg of settlement money they now had, led a number of relocatees to take the plunge of home ownership despite their lack of good, regular income.

Ten of the household heads living in "Big Town," the area of Africville in which the hard-drinking and boisterous people of the residual grouping were concentrated, used part of their settlement money as down payments on modest homes. Within a year or two, relatively isolated from their former friendship networks and overwhelmed by financial pressure, four of the families had lost their homes and the others had continuing financial and personal crises. One of the household heads still struggling to maintain his home bitterly denounced the city and vowed that if he lost his home he would get revenge by deserting his family, thereby forcing the city to support it through welfare.

Of the remaining relocatee homeowners, one person had lost her home and several were struggling under heavy financial pressure but most (eight or nine) were making out well and expressed considerable satisfaction with their relocation. These were usually the relocatees who had received the largest settlements, several obtaining more than ten thousand dollars for their Africville properties (six of these were mainliners). One such relocatee, a mainliner, commented:

> My children, they come to visit us and they like the home
> and hate going back to Montreal. This is an ideal place for
> an old couple to retire. We have all the conveniences. The
> neighbourhood is friendly and the scenery is beautiful. We
> have to pay twice as much now to live; we have the same
> amount of money as we did in Africville but it's well worth
> it.

The category of relocatees with fewest resources and receiving least attention were the renters who moved to private dwelling, or city-owned houses in the north-central redevelopment area of Halifax, which provided only temporary shelter. Almost one-quarter of the pre-relocation Africville population was rehoused in this manner. Their housing, while on the whole an improvement over Africville accommodation, often was neither safe nor decent. Many of these buildings were ugly and slum-like in appearance. They were the kind of mid-town city dwellings to which Africville residents, prior to relocation, had favourably compared their own dwellings. Only a few of these buildings could pass a strict application of city ordinances. Several buildings were unheated, a few others were impossible to heat effectively and economically, and shared bathrooms were common. Several of the buildings were condemned shortly after the relocatees had been placed there. The relocation social worker pointed out that in a few instances relocatees accepted this kind of housing against his advice. In other cases he placed people there supposedly on an interim basis while waiting for better accommodation in public housing and elsewhere to become available. Obviously the pressure of time to complete the relocation project was an important consideration. Many Africville relocatees complained about this rehousing practice; one relocatee commented: "Wherever they could squeeze you in, that's where you landed." Of the relocatees rehoused in rental accommodation in these redevelopment areas, a significant number had moved as many as three times since leaving Africville.

The relocatees most likely to be placed in the type of housing described above were the marginals/transients. Besides these persons, people without resources or considered unacceptable for public housing were commonly relocated in this "interim" inadequate housing. These relocatees received from the relocation little beyond temporary welfare assistance; they were often the hard-core, multi-social-problem cases.

Employment

A 1962 report dealing with socio-economic conditions among blacks in Halifax city stated:

> No matter what one uses as an index of a poor employment situation (low average income, large numbers of weeks unemployed, fewness of people in the more skilled occupations) Africville Negroes rank worse than Halifax as a whole and in general worse even than the mid-city Negroes.[13]

No serious creative employment program was developed by city officials during the basic relocation period, 1964-67, dispite the fact that this was a critical, if not the most critical, rehabilitative and opportunity-creating aspect of the relocation rhetoric. During the basic relocation period members of the Africville Subcommittee often expressed concern about relocatees' employment prospects, and a few Africville residents were induced by the relocation rhetoric to raise their aspirations. The relocation social worker did not have an employment program with which to work and was fully engaged in settlement negotiations and other aspects of the relocation program. Beyond arranging for an adult-education course (which proved unsuccessful) and attempting to secure employment for a few relocatees through the Longshoremen's Union (again unsuccessful), the relocation social worker did not spend significant time securing employment opportunities for the Africville people. He sent unemployed or underemployed relocatees to an employment officer who had been assigned by the provincial department of public welfare to concern himself exclusively with the placement of blacks in the metropolitan area. No special consideration in employment placement was given to Africville residents. The employment officer worked with many relocatees and their grown children, especially in the post-relocation period, but was unable to secure regular, well- or average-paying employment for most of them. One young relocatee observed that "what we needed was steady jobs. Two days work was no help to us. I can get casual jobs myself."

In a follow-up proposal that the social planning department submitted to city council (March, 1969) it was observed that, with reference to both permanent and temporary work, vague records indicated that employment opportunities may have been found for twelve to fifteen people. Even this small figure seems too high. Only six relocatees indicated that they used the employment service made available by the city during relocation and only an additional fourteen people indicated awareness that the service was in existence. The relocation may have done more harm than good to relocatees' employment opportunities; in the 1969-70 survey sixteen percent of the relocatees reported that they had experienced job problems as a result of relocation.

In the second phase of the relocation, when the social planning department became involved in the plight of the relocatees and the latter formed the Africville Action Committee, there was renewed concern for the employment of Africville relocatees but only modest concrete achievement. In late August, 1969, a general meeting of Africville relocatees was called under the auspices of the city's social planning department to consider suggestions for employment. A committee of relocatees emerged from the meeting, but there is no evidence of subsequent action. In early 1971 the department, representatives of the Africville Action Committee, and a Canada Manpower official formed a special committee to inquire again into problems of employment among Africville blacks and to develop and coordinate assistance programs. Several important observations emerged from these discussions: (1) it is extremely difficult, within existing social arrangements, to provide real economic opportunity for Africville relocatees; (2) many of the relocatees are virtually impossible to place in employment because of age, infirmity, family responsibilities, or behavioural disorders; and (3) many of the out-of-school children of relocatees are without economic prospects. In view of these observations and the achievements of the basic relocation program, the rhetoric of liberalism that accompanied the Africville relocation seemed empty, if not perverse.

Assessment of Life Conditions

The Africville relocation, in structure and rhetoric, was a liberal-welfare program of planned social change. Clearly, though, the rehabilitative and opportunity-creating aspects of it did not dramatically improve life conditions for many Africville residents. One relocatee spoke of "the shiny future which never came." Most, but not all, relocatees did obtain better housing and more services; property owners do appear to have received better than the then market value for their individual properties; more residents who were in need of social assistance while in Africville received welfare in their new environment.[14] At the same time, these gains have to be qualified. With better housing have also come higher costs, more financial worries, often a change in status from homeowner to renter, and sometimes a valid enough feeling of less freedom to adjust the physical environment to one's needs and wishes. Increased social assistance in some cases has been necessitated by the relocation itself; it has caused some recipients to feel more dependent and regulated. Moreover, it is difficult to see welfare assistance as more than a short-term solution, albeit an important support, as testified to by a relocatee who observed that "with the help of God we'll get along with welfare." In addition, although individually Africville residents may have received a good deal for their properties, it is less certain that collectively they could be said to have fared as well.

Interviewed in 1969-70, approximately sixty percent of the relocatee respondents claimed that the relocation produced a personal crisis for them. Yet it is clear from the following tables that, apart from money worries, the crisis problem was less one of what the relocation produced than of what it took away.

Table 7.5 indicates that virtually three-quarters of the relocatees reported increased money worries as a consequence of relocation. In the light of the inadequate rehabilitative program and the disruption and inappropriateness of pre-relocation coping behaviour, the above fact is entirely predictable. A less common but significant result of the relocation which affected about forty percent of the relocatee respondents was that it produced changes in household composition.

In several instances older married children and unmarried daughters with children readily took advantage of social assistance proffered by the city to set up their own households; in other instances such a change was

Table 7.5
Relocatees' Perception of Changes Wrought by Relocation (N=140)

	% Yes
Job Problems	16
Household changes	40
Marital strains	17
Money worries	72
Strains among relatives	12

undertaken as a means of getting something out of the relocation program, given the policies and rules established by the relocation social worker, the welfare department, and the public housing authority.[15] Whereas formerly unmarried daughters with children would have continued to live with or at least adjacent to the parental family and, accordingly, be embedded in a larger, supportive extended-family system, after relocation the single-parent family was comparatively on its own and dependent on welfare.

In a general sense, the relocation had an *embourgeoisement* effect on family structure and relations; Table 7.6 indicates that there were fewer children and other relatives in the post-relocation households. An unusual and striking instance of this pattern was reported by one relocatee: "I had fifteen children when I left Africville and I had to give several of them away when I came to live in [public housing]. We just couldn't afford to keep them. My sister has one, another is somewhere else." The extended-family form was too expensive and inconvenient in the new environment. Especially among older relocatees there was grief over this stripping away of kinship intimacy. One relocatee, who in Africville had housed her brother, a son, a nephew, and a boarder, observed that she tried to bargain for more money in her property negotiations because she wanted to have her "family" with her. In Africville it had been common for older people to have a young grandchild or other relative in their households. Only in two cases among the post-Africville households was this pattern carried over.

There was a peculiar irony concerning the post-relocation households; while the extended-family form was severely disrupted because of cost, inconvenience, and public policy, there also was a slight tendency for more

Table 7.6
Relocatees' Perception of Household Changes Since Relocation (N=140)

	% Yes
Children left home	26
More or fewer boarders	11
More or fewer other relatives in home	22
Family sickness	28

post-Africville households to take in paying boarders, non-relatives, or welfare cases for whom a guardian payment was received. This pattern was common among the relocatees who were struggling to meet mortgage obligations. Clearly something is amiss when, partly because of public social policy, the poor have to abandon warm and supportive kinship intimacy, on the one hand, yet on the other hand have to accept inconvenience and lack of privacy by performing services for the same welfare system in order to survive adequately.

A number of relocatees reported marital and kinship strains that they perceived as traceable to relocation. About fifteen respondents pointed to difficulties and animosities among relatives which were by-products of the scrambling and *sauve-qui-peut* nature of relocation negotiations. Table 7.5 indicates that approximately twenty-five relocatees reported marital strains; there were at least five cases where the marital relationship did not survive the relocation change and in several other instances the relationship assumed an "on-again, off-again" nature. About half of the marriages that broke up had been common-law, and a majority had a history of instability in Africville. But it seems clear that post-relocation difficulties were significant factors, for despite the instability and common-law character of the relationships, the couples had remained together while in Africville. In the majority of cases of severe strain and marital break-up the couple had been struggling financially or were living outside the city, relatively isolated from their former Africville friends and relatives. One city official who was familiar with the Africville situation observed:

There has been considerable marital discord and family break-up since the time of relocation and this has involved

Table 7.7
Relocatees' Perception of Trouble Making Ends Meet Since Relocation (N=140)

	% Yes
More trouble	66
About the same	22
Less trouble	12

some violence on the part of the husband toward the wife and children; several persons had commented that when the family was living in Africville there were certain built-in controls on this kind of thing: when _____ had a temper tantrum and became violent with his wife, the neighbours, even if it was four o'clock in the morning, would take this individual and dunk him in the harbour to cool off and things would be fine; this family now lives [isolated from] other relocatees.

This account, while perhaps somewhat fanciful in specifics, is essentially valid in emphasizing the built-in controls of kinship ties within the community of Africville.

As indicated in Table 7.7, two-thirds of the relocatees reported in 1969-70 that they were having more trouble making ends meet than they had had in Africville. Only approximately twelve percent of the respondents reported improvement on their pre-relocation coping behaviour. About twenty-five relocatees indicated that they experienced job problems as a result of the relocation (Table 7.5), a number significantly larger than the few who claimed to have received employment assistance through the city's "rehabilitative" program. Many relocatees apparently never fully realized how expensive they would find it in the post-relocation environment; some Africville residents in their poverty were awed by the cash settlements offered by the city during the relocation negotiations; one relocatee observed that "there were too many people who were anxious to get the money. They thought that two thousand dollars would last them the rest of their life. They didn't realize the value of money." In a small but significant number of cases relocatees invested their cash settlement unwisely

Table 7.8
Relocatees' Contact with Social Agencies Since Relocation (N=140)

	% Yes
Social Agency:	
Social planning department	25
Seaview Credit Union	28
Canada Manpower	20
City welfare	49
Provincial welfare	16

and very soon after they had been relocated the money was spent.[16] In the majority of cases the problem, however, was quite simple and predictable — the relocatees just did not have the resources — nor did the city provide them — to cope with the reality of new and increased expenses. One relocatee observed: "Pretty hard to get used to paying out all your money on rent and bills when you didn't have to pay these in Africville."

Table 7.8 reveals that a large number of relocatees sought assistance in meeting post-relocation difficulties by contacting social service agencies. Fifty percent of the respondents in 1969-70 had applied for assistance to the city's department of welfare and almost all the relocatees who had moved into Halifax County had applied to provincial welfare authorities. About a quarter of the respondents had contacted the city's social planning department, which was established subsequent to the relocation and charged with considering what might be done to assist relocatees. Slightly more attempted to obtain assistance from the Seaview Credit Union set up in 1969 by the city in conjunction with the province to make available low-interest loans to the former Africville residents. A small number of relocatees also reported that they had received assistance from the Red Cross. Clearly the majority of relocatees became heavily dependent on welfare to maintain themselves. In some ways this dependency could be considered an improvement on the pre-relocation situation since people then needing assistance were not given it. A number of relocatees expressed satisfaction regarding the consideration and assistance they were receiving from city officials. On the other hand, other relocatees reacted

Table 7.9
Relocatees' Mobility Since Leaving Africville (N=140)

	% Yes
Lived in one home	60
Lived in two homes	30
Lived in three or more homes	16

angrily to their welfare dependency and the rules and invasion of privacy associated with seeking assistance. Some former residents believed that welfare support was part of their relocation settlement and were upset upon realizing that they were going to be treated like any other applicant would be. One male relocatee summed up the feelings of many others concerning this welfare dependency when he observed: "You didn't need nobody in Africville. Now the people are all broke up. You got to suckhole to make a living."

It has been noted earlier that a number of relocatees lost their new homes or were placed in inadequate interim housing or were evicted from public housing. These facts, plus the efforts of the city's social planning department to obtain better housing for relocatees, account for the patterns revealed in Table 7.9 in which thirty percent of the respondents reported that they had lived in two places since leaving Africville and approximately fifteen percent that they had lived in at least three different homes. The marginals/transients, most of whom had been placed in housing in the city's redevelopment area, exhibited the greatest mobility.

One relocatee's moves illustrated this pattern: a hard-drinking, fun-loving, generous, elderly oldliner referred to by other Africville residents as "Mother Africville" had, upon being relocated, been placed in a flat in the redevelopment area; the home burned down and she was then placed by the city in another flat which one of the study's interviewers described as follows:

> ...showed me through the rooms which she has the use of.
> They were a front room which is the only room she uses, a
> kitchen in which the sink and cupboards are torn out, and
> another room which is empty. The rooms were all clean.
> There is a bathroom upstairs but the plumbing does not

work. She uses a bed pan instead of a toilet, and gets water from the house next door. There is a bed, a couch, a refrigerator which doesn't work, a fireplace, washing machine, and table in the front room. The building is not heated.

Fellow relocatees expressed considerable shock and indignation over the housing "Mother Africville" received; from oldliners to marginals/ transients came angry condemnations of the city. Subsequently she obtained better housing from the city's social development department.

As most Africville residents were relocated within walking distance of the Africville site, there was no profound change in the contact they had with relatives and friends; they were already familiar with the neighbourhood. Tables 7.10 through 7.14 bear out this expectation. A large majority of the relocatee respondents reported themselves to be quite familiar with their new area of residence (Table 7.11) and a majority reported that close contact was retained with former close friends from Africville (Table 7.10). It was also found that most relocatees were aware of the new addresses of their former fellow Africville residents. A large majority of relocatees reported that they had some feeling of belonging in their new neighbourhood and almost fifty percent (Table 7.13) identified very strongly with their new neighbours. Table 7.13 reveals that ninety percent of the relocatees described their new neighbours as at least somewhat friendly and over seventy percent characterized them as at least somewhat trustworthy; almost forty percent of the relocatees reported (Table 7.12) that they could count on their neighbours if they were in need. It could perhaps be expected that in time the relocatees' positive assessment on these matters would gradually approximate their stated attitudes towards Africville living; the data in Table 7.14 points in this direction. Nevertheless, when interviewed in 1969-70, on the average three years after their relocation, they still indicated a slight preference on the grounds of general living and a larger preference for the sociality of their old Africville situation.

There were significant variations in relocatees' assessment of their new environment. Surprisingly there was a tendency for young adult relocatees, those aged between twenty and thirty-nine years, to be more negative about living conditions in their new environment than were relocatees fifty years of age and more; a slight majority of the latter indicated that living in their present neighbourhood was the same or better than living in Africville

Table 7.10
Relocatees' Perception of Contact with Former Close Friends in Africville (N=140)

	% Yes
Regular contact	53
Reduced contact	20
Little contact	27

Table 7.11
Relocatees' Perception of Familiarity with New Environment (N=140)

	% Yes
Know area well	77
Somewhat familiar	18
Not at all familiar	3

Table 7.12
Relocatees' Perception of Being Able to Count on Neighbours if in Need (N=140)

	% Yes
Can count on	37
Cannot count on	58
Do not know	5

whereas only forty-five percent of the young adult relocatees held this view. While it appears that the young, in their assessments, were reacting to unrealized expectations induced by the relocation rhetoric, there was an objective basis for their greater negativism; they had profited least from the relocation and with few resources were struggling to cope with new expenses and difficulties.

Among the social groupings, the mainliners stand out as being much more likely to report that present neighbourhood living conditions are at least the same if not better than living in Africville; almost eighty percent of the mainliner relocatees held this view. Mainliners, too, were the most

Table 7.13
Relocatees' Perception of Africville and New Neighbourhood (N=140)

	New Neighbourhood % yes	Africville % yes
Feelings of belonging		
Really belong here	45	87
Don't belong as much as others	20	6
Don't belong at all	30	4
Friendliness of neighbours		
Very friendly	45	80
Somewhat friendly	45	18
Unfriendly	8	1
Trustworthiness of neighbours		
Very trustworthy	28	56
Somewhat trustworthy	45	39
Not trustworthy	18	2

Table 7.14
Relocatees' Perception of Adequacy of Living Conditions in New Neighbourhood (N=140)

	% Yes
Better than Africville	38
Same as Africville	16
Worse than Africville	43

likely (sixty percent) to report that they felt that they really belonged in their present neighbourhood. Among the oldliners, residuals, and marginals/ transients there was more collective ambivalence; in each grouping the relocatees were about equally divided concerning whether or not present neighbourhood living conditions were better than those in Africville. Predictably oldliners had the greatest investment in the kinship and friendship networks that had been disrupted by the relocation. They most frequently grieved over reduced contact with their former friends and relatives and were more likely than respondents in other groupings to report that they felt they did not belong in their new neighbourhoods. One oldliner commented that:

> When we had to move and live in Halifax County permanently, I couldn't stand it. I mean, if we were in the city or near a town, okay, but we're in with a bunch of rotten neighbours who watch us because we're from the city. They're not friendly to us. I had to get out.... In Africville we had neighbours all around us; we was as one.

Some oldliners, while regretting the loss of community, nevertheless reported that because of water and sewerage they believed that living conditions in the new neighbourhoods were better. Other oldliners, more positive about their new environment, seemed to accept, more or less reluctantly, that its price was the loss of former close associations. As one oldtimer observed:

> *Relocatee:* "This is a better neighbourhood. People are very friendly and visit us often. Have established new friends. I fixed this place up, put new gutters and driveway, landscaped the backyard and put in a retaining wall. People come and tell me how amazed they are at what I've done to this property in such a short time. Of course, I have to make a good impression."
> *Interviewer:* "Why? Is it because you're coloured?"
> *Relocatee:* "Well, you know how it is. I have to make a good impression. The neighbours will not think a person from Africville lived here. I can't have my friends dropping by anymore. Don't hardly see any of my friends. You can't make any noise. You know how it is. They're liable to start drinking and might forget themselves and piss in the yard. I couldn't afford to have that happen."

Of course a few oldliners, like many of the mainliners, perceived the relocation not only as a means of obtaining better facilities and conveniences but also as an opportunity for dropping a lot of "old friends" and associations. One such oldliner who received a good property settlement and purchased a home in an "all-white" block reported "no losses I can think of" from relocation. He believed that the city officials and the relocation social worker had done a good job in the relocation. Prior to the relocation, this oldliner had expressed a desire to move out of Africville. He disliked the stigma of living there and what he perceived as the ghettoization of Africville residents. He dissociated himself from other residents, many of whom he considered have-nots and unambitious. The anxiety that his life in Africville generated is indicated in his comment:

> Suppose you had to come to visit me in Africville and you asked me for a drink of water or you asked me to use the bathroom; then you would have to go outside to use the bathroom; you even had to go outside to get water. Here I have running water and I have a clean bathroom and I'm quite happy; I'm not afraid. I'm not embarrassed by people here.

This relocatee, like a small minority of others, saw himself as living a new life in a new neighbourhood and did not wish to continue contact with his previous life.

The marginals/transients were virtually all rehoused in the poor, redevelopment area of Halifax. Among the social groupings they were the least likely to report that they felt they "really belonged" in their new neighbourhood. Yet they did not report as frequently as the oldliners that they felt they did not belong at all. But the marginals/transients had always been outsiders, never really belonging but not out of place in poor and deprived neighbourhoods. The residual grouping had an intermediate position concerning their new neighbourhoods. Among the more disgruntled members of the residual grouping were those "Big Town" area relocatees who had broken with their Africville associations and purchased homes outside the city; struggling in the post-relocation situation with heavy and unexpected expenses, they often found their isolation from friends and relatives to be a significant cost of relocation.

The relocation promise of dramatically improving life-opportunities for Africville residents fell far short of realization. Roughly fifty percent of the respondents stated that they were "not at all pleased" with their post-relocation conditions and slightly more than forty percent reported that "things were going badly" for them. Only twenty-five percent reported themselves as "very pleased" and indicated that "things were going well."

Older relocatees, those aged fifty years or more, were, surprisingly, more likely to report that they were at least somewhat pleased with post-relocation conditions and a slight majority of the older relocatees believed that at least things were "going okay" if not well. On the other hand, a slight majority of the younger relocatees reported that they were not at all pleased with the post-relocation life and that "things were going badly" for them. These unexpected age patterns seem to be accounted for by two factors; first, the older relocatees objectively appear to have gained more from the relocation and, secondly, the two age categories held different expectations concerning relocation. Older relocatees had been less willing to relocate, but it appears that many found post-relocation conditions to be better than they expected; despite considerable grief concerning Africville, the older relocatees appreciated the better facilities and conveniences. The large minority of older relocatees who were not at all pleased with post-relocation life appeared to place more value on their former Africville involvement and reported themselves as relatively isolated. The young adult relocatees, it will be recalled, were the least unwilling to relocate; clearly post-relocation life did not measure up to their expectations and, retrospectively, many of them began to appreciate the freedom, autonomy, lower costs, and community feeling they had taken for granted in Africville. One young relocatee expressed the general point with the comment: "If they were to give them Africville back now that they've tasted bitterness, they'd realize that all along they had it so sweet."

Table 7.16 reveals that the relocatee respondents, interviewed two to three years after relocation, still felt considerable grief over the destruction of their community. Over seventy percent reported that they missed Africville very much and a slight majority have often returned to the Africville site. A number of residents claimed that family sickness since relocation was traceable to relocation anxieties and pressure. Generally relocatees contended that the older persons had experienced the greatest grief and heartbreak, in some cases to such an extent that they attempted not to think of Africville and did not visit the site. One elderly relocatee stated: "The city took it from us; it's gone. It's no good for us now. I've put it out of mind so I can't really talk about it." The older relocatees often pointed out that what they missed most was their church, clearly a concrete symbol of the community. Most of the respondents, who, in Africville, had been heavily involved in church affairs, contended that their church had been unique and that they found churches in their new environments to be less meaningful for them. One relocatee commented:

Table 7.15
Relocatees' Perception of General Situation after Relocation (N=140)

	% Yes
How things have been going.	
Good	26
Indifferent	30
Bad	42
Overall are you pleased with things since relocation?	
Very pleased	25
Somewhat pleased	28
Not at all pleased	47

Table 7.16
Relocatees' Grief Concerning Africville (N=140)

	% Yes
Have you returned to Africville since the relocation?	
Yes, often	54
Yes, a few times	26
No	20
Do you miss the Africville life?	
Very much	73
Some	7
Little or none	17

"There are more rules in this [new] church; there is no handclapping and no feeling of pouring out your heart."

Overall, it is clear that the Africville relocation was not seen as a dramatic improvement by the relocatees. They did not believe that they had obtained a fair deal from the city and roughly half the relocatees were displeased with post-relocation conditions. Considerable grief regarding loss of community was expressed by a significant majority of former Africville residents. In retrospect many relocatees believed that if they had bargained collectively they might have retained their community on its old site or elsewhere. Housing improvement and individual property settlement were the key benefits of relocation. What was taken away from the people — land, community, freedom, and intimate social involvement — loomed large in their minds when set against the expense and other difficulties of post-relocation, and despite the fact that most were relocated within walking distance of Africville.

What happened to Africville residents as a result of relocation could be reasonably predicted; perhaps this is the main reason for judging the relocation to have been a failure. The relocation is unique in that the relocatees' long occupation of and commitment to their community was considerable. Africville relocatees appear to be somewhat unusual in their prolonged grief for their community. They exhibited, on the whole, a non-optimistic outlook as reflected in the fact that the percentage giving adverse responses to the five items on a standard sociological alienation scale were respectively seventy-five, eighty, eighty, eighty-three, and eighty-eight percent.[17] Most relocatees did not accept the view that the relocation was the result of the city's concern with social problems, although only a minority shared the sentiment of one elderly oldliner who observed: "I bet you in a few years you will see the rich in our old land in Africville."

There were few differences between males and females in response to relocation. Perhaps the only significant variation by sex was that males were more likely than females (fifty to forty percent) to report that "things were going badly" for them in the post-relocation period. Welfare dependency, as is well-known, often generated an emasculating process; one male household head, now dependent on welfare to maintain his family in admittedly improved housing conditions, observed that "there was always something for a man to do [in Africville]; fish, gather wood, search the dump." Age differences were clearly much more important. There were, as noted above, important differences by age in terms of initial orientation to relocation, benefits obtained, and post-relocation satisfaction. Unexpectedly, the young adult relocatees exhibited significant grief over the loss of community and were more displeased than older relocatees with their post-relocation living conditions.

During the relocation planning phase and throughout and after the relocation, city officials often emphasized that a major benefit of the relocation would be the long-run advantage to the relocatees' children as a result of integration. Some relocatees did mention integration as one of the positive aspects of the relocation, but the majority did not see this as an important consideration. They now mistrust the rhetoric of liberalism.

When the Africville school was closed in 1952, and the children transferred to racially mixed schools outside the community, long-run advantages were predicted, but many of the children went into auxiliary classes and many now as young men and young women are unemployed and frustrated. Vague hopes are a poor substitute for detailed planning and serious commitment.

Notes

[1] In the post-relocation survey, approximately fifty percent of the marginals/transients and fifty-five percent of the mainliners reported having considered alternatives to relocation; on the other hand, about seventy percent of the oldliners and residuals had alternatives.

[2] It was also surprising that fifty percent of the mainliners were unwilling to relocate. This is somewhat inconsistent with other data on their orientation to Africville and to the relocation program.

[3] Surprisingly, younger oldliners were as likely as elderly oldliners to have reported that they had fought hard against relocation; in both cases, however, only a handful of residents characterized their orientation towards relocation in this fashion.

[4] It was true that the city did provide a lawyer from its own staff, but although few relocatees were aware of the fact, the city had also agreed to pay the legal expenses of residents who obtained private legal assistance.

[5] It should be noted that relocatees were asked to judge whether they could influence the relocation social worker "very strongly," "somewhat," or "not at all;" if the respondent gave either of the first two responses he was considered to have perceived that he could influence the worker.

[6] Whereas about sixty percent of the relocatees reported that the city used the threat of expropriation to get the people to relocate, only twenty percent indicated that the relocation social worker used this threat.

[7] The authors read several letters sent to relocatees by the relocation social worker, which in a vague and ambiguous way did promise financial assistance to them in their new housing situation.

[8] In a few cases the household head allowed a son or daughter to claim a parcel of property or a shed and thereby establish a property claim. Such a claim might yield $500 or more depending on the bargaining skill of the claimant, his social characteristics, and the sympathy of the relocation social worker.

[9] "Women Fined for KKK-Type Threat," *The Mail-Star*, Halifax, N.S., February 22, 1966.

10   These designations are used, despite the fact that the district has more whites than blacks. With the elimination of Africville, however, the district now has the largest concentration of blacks in Halifax.

11   Six additional applications had been rejected for a variety of reasons; and three applicants subsequently were no longer interested in moving into public housing.

12   The Africville Subcommittee had earlier expressed concern (October 20, 1965) about the unsatisfactory rehousing of relocatees and requested that consideration be given to establishing a housekeeping course for some of them. The request was referred to the relocation social worker, but action was not taken.

13   *The Condition of the Negroes of Halifax City*, Nova Scotia, op. cit., p. 13.

14   In the questionnaires that the relocation social worker completed on each adult relocatee, he estimated that sixty-eight percent of the relocatees gained better living conditions and fifty-nine percent obtained better services; beyond these two benefits from relocation, he considered that the chief benefit Africville residents received was financial, which in his estimation applied to about forty percent of the relocatees.

15   Because of the regulations of the public housing authority, a daughter who had illegitimate children was usually forced to establish a separate household to qualify for Mother's Allowance.

16   In several instances much of a relocatee's cash settlement was spent on a prolonged "good time" and drinking binge. In a few other cases the grown children of relocatees receiving a cash settlement borrowed the money and spent it on personal items such as automobiles and clothes.

17   See Clairmont and Magill, *Africville Relocation Report*, p. A120. The items were taken from Melvin Seeman, "On the Meaning of Alienation," *American Sociological Review*, XXIV (December 1959), pp. 783-791.

The Implications of
Africville Relocation

There is a dialectic of disorder at work in the world. It is a dialectic every bit as ruthless in its impact on human hopes and values as any Hegel ever dreamed of. It spares no society, and few people. It is impartial in the way it defeats the plans of both dropouts and presidents. And the misuse of the rhetoric of liberalism has contributed in no small measure to the operation of that dialectic.

For even empty rhetoric generates aspirations among people who take it seriously. Aspirations kindle new and concrete hopes. But then the emptiness of the rhetoric is revealed in the paucity and perversion of the complementing programs. Thus expectations are not fulfilled, and frustration and bitter anger result. The expression of this anger differs, depending on the intensity of the expectations and the extent of the gap between program and fulfillment.[1]

—Arnold S. Kaufman

Why was Africville Relocated?

This book has raised a number of questions: Why were the people of Africville relocated? Were the underlying reasons humanitarian, intended to improve socio-economic conditions among the residents and to end segregation; or, primarily, did Halifax politicians and development officials want Africville land for industrial or residential development? Was the purpose of the relocation to further the economic interests of Halifax? Reason analysis, whereby one attempts to find the basic motivation behind social action, has many pitfalls; nevertheless, it is necessary when examining planned social change. If one is to characterize the Africville relocation as liberal-welfare type or development type, one must refer to the motivation and ideology of the decision-makers as well as to the organizational aspects of the relocation project. Moreover, the success of a relocation as a particular type of planned social change depends partly on the strength of the underlying motivational and ideological orientation of the key decision-makers.

As noted earlier, relocation of Africville was long considered by city officials and planners. Two explanations for why it took place in 1964 emerge clearly from interviews with the caretakers, politicians, and city hall officials associated with the relocation: distaste for adverse publicity and humanitarian concern. These factors created pressures that forced a decision for relocation, but the date suggests that there were additional significant factors.

The major adverse publicity consisted of articles in two national publications, *Maclean's Magazine*[2] and the *Star Weekly*,[3] a report in *The New York Times*,[4] and the Dalhousie University study[5] that described the socio-economic conditions of Africville. However, all three of these publications appeared after, not before, the city development department report recommending relocation,[6] that is, after the stage had been set for relocation. The publicity disposed the average Haligonian to accept city council's Africville policy. As the assistant archivist, Public Archives of Nova Scotia, stated:

> It is my personal opinion that there may have been some aldermen and businessmen who wanted Africville land fully developed by industry and paying higher taxes, but that the average citizen supported relocation of Africville families because they were sick of such publicity as that of Stein in *Maclean's* and the others, focusing attention on how badly the Negroes were treated in the Africville ghetto.[7]

The humanitarian concern to relocate Africville residents related to two matters: the improvement of living conditions and the racial integration of Africville residents. The segregated black community and the poverty of its residents had, however, existed for many years prior to the events of 1962-64 and the final decision to relocate. Previous chapters have documented the numerous petitions from Africville residents, the many times prior to 1962 that humanitarian concern was expressed on their behalf, and the abortive city policies formulated to rectify deprivation in Africville. Why did the humanitarian concern crystalize at this time as a factor urging relocation? Sylvia Fraser's pithy analogy speaks to this question:

> For 150 years [the Africville residents] were nourished on neglect. Now everyone professes an interest in them. The community of Africville is like a patient that has shivered for weeks in the corridor of a hospital and then is suddenly whipped into a private room where a squadron of nurses fight to take her temperature and feel her pulse.[8]

Explanation of the intensification of concern lies in the convergence of an improved ideological climate and a desire by city officials in land-scarce Halifax to redevelop Africville as part of a larger scheme of industrial and commercial development. The changing ideological climate in the late 1950s and early 1960s was characterized by the development of urban-renewal policy in Canada,[9] the growth of the civil rights movement in the United States and in Canada, and local criticism of social policy by both blacks and whites. In Nova Scotia this was reflected in the achievements and new leadership of the Nova Scotia Association for the Advancement of Coloured People[10] and in the formation of "ginger groups" for social action such as the short-lived Joseph Howe Society.

There were two more specific developments in the 1950s that proved to be significant for Africville. One was the increased participation by organized labour in the general struggle against racism and poverty. It may be recalled that when Africville residents sought outside assistance in the early 1960s they contacted persons associated with the Canadian Labour Congress. The other development was the formation of a "ginger group" within the local Halifax branch of the Community Planning Association of Canada. This group pressed for housing reform and encouraged the city to bring in a noted planning authority to examine Halifax problems; one of its 1957 recommendations was that Africville be relocated. It should be noted that, while Africville residents were being relocated, larger redevelopment projects in the north and central areas of the city were being completed. It is difficult to determine precisely how much weight should be given to the change in ideological climate as a factor in the Africville relocation. Prior to 1962 there was no sustained effort based on this factor to rectify neglect and oppression in Africville.[11] The "problem" of Africville surfaced periodically and was brought to public attention but soon faded away. It does appear, however, that the changes in social climate referred to above were relevant to the Africville relocation. Groups and organizations came into existence, pressuring for social change and ready to be mobilized in projects such as the Africville relocation.

While the improved ideological climate was an important factor in public responsiveness to the relocation project, land-use considerations appear to have precipitated the chain reaction of events leading to the Africville relocation. A former mayor of Halifax recalled that, unless there was some clear advantage for Halifax as a whole, the city would have been quite cautious about relocating people who did not want to move. In 1962, as part of a more comprehensive plan of development, the North Shore Development Plan proposed that the Africville land be used for a limited-access expressway. The plan was publicly released in February, 1962. By August the development department report recommending relocation was released to the press and, seven days later, rejected by Africville residents. That same month A. Alan Borovoy visited Halifax and discussed the city's relocation proposal with Africville residents and other concerned Halifax citizens. Following his visit a white-black caretaker alliance was formed. By October Africville residents had resigned themselves to the relocation, and city council adopted relocation as official policy. For sixteen months the caretaker members of the Halifax Human Rights Advisory Committee explored alternatives to relocation. In January, 1964 the Rose Report's recommendations for relocation reinforced city council's existing policy, and the caretakers accepted the fact of relocation.

Interviewed in 1969 the caretakers, politicians, and city officials associated with the decision to relocate stressed humanitarian reasons for their involvement. Undoubtedly their concern was genuine. Clearly, too, this mobilization of concern was directly related to the city's 1962 announcement of the North Shore Development Plan. In his 1962 letter to the Halifax Human Rights Advisory Committee, the development director stressed that the primary consideration in deciding to relocate was the "betterment of housing conditions." He indicated to the committee that Africville land was proposed for expressway, industrial, and commercial use. Commenting on the compensation value of Africville land, he wrote that industrial lands are not normally of high value; however, "the economic well-being of a community depends upon a vigorous employment factor and industry creates this."[12] Ironically, after a century of neglect, the residents of Africville were to bear the added burden of subsidizing the economic growth of a city of which they were never truly a part.

The relocation was, thus, the result of the reactions and counter-reactions engendered by a plan that was intended to further the economic development and further growth of the city while at the same time removing the "blight of Africville." For this reason it would be difficult to decide, solely on motivational-ideological grounds, whether to classify the Africville relocation as a liberal-welfare or a development type of relocation. Only when one considers the structure and organization of the relocation project does it fall more unambiguously into the former category.

There is further irony in the fact that apparently the Africville land will not be used for the purposes outlined in the 1962 North Shore Development Plan. A senior planner of the city development department explained that the plan was studied further and considered unfeasible.

In 1974, when the first edition of this book was published, the Africville land lay vacant.[13] It had been altered by construction of a highway approach to the nearby A. Murray MacKay Bridge, which crossed the Narrows between Halifax and Dartmouth. Halifax city officials were opposed to the bridge site; during a 1969 interview, the incumbent mayor of Halifax explained that the cities of Halifax and Dartmouth had disagreed about the location of the bridge and that its present location had been decided, in 1966, by the premier of Nova Scotia.

In February, 1969 the city of Halifax commissioned project planning associates and their architect affiliates to formulate development proposals for an area which included the former Africville site. Dr. Albert Rose, who had earlier advised the city with reference to the Africville relocation, was engaged as a consultant in the study of city prison land. In a June, 1969 report, without acknowledging his own role in the relocation, he wrote:

> Nova Scotia contains perhaps as many as forty per cent of Canada's total black population, that is, 20,000 to 25,000 out of an estimated 60,000. The experience in the elimination of Africaville [sic] from 1964 through 1967 has left a number of bitter legacies. **The white population realizes that it sanctioned the elimination of a black ghetto**, yet at the same time, it

has not developed any appropriate use for the Africaville [sic] lands and they remain at the present time a mass of rubble extending for a considerable distance to the north of the prison lands. **To a very real degree Africaville [sic] stands for destruction without long range planning or, at best, a degree of planning without goals for the implementation of sound social objectives**. (Emphasis added)[14]

On October 14, 1969 an "area conceptual plan" was submitted to the city's development director.[15] The Africville land was designated for a district city park as well as for industrial, warehouse, and highway use; however, these plans did not materialize. In 1999, where Africville once stood, is the Seaview Memorial Park. To the north of the park is the Fairview Cove Terminal. Arching high above the former community site is the A. Murray Mackay Bridge; its approaches and roads utilize the inland boundary of Africville.

The Racial Implications of the Africville Relocation

Many observers of relocation programs in contemporary North American society have likened this form of planned social change to the violent removal of Indians during the period of colonization. They have referred specifically to urban renewal as a race/class war since urban renewal projects have usually displaced the poor and the minority-group members without significantly improving their life conditions. Such critics have attacked the liberal-welfare rhetoric that has accompanied typical relocation programs since the Second World War as a subtle cover for the class interests of monopoly capital which "pulls the strings" of the welfare establishment.[16]

The Africville relocation, as noted earlier, was accompanied by the rhetoric of liberalism. The relocation was presumably to represent a step forward in improving race relations. The Halifax Human Rights Advisory Committee was given a role in implementing the relocation, and the relocation policy was to include provision of educational and economic programs designed to present new social opportunities.

In the beginning most blacks in Nova Scotia either accepted the relocation as desirable or were silently critical of its policy. White officials and citizens interpreted relocation as positive social change. Since the relocation of Africville families, however, there has been a change in these evaluations. Many black Nova Scotians have become very critical of the relocation program and consider it to have profited the city much more than the relocatees. Extrapolating from the Africville instance, some black leaders have begun to suspect that relocations of this kind may indeed be a form of race warfare. Among city officials and informed citizens, there has been a similar, though less profound, disenchantment with the Africville relocation.

The White Community and The Africville Relocation

Initial evaluation of the Africville relocation by the local and international press and by city officials was positive. The relocation was publicly defined as symbolic of a new and more progressive era in race relations. The editors of *Time* magazine observed:

> The bulldozing of Africville exemplifies a determined, if belated, effort by the municipal and provincial government to right an historical injustice.[17]

While an article in the national *Star Weekly* described "the slow and welcome death of Africville,"[18] city officials postulated that considerable benefits would ultimately be reaped by children of relocatees now that Africville was phased out and the children could be raised in a more healthy and integrated environment.[19] An article in *Maclean's Magazine*[20] suggested that "a fear of integration" on the part of community residents was an unfortunate and irrational obstacle to necessary and desirable relocation. Throughout relocation implementation, the local press issued progress reports on the number of families relocated and encouraged a faster phasing-out of the community. Selective publicity, emphasizing the contentment of relocatees,[21] resulted in good press for the relocation and assured the public that a creative program was being achieved. The tone of the local press coverage is indicated in the following editorial summation of the relocation:

> [The relocation social worker] never swerved from his goal of securing not only much better housing for the families of Africville but, equally important, of ensuring that the children of the relocated families would have the benefits they had so obviously missed.

> Soon Africville will be but a name. And, in the not too
> distant future that, too, mercifully will be forgotten.[22]

Since the apparent termination of the basic relocation program with the departure of the relocation social worker in late 1967, there has been a changing evaluation of the Africville relocation among local government officials and informed citizens, as well as in the local press. There is still a consensus that Africville residents should have been relocated and that, eventually, integration will bring numerous beneficial by-products. On the other hand, there is also a greater realization that Africville relocatees are not satisfied with the relocation and that much of the rhetoric accompanying it did not lead to the benefits anticipated and desired.

Much of the criticism in the white community relates to the lack of adequate follow-up to assist relocatees in coping with life in their new environment; another major point of criticism, which reflects both a shift in societal values and a restrospective idealization of Africville, is focussed around the issue that the relocation broke up a community but did not provide an adequate substitute for the relocatees. The changed evaluation is a result, in part, of public criticism expressed by an Africville Action Committee (formed in 1969) and the interest in relocatees expressed by the city's social planning department (created in 1968). Several television programs have discussed the socio-economic conditions of relocatees, and the local press has carried several accounts of officialdom's "sympathetic" response to criticisms expressed by the Africville Action Committee.[23] The city's dishonourable mishandling of "Pa" Miller, the last Africville resident to be relocated, occurred after criticism of the relocation had begun to mount. This incident, creating an inept and shameful ending to the relocation, added to the criticism.

There is still a critical appraisal of the Africville relocation in the white community and even among certain city officials. One of the white caretakers, looking back on the relocation, wondered if, in the light of the black militancy in 1973, Africville would have been handled the same way. It appears, however, that criticism has not been channelled productively and that no clear, widely held lesson has been drawn from the relocation. Some city officials, annoyed by criticisms of the relocation, hold the view that the relocatees have already received more than strict justice would demand; in effect, the officials themselves have discounted much of the rhetoric originally associated with the relocation.

Blacks and the Relocation: Phase One

It appears that among Nova Scotian blacks the Africville relocation was initially regarded as both inevitable and acceptable. Numerous blacks living elsewhere in Halifax and in surrounding communities believed that Africville was a slum of the worst sort; its reputation as a deviance service centre, exaggerated by bad publicity, had led many blacks to believe that Africville's continuing existence was unwarranted and made them receptive to the liberal-welfare rhetoric that accompanied the relocation announcement. That living in Africville was perceived as a stigma by blacks as well as whites was attested in numerous interviews.[24]

Several black Haligonians recalled that, when younger, they were warned by their parents against ever going to Africville. Others were quick to point out that they were born and raised in Halifax proper, pointedly dissociating themselves from Africville. Even the black ministers who had served the community in the decades preceding relocation, while pointing out positive attributes of the community and discounting much of its notoriety, indicated that oppression and discrimination had over the years exacted a heavy toll on the community's morale and solidarity. The few black Haligonians who dissented from this view of Africville were exceptions. One man, for instance, noted that he regularly visited Africville and argued that the bad image of the community was, more or less, the creation of the city conspiring to obtain the Africville lands; he acknowledged, however, that "there are very few black people in Halifax County who would look upon Africville in the way that I do."

Although many black Nova Scotians accepted the public assessment of Africville and of the relocation program, and supported the need for planned social change, there were some who also understood the causes of Africville's peculiar development. They expressed concern that, at least in relocation, Africville residents would be treated fairly and generously by the city. A few black leaders urged that a section of the city be set aside for Africville families and that a new and well-serviced community be constructed; various possibilities of low-cost housing were advanced.[25] Implicit in these comments and suggestions was the belief that there was something valuable in the Africville community and that it would develop and flower if, under new opportunities, the residents were able to re-establish themselves elsewhere. Other black leaders, while not sharing these assumptions, recognized that Africville residents had long been oppressed. They sought to guarantee that relocation would bring real opportunity and not be simply another, and perhaps more subtle, example of city mistreatment. As one of the black caretakers on the Halifax Human Rights Advisory Committee put it:

> There was no doubt in many of our minds that the city had intended to take in that land and we were afraid compensation would not be accurate and adequate and that is why a group of us got together and started working.

At the beginning of the Africville relocation most Nova Scotian blacks were aware of the relocation program's existence and some leaders had made public their concern about, and suggestions for, the residents' future. Africville was by no means, however, a rallying point for nationalistic and militant voices in the black community. Black organizations, on the whole, did not participate significantly in advising and assisting Africville residents or in defining operational terms of the relocation.

Beyond some public expression of concern and quiet urging of city benevolence, black leaders and organizations were involved in the Africville relocation only to the extent that several blacks participated in the Halifax Human Rights Advisory Committee and, subsequently, in city council's Africville Subcommittee. There are several reasons accounting for what appears in retrospect to have been a low level of involvement by the broader Nova Scotian black community.

First, as noted above, there was a stigma associated with Africville by blacks living elsewhere and a belief, considerably influenced by scandalous newspaper accounts of life in Africville, that the community was not viable. Moreover, Africville was not an integrated community and so was difficult to organize. The church clique, with whom outsiders attempting to work for social change would normally associate, was old, somewhat withdrawn, and conditioned to seek allies among white liberals. Then, too, even the strong, stable residents were vulnerable in that employment was irregular and property claims were questionable. Several black leaders reported that they had tried, without success, to go into the community to organize and otherwise assist residents.[26]

Another reason for the insignificant participation of black leaders and organizations was that the existence of the Halifax Human Rights Advisory Committee may have created the impression that additional outside involvement was unnecessary. Apparently it resulted in those black leaders, not desiring to participate in the committee, being discouraged from involving themselves in Africville affairs lest they be considered troublemakers.[27] Since the Halifax Human Rights Advisory Committee was committed to the realization of general or universal human rights, there was little justification in its frame of reference for the celebration of Africville as a black community or for rallying strong black sentiments around the relocation. Finally, in the early 1960s, the Nova Scotian blacks did not have the sense of unity and identity nor the more articulate and effective militant leadership and organization that developed later in the decade. Thus, not only was there little likelihood that Africville affairs would strike a responsive chord in the broader black community but there was also slight motivation on the part of Africville residents to seek allies there.[28]

Since no Africville organization participated in relocation decision-making, and no Africville resident was privy to the deliberations of city council's Africville Subcommittee, participation of blacks in relocation policy and mechanics was limited virtually to the three black caretakers from the Halifax Human Rights Advisory Committee. These three men spent considerable time and effort defining the terms of relocation, examining alternatives, meeting with Africville residents, and obtaining information from residents and city officials. They saw their role essentially as advocates and bargainers for the relocatees. By their very presence on the subcommittee, as well as by their advocacy, the black caretakers were able to make black experience in Nova Scotia a consideration in relocation decision-making. On the other hand, bargaining within narrow terms of reference was an ineffective means of realizing the presumed ends of the relocation program; that is, decisively to redress injustice against Africville blacks and to provide new and real opportunities for them.[29] Such ends are long-term in nature, difficult to measure, and tend to be shunted aside in the day-to-day quest for equitable and reasonable individual settlements and temporary welfare assistance.

Blacks and the Relocation: Phase Two

In the years since relocation, Africville has acquired a new symbolic meaning in the black Nova Scotian community. Winks observes:

> By January of 1967, when the last building fell to the bulldozers, Africville was more than a designation on the city's old maps, however — it was a word to which militant black Nova Scotians now rallied....[30]

With the creation of new black organizations such as the Black United Front (BUF) and the Afro-Canadian Liberation Movement (ACLM), as well as the growth of infrastructure requisites such as social clubs, stores, and publications for a vibrant black subculture, a more visible unity and integration has developed among Nova Scotian blacks.[31] A new mood has become pervasive in the black community, a mood which is more militant, more protective of its uniqueness, and more conscious of its possibilities than previously existed. In this new context increasing criticism has been directed against the Africville relocation and, as a symbol, the relocation has generated considerable cynicism among blacks as to the motives of government and a suspicion that relocation may be a tool for continued exploitation. With reference to Africville, one black leader observed:

> Black people are bitter and hostile and a lot of black communities now learned of the necessity for them to get together when the man comes out and starts talking relocation.

An influential militant and politically radical black leader expressed the cynicism that has become relatively common among blacks, about the liberal-welfare rhetoric accompanying the relocation:

> I think the man got what he wanted — that land. It was as simple as that. People were allowed to stay there the same as black folks anywhere; they could stay until the white man decided. Okay, now I want my land back. And the time came, and he said 'Okay nigger, get out!' And all the black folks had to get out.

That Africville, although now non-existent, has become something of a rallying symbol for blacks is illustrated by the remarks of one black leader heavily involved in community organizing among Nova Scotian blacks. When he enters a new community to organize the residents there, he discusses the plight of Africville relocatees who lost their community and their land and got little in return. He urges the residents, "Let's pull together, or else we'll be another Africville!"

This cynical, critical perspective among many blacks reflects more than institutional and attitudinal changes in the broader black Nova Scotian community. As the dust of relocation has cleared, it has become evident to many that the relocation achievements fell far short of the accompanying rhetoric. Beyond real estate considerations, city officials did not make a sustained creative effort to provide the new opportunities promised to relocatees. This fact has become public knowledge due to the protests of the post-relocation Africville Action Committee, the word-of-mouth communication among blacks concerning the hardships of some relocatees, and the publicity given city hall machinations in dealing with "Pa" Miller, the last relocatee. Consequently, many blacks have concluded that the city must have been primarily interested in obtaining Africville land. Most of the black leaders interviewed believed that Africville was choice real estate of considerable value to the city. One black minister reasoned as follows:

> [the Africville relocation] was something that was planned for years. That's a very ideal locality and I think in the long-range planning of the city of Halifax they looked forward to the day when they were going to move those Negroes because they wanted the area. They didn't do anything to help those people do anything for themselves. It was planned, it was deliberate, and when the time came for them to move them, they moved them.

On the other hand, a black city official and community leader who came to Halifax after the relocation discounted both the alleged value of the Africville lands and the argument that residents received inadequate compensation:

> I am in a position to state...that the city did not take the land because they needed it. The city took the land, Africville was removed, because it was a bloody embarrassment. Up to today [September 9, 1969], we have not been able to use that land.... Only if containerization goes to Bedford Basin instead of Navy Island will part of that land be of any economic value....
> A substantial number of people had no title to the land and the city gave them settlement far and above a fair market value and the equity situation.

Most black leaders refer, however, to the collective and potential value of the land. It is argued that as long as relocatees held property in Africville, they possessed a scarce waterfront area that could become increasingly valuable as Halifax developed. Not only have the relocatees not received benefits and opportunities commensurate with their needs but as a collectivity they have lost identity, traditional security, and a potential bargaining resource, their lands, with which they might have been able to revive their own sense of community.

This conception of the relocation, in which the city is the party that profited, has been deepened by changes in the Nova Scotian black community and throughout society. The rise of a counter-culture in the broader society and the demand for meaningful citizen participation have influenced the ordering of criteria on which the Africville relocation is now being assessed by Nova Scotian black leaders and other citizens. More positive value is being accorded to the small community and to lifestyle differences. Accordingly the relocatees are perceived as having lost much and received little. It is in the light of such considerations that one must understand occasional exaggerations concerning land value and occasional idealizations concerning Africville as a community.[32]

At the time the Africville relocation was being planned and implemented, less intrinsic value was ascribed to the small community style of living. Higher value was placed on racial integration per se, and greater stress on universal application of standards. This was the era of the Civil Rights movement, when the rhetoric of liberalism was very persuasive and the Africville relocation could be credited as a laudable achievement: a segregated slum community was obliterated and most property owners received better than market value. It is not surprising that some blacks listed as a significant achievement of the NSAACP the latter's limited participation in the Africville relocation.[33]

In the first part of the 1960s, few black leaders used the evaluative criteria now common in assessing relocation planning and implementation. Nationalistic black control of voluntary associations oriented to social change and relegation of racial integration to a position subordinate to economic and cultural considerations were rare.[34] As leaders having the new outlook have become more common, a corresponding higher valuation has been accorded the black community in general, and a greater protectiveness given to its resources. A critical community resource is land. Traditionally, due to racism, blacks settled on the edge of white towns and villages in Nova Scotia; typically, the black enclaves were neglected by government. Nowadays, with developing industrialization in certain areas of the province — especially in Halifax County — many blacks are apprehensive lest their lands be expropriated. Africville is instructive here, not only because of what blacks perceive as an unfair settlement favourable to the city but also because in some black communities there is, as there was in Africville, a common lack of legal title to land. One black leader from Preston pointed out the lesson of Africville:

> Some [people in the community] are learning from [the Africville relocation]. Some of them realize that if they don't pull up their breeches and look to their needs and get their businesses in order the same thing could happen here that has happened in Africville.
>
> Halifax cannot expand any further. If there is any expansion in this area, it is going to be in the Dartmouth area and here on number seven highway, and we have a number of black homes on the main highway; in fact, I think we have one of the few Negro communities in Nova Scotia where black people are still living on the main highway. If the area expands, if those black people don't get themselves in order, they are going to be pushed onto the roads.

Some black leaders contend that a relocation along the lines of the Africville relocation will never occur again in Nova Scotia. Their argument relates not only to the settlement terms of the Africville relocation but also to the fact that the black communities have been developing stronger community organizations; consequently, it is held that the process of future relocations would be materially different. The Africville relocation is seen by the black leadership as having been decided upon and implemented by outsiders, chiefly white city officials. One black Haligonian, in commenting on the development of community organization, remarked:

> I feel sorry for the power structure or any white group that would go [into the black communities, attempting to relocate the people]. This was attempted in Beechville and it was clearly defeated there. I would not want to see a person go into Preston; I think you would have a lot of [aroused] black people, not only in Preston but all over Nova Scotia. This could not happen again.

The Africville relocation did present the city with an opportunity to redress previous injustice to blacks. The relocation has been hailed as a step in that direction, but clearly it has not been perceived as such by many members of the black Nova Scotian community. It would be a considerable exaggeration to claim that the relocation effected a new climate either for better or worse in race relations. For one thing, changes in climate in recent years have had other important causes; the new perception of the Africville relocation is more an effect than a cause. Furthermore, in organizing data around one issue and relating it to other themes and developments, there is usually a tendency to overemphasize the data's total significance. Nevertheless, it is not an exaggeration to say that the Africville relocation has angered many blacks and, by making them sensitive to the rhetoric of liberalism, has contributed to their sense of urgency in organizing themselves. One black leader succinctly expressed the Africville relocation's key symbolic importance for Nova Scotian blacks:

> This is one of the things that causes us to move, because it is my feeling that many of the black communities are threatened by development, and development is in, here in Nova Scotia. I am not satisfied that our master plan takes into consideration the black community; all of the maps or plans that I have studied always seem to skip the black communities. They are not included in the overall planning, as a consequence they are left barren and become the municipal dumps, and once they are depreciated to that extent they are bought for little or nothing and the black people are moved off. So the planning of our people (any program that we set up) must include this whole business of community planning and people who are knowledgeable about the long-term planning…so that our communities can be included in the development processes. As the land values [increase], so the land values of the black land should increase. You see all over the world this whole business of squatters; the land is allowed to depreciate and people are allowed to do whatever they like. Building codes are ignored and health regulations are ignored, until development comes, and then all of a sudden there is a push and they are pushed off. Sometimes it is difficult to awaken people who have lived this easy way, to warn them of what is coming.

Planned Social Change:
Policy Implications of the Africville Relocation

The Africville relocation, as rationalized in city council's acceptance of the Rose Report, was supposed to have effected a planned and comprehensive social change. In that perspective the relocation was an opportunity to restructure the lifestyle of a particular group of people, to redress long-standing injustices against them, and to bring to bear on their problems a coordinated set of welfare solutions. The planned social change, as we have seen in previous chapters, was less than satisfactory.

Relocation, as planned social change, can have a variety of goals, strategies of implementation, and criteria of assessment. Order can be imposed on diversity in any specific instance by identifying the operative relocation model. The Africville relocation, in intention, rhetoric, and administrative arrangement, clearly is an example of the liberal-welfare model. The relocation's lack of success in effecting significant and positive social change among Africville residents needs to be examined for the insight that it can yield into problems in welfarism and the liberal-welfare approach to social change. Three of these policy limitations are the formulation and attainment of goals, bureaucratic constraints, and problems of advocacy.

Formulation and Attainment of Goals

One of the most important weaknesses in the Africville relocation was the lack of adequate discussion of the problem situation and the absence of strategy for effecting significant social change among Africville residents. In the Rose Report and other relocation reports, mention is made of educational, occupational, and consultancy programs, but no guidance is provided concerning design or implementation of programs and no analysis that would link specific actions to measurable goals. Yet it is very difficult to alter the life conditions of the poor and the disadvantaged. The problems of such relocatees are usually multi-faceted, historically and structually rooted, and hard to redress. It is easy to rationalize away failure in terms of the attributes of the disadvantaged or their lack of cooperation and unwillingness to change. It is convenient to use temporary expedients or to dodge responsibility. For these reasons a detailed, legally binding plan of action is often imperative. In the absence of this kind of guidance, the Africville relocation program became essentially a matter of real estate negotiation and temporary welfare assistance. In its relocation contract, the city committed itself to extraordinary measures expressed in an empty rhetorical fashion. Expert legal opinion has advised us that, in undertaking the relocation, the city did not commit itself legally to provide educational, occupational, and consulting programs.[35] Given that lack of legal commitment, success in achieving the larger ends of relocation, assuming that such an achievement is fully possible within the institutional structure that created the problem in the first place, depended either upon building a strong power of advocacy into the public agency responsible for carrying out the relocation, or upon mobilizing external pressure to counterbalance the ultimately legalistic orientation of the city administration. The Africville relocation failed on both counts.

Bureaucratic Constraints

The liberal-welfare approach to planned social change invariably confronts the power and conservatism of bureaucracy. The administrator is charged with specific powers by elected officials; it is his or her task to separate the wheat from the chaff, the specific commitments interpreted legalistically from the emotional and often deceptive rhetoric of policy announcements. In performing this role the bureaucrat, if competent and aggressive, commands considerable day-to-day direction over policy. As one elected city official reported in attempting to account for the gap between rhetoric and achievement in the Africville relocation:

> The elected people are amateurs; they tend to respond to crises and to what is placed before them in terms of staff reports and recommendations. They tend to assume that [the city] staff are looking after implementation of policies previously adopted.... There is a certain lack of consistent pressures from the community. As I said earlier, I think that those of us who thought about [follow-up] at all, assumed that the welfare operation of the city was responsible for looking after the needs of people wherever they were.

In some instances bureaucracy may subvert publicly announced intentions, but usually it performs its legitimate task more or less efficiently. Criticism of the welfare approach and welfarism when directed against bureaucrats is often merely a way of finding scapegoats to deflect attention from the political system itself and the interests of a power elite.

In the implementation of welfare policies, experts and services alike are coordinated and directed by the responsible government departments. These have their established routines, and acknowledged friends and detractors, and, typically, zealously guard against or try to absorb outsiders. On the grounds that the bureaucracy, given its legal or quasi-legal mandate, does not effect the maximal change possible, a critic might well speak of the "dead hand of bureaucracy" subverting social policy oriented to significant social change. Legislation virtually always allows some scope for policy innovation within administration. As Doern and Aucoin note:

> [Policy] outputs can be altered not because the bureaucracy is 'inefficient' nor that these outputs are merely the accidental results of the clash of bureaucratic forces. They are often 'rationally' contrived; that is, related to a different set of goals or assumptions later inserted by policy actors, which are just as effectively 'policies' as were the original general statements made by politicians.[36]

How the bureaucracy will cope with this innovative possibility depends on its particular guiding philosophy, its existing political realities, and its established routines. Although internal change may occur within government departments through change in leadership and in the disposition of other personnel, the most common source of change is external. Indeed, changes intitiated by internal considerations usually have to be justified in terms of external pressure; for example, a new leader or director may justify, in terms of outside demands, a new policy or new departmental structuring.

In the case of the Africville relocation, the city's welfare office had little to do with relocation planning and execution. That agency developed, over the years, a model of Africville and Africville people that virtually precluded any real change in their life situation. Its director was opposed to the relocation; the policy line (or recommendation) was to urge, although not strongly to fight for, extension of regular city services to the Africville community. Welfare assistance, when given, was doled out with a heavy paternalism. There was approval of the resourceful Africville residents who could "scrounge out" an existence amidst the squalor of the garbage dump. Consequently, impetus for the relocation of Africville did not come from the welfare office; nor, under the circumstances, was there much likelihood that it would be charged with significant responsibility for relocation.

The city department most interested in the relocation of Africville was the newly established development department. Seeing Africville as an environmental disaster as well as the site of scarce waterfront property important to the city's future growth,[37] it provided the impetus for relocation and coordinated all aspects of the relocation program. The relocation officer, a trained social worker hired because of his ability to get along with people, was assigned to the development department and placed under the immediate supervision of the development officer. He coordinated the real estate and welfare components of relocation. The tactic of centralizing under the one city department the relocation administration had, from the point of view of planned social change, several practical advantages. Not only did it appear to offer more creative possibilities than working through the existing welfare office but, by facilitating the potential coordination of services and agency functions under the relocation social worker, it made possible a concerted effort to effect change. The relocation social worker dispensed welfare, arranged relocation transportation, and acted as liaison in making real estate, legal, and other city services available to Africville residents. On the other hand, given the nature of the task discussed above, centralizing the relocation under the development department had certain limitations for social change. The development department saw the Africville relocation as a short-term, three-year project; special responsibility for the relocatees once the land was cleared of people was not built into the frame of reference or guiding philosophy of the department. Moreover, the development department was, by fixed terms of reference established by council, a professional entity, staffed by experts and oriented to the interests of the city as a whole. Ideologically, its commitment was to the development model of relocation implicit in these terms of reference. In the case of the Africville relocation, for very good reasons, planned social change was not handled through welfare-oriented agencies and therefore became the responsibility of a different governmental bureaucracy which, while oriented to change, was not likely to emphasize special client interests, citizen participation, or a long-term commitment to the relocatees' socio-economic conditions.[38]

Given the bureaucratic arrangements of the Africville relocation and the normal tendency for a bureaucracy to hover close to its legal responsibilities, it is not surprising that the emphasis of the development department was on the clearing of land and on real estate negotiations. The relocation social worker became, in effect, more an employee of the development department than a liaison officer representing clients in negotiations with a bureaucracy. Initial plans to maintain a separate office at Africville for the social worker were abandoned; he used an office in the development department, at city hall. Relocation transactions were discussed by the social worker and the development officer, and the city's position communicated to Africville residents. Almost all of the relocation social worker's reports to the Africville Subcommittee were first discussed and approved at meetings between him and the development officer. In the eyes of most relocation participants, the latter was the relocation social worker's employer. A major problem of the welfare approach in the instance of the Africville relocation was to build into a non-welfare-oriented agency a commitment to special client interests. A major task of the relocation social worker was to bring this about while in the ambivalent position of being an employee of the agency. Failure to deal successfully with this problem is seen in the lack of effective programs to create new opportunities for relocatees. The relocation became largely a real estate operation, with welfare payments thrown in to satisfy the caretakers and to meet community concern that a long-neglected and oppressed people be treated equitably. One city official observed:

> A certain kind of pressure was brought to bear [on Africville relocatees]...in relation to the use of social assistance funds which were available to [the relocation social worker] on some kind of special-arrangement basis. He was able to meet requests for financial assistance. I think in many cases the effect was to soft-pedal or soft-pad the transitional period, to perhaps conceal from people really the full impact of the economic burden and so on which they would have to encounter, making the entire relocation more acceptable to the people and in many respects unrealistic because these funds were terminated with the termination of [the social worker's] employment.

Problems of Advocacy

The other way of achieving the larger ends of relocation while operating within the terms of reference established by city council was to mobilize external pressure that would counterbalance bureaucracy by demanding maximal achievement of the city's moral, if not legal, commitment. Perhaps, too, such pressure could lead to new council policy and formal adoption of additional explicit responsibilities should the relocation experience demonstrate that this was necessary in order to realize welfare goals.

In the Africville relocation, external pressure was expressed institutionally through participation of the three black caretakers from the Halifax Human Rights Advisory Committee on the Africville Subcommitttee. Their participation and the prior involvement of the larger committee were significant structural features in the planning and implementation of the Africville relocation and served to define the relocation as a liberal-welfare model, although it did not result in achievement of the larger welfare goals of the relocation. The formation of the Halifax Human Rights Advisory Committee and its role in examining the city's relocation plan, suggesting alternatives, and seeking expert welfare advice have been discussed at length. Certainly the committee's involvement in planning for the relocation did much to ensure that a liberal-welfare rhetoric would characterize the relocation program, and that the city would commit itself to developing related programs for effective social change. The Halifax Human Rights Advisory Committee, and especially the black caretakers, rendered an important service to Africville residents in terms of relocation settlements, temporary welfare assistance, and city concern for Africville residents awaiting relocation. But once actual negotiation began between the city and relocatees, the external pressure for change was absorbed into day-to-day concern with specific individual settlements and crises. There was little time to focus on the larger picture of relocation and to create programs oriented to long-term objectives. There was no available mechanism by which an Africville opinion or voice could be readily identified and assessed. The caretakers and other members of the Halifax Human Rights Advisory Committee, involved on a part-time, voluntary basis and possessed of few independent resources, naturally relied upon staff reports.

They found themselves, rather than taking initiatives of their own, responding either to those of the city or of the few Africville residents who sought their assistance. Given the absence of a strong indigenous Africville organization and the non-involvement of other external organizations, individual problems, requests, and crises could not be channelled effectively through the caretakers into new programs or policies. Their difficulty in not being able to see the forest for the trees nor to keep abreast of relocation developments is illustrated by their subsequent acknowledged surprise at the absence of a relocation follow-up.

Apart from lack of time, energy, and resources, the most important reason for the inadequacy of institutionalized external pressure in closing the gap between rhetoric and achievement was the weak linkage to the Africville people themselves. There was little organized Africville involvement in any phase of the relocation, and virtually none once relocation negotiations began. The majority of relocatees had no sense that their individual or collective interests were being advanced by the Halifax Human Rights Advisory Committee. Many more relocatees reported that they depended on the relocation social worker's help or on their ability to bargain well with him. These facts raise important issues concerning the manner in which sources of pressure external to the city government were marshalled in the Africville relocation.

It is usually difficult to achieve organization among the poor, for their poverty obstructs the development of ramifying and consolidated exchange systems. This often means that the infrastructure requisites for effective indigenous organization are lacking and, accordingly, poor and oppressed groups seek assistance from middle-class liberals. The pattern was especially evident in the Africville situation, where residents had the additional liability of being black in a somewhat racist society and where they experienced a clash of different social styles within Africville itself. The natural bias, as far as the mobilizing of pressure was concerned, was therefore towards an integrationist-collaborationist strategy. This strategy was encouraged by the civil rights leaders who responded to pleas for assistance from a few residents.

The middle-class professionals who, with the support of a few Africville residents, guided the strategy of mobilizing pressure made some crippling presumptions about life in Africville and about how significant social change could be achieved. That such presumptions were made is related to the ideology of the times, as well as to the scant time, energy, and resources they could devote to the Africville case. One set of presumptions concerning the nature of Africville (that it was a slum, that as a segregated community it had become atavistic, that the people were squatters and transients), while not without some foundation in fact, was selective; Africville was not seen as having much value for its residents. By not giving as much weight to positive considerations (such as *the potential land value*, the fact that a number of people owned their own homes, and many residents' sense of historical continuity) the well-intentioned outsiders failed to see the Africville people as having a strong base which, if they were well organized, would enable them to bargain from a position of power.

The Implications of Africville Relocation 269

A second and related set of presumptions dealt with how to effect social change, given the nature of the Africville community. It was considered valuable to have middle-class people associate with Africville residents and apply strong moral pressure on the city; in other words, to make sure that the poor had sound, articulate, middle-class spokespersons. Middle-class professionals may well be helpful in developing organization among the poor. It does appear that, prior to involving the poor in a larger structure of middle-class people and organizations, it is important that the poor's own organization be strong and viable. Otherwise what happens is precisely what occurred in the Africville case; as residents saw in the larger organization a veering away from their own specific concerns and their own perceptions of problems, they allowed others to do things for them and simply dropped out. The result was lack of identification of relocatees with the caretaker group so that organized external pressure in the relocation was exerted by a group without roots in Africville and without an Africville mandate.

Gauging the Success of the Africville Relocation

Good social policy for planned social change depends upon an accurate assessment of the problem situation; a set of goals defined precisely enough that one can know whether one has achieved them (and to what degree); a strategy which maps out the instrumentalities of a highly probable way of effecting the desired change; and a mobilization of advocacy which sets the planned social change in process and monitors its development. In the Africville relocation program all these components of social policy, as noted above, were inadequately attained. If the Africville relocation were framed in terms of the development model of planned social change, the relocation might very well be considered successful — land was obtained by the city, in keeping with the needs of a proposed redevelopment program. By relocating Africville residents, the city has rid itself of what some have considered an "environmental disaster" and has overcome the embarrassment of having within its boundaries a distinct, segregated, black community. While this public benefit presumably has been achieved, the city can claim also to have treated the relocatees fairly, and even generously, from the standpoint of the market value of individual properties in the period 1964-67. But if the relocation is framed in terms of the liberal-welfare model of planned social change, as its intention, rhetoric, and structure would indicate, it can hardly be called a success and in none of the four components of social policy does it signal new creative ways of intervening to alter radically the life-opportunities of the poor and deprived.

Within the general framework of the relocation program, several modifications would have increased the probability of an acclaimed success. For one thing, it would have been useful to eliminate some of the ambiguity in the relocation social worker's role and to strengthen his internal advocacy function by giving him a freer rein and independence from any specific city department. Clearly, too, the external advocacy of the caretakers would have been more effective had further resources been available to them such that they would not have been dependent upon initiatives from the city bureaucracy. Also, a greater effort to involve an indigenous Africville organization would have produced different results.

As it is difficult to generate and maintain representative community organization among the poor, collaboration with well-intentioned, middle-class citizens is usually necessary since the urban poor often lack resources for effective mobilization and perceive their poor neighbours as powerless, useless allies. Dependency upon the advocacy of citizens-at-large, even when they are provided with resources, is inadequate. The notion of larger citizen involvement is central to liberal-welfare social change since it is consistent with assumptions of consensus and reasonableness which underlie this model; clearly, though, what gets defined as a reasonable societal commitment by citizens-at-large is usually inadequate for dramatic improvement of the life-opportunities of the poor.

In recent years oppressed minorities have been demanding reparation; in effect they have been saying, as some Africville relocatees said, that one cannot simply look at the end-product of an historical development and compensate generously on that basis (in the Africville case, on the basis of current market value of land) but rather one's notion of reasonableness must take into account and compensate for the historical development itself. In the case of Africville, without the historical patterns of discrimination and city neglect, it would have been a quite different community. Indigenous organization among the urban poor is critical in providing this additional dimension to the idea of a reasonable societal commitment. It seems to be virtually a law that such organizations manifest an historical consciousness and celebrate the good aspects of the community and those coping behaviours contributing to its survival. A side benefit associated with community organization under these circumstances is that the urban poor tend to become more positive about themselves and their community, a development of considerable significance in the restructuring of their lives.

Developing a representative organization among the urban poor in relocation and rehabilitation programs will take time, energy, and funds. But if the rationale of the relocation is liberal-welfare, investment of the necessary time, effort, and money cannot be considered wasteful. The demand for citizens' organizations and participatory democracy has both normative and pragmatic aspects. It is not only a response to failures in planned social change; it is based on the premise that involvement in decision-making will make relocatees better citizens. If the inefficiency and squabbling of such structured participation produces clear hazards to living or threats to the general city interests, a redefinition of the relocation situation with a different and appropriate relocation rhetoric and administrative structure might well be required. Certainly there are different models of planned social change appropriate to different circumstances.

The modifications discussed above concerning internal advocacy, external advocacy, and indigenous organization all bear on the one component of social policy, the mobilization of advocacy. The implication of such modifications is tantamount to positing structured conflict as endemic in society because of different interests associated with different classes, strata, and other groupings. The assumptions and strategies of the political model of relocation appear more appropriate than those of the liberal-welfare model in cases such as the Africville relocation; in these instances — where the purpose of relocation is ostensibly to improve the relocatees' life-opportunities — it is reasonable, for example, to contend that the potential relocatees should be able to exercise veto power regarding relocation programs.

The instability of the liberal-welfare approach to relocation in instances such as Africville is also evident in the other components of social policy. Especially with regard to the component of strategy this approach seems inherently inadequate. To change the life-opportunities of the poor is very difficult. While it is certainly possible to draft a better and more detailed intervention strategy than was done in the case of Africville (lack of post-relocation follow-up programs was proof of this), the overall record of relocation programs oriented to this set of goals has not been very impressive. A more political approach seems necessary not only because of the political nature of the root problem — income and resource distribution in society — but also because it appears imperative that the poor and deprived have a factual basis for the perception that they themselves can do something about their present situation and future prospects. In many relocations, as in the case of Africville, a large number of relocatees are, more or less reluctantly, written off by relocation officials as impossible to rehabilitate; in the case of many other relocatees, the officials, using vague and factually dubious extrapolation, justify their contention that the future will be better on the grounds of housing or some other modest improvement. Typically, the relocatees profiting most significantly from liberal-welfare relocation programs have been the politically active, mobility-oriented residents least committed to and dependent upon neighbourhood associations.

In terms of goals and definition of the problem situation, the liberal-welfare approach to planned social change also exhibits some basic inadequacies. Since the model is premised on consensus and a constricted conception of reasonableness, it carries the implication that experts and technocrats are best able to define the problem situation and to articulate the underlying, common goals of the society. In the Africville relocation, ouside experts with scant knowledge of Africville and minimal contact with its residents exercised considerable influence in both these regards. But even where the experts and technocrats are well-informed one can expect fairly profound differences between them and the potential relocatees concerning what is desirable and valuable and what the most crucial aspects of the problem situation are. In the case of Africville, the residents placed considerable value on the historical continuity of the community, on the church, and on the possession of homes which they could leave to their children; none of these considerations appeared especially significant from the point of view of the experts and technocrats. Furthermore, for the latter, a significant aspect of the problem situation was the fact that Africville was a segregated black community; accordingly, a basic goal of the relocation was integration, but only a small minority of the residents placed an equal emphasis on this factor.

As noted in Chapter Two, very poor urban areas such as Africville are characterized by considerable social differentiation. The different social groupings tend to respond to relocation in diverse ways and have different problems with which an intervention strategy must deal. Usually there is a minority, pre-disposed to mobility, who do better than others in the relocation exchange; in Africville this group was the mainliners. Generally, too, older relocatees express the greatest grief upon being relocated, but, as was the case in Africville, older persons probably adjust to their new environment better and more easily than they had anticipated. Young adult and middle-aged relocatees, especially males, may in the long run become the most disgruntled as they become more aware of the failure of the relocation promise. The opportunists and marginal types tend to be relatively untouched by the relocation experience. But despite their different problems and reactions, the Africville experience leads us to think that, with time, effort, and funds, the residents could have developed a collective response based upon common interests. The relocatees did display a sense of distributive justice and their view that relocation benefits were not distributed fairly among the people was largely a function of misinformation about what different people received and cynicism due to the fact that relocation negotiations were carried out on a private and individual basis.

The Africville relocation has been a useful example of planned social change to study. It is typical of many liberal-welfare relocation programs carried out in North America. It might, however, be less instructive for future planned social change, as the social and cultural climate has altered. Given the re-emphasis on the importance of the small community in recent years, the revitalization of concern for subgroup collective identities, and the new emphasis on rehabilitation rather than relocation, what possibility is there of another Africville relocation? The development director for the city of Halifax did not think the possibility was high as indicated in the following interview:

> *Interviewer*: [If you had the opportunity] "would you make any significant changes in the way the Africville relocation was carried out?"
> *Development director*: "Personally, no. I think this is the only way in which you can approach this type of community, be it black or white. I don't know, however, that the times haven't gone to a point where it is almost impossible to tackle these problems."
> *Interviewer*: "I'm not sure what you are referring to."
> *Development director*: "The age of dissent has reached the point — can you solve these problems?"

One Africville relocatee, on the other hand, wished that the "age of dissent" had come ten years earlier; she commented: "What happened in Africville won't happen again, but how in hell does it help us."

Notes

1   Arnold S. Kaufman, *The Radical Liberal: The New Politics: Theory and Practice* (New York: Simon and Schuster, 1970), p. 13.

2   Stein, op. cit.; Susan Dexter, "The Black Ghetto That Fears Integration," *Maclean's Magazine*, July 25, 1965, p. 16, *passim*.

3   Sylvia Fraser, "The Slow and Welcome Death of Africville," *Star Weekly*, Toronto, January 1, 1966, pp. 1-7.

4   Raymond Daniell, "Nova Scotia Hides A Racial Problem," *The New York Times*, June 14, 1964, p. 64.

5   *The Condition of the Negroes of Halifax City, Nova Scotia*, p. 13.

6   The development department report appeared in *The Mail-Star* on August 1, 1962. The Dalhousie University publication was released to the press on October 3, 1962. National and international publicity appeared as a response to city council's relocation policy: Stein, October, 1962; Dexter, 1965; Fraser, 1966; and Daniell, 1964.

7   Personal communication from Miss Phyllis R. Blakeley, Assistant Archivist, Public Archives of Nova Scotia, Halifax, April 1970.

8   Fraser, op. cit., p. 6.

9   See Stanley H. Pickett, "An Appraisal of the Urban Renewal Programme in Canada," *Urban Renewal*, (Toronto: Centre for Urban and Community Studies, University of Toronto, 1968).

10   Clairmont and Magill, *Nova Scotian Blacks*, pp. 34-35.

11   The Halifax *Mail-Star* had an editorial practice of reporting the relocation of Africville residents. Prior to 1962 only sporadic articles about Africville were published. Most of the *Mail-Star's* articles appeared during the relocation decision-making (1962-64) and the relocation itself (1964-67). A former reporter for the *Mail-Star*, in a tape-recorded interview, commented about the possible influence of the newspaper's publicity on the average Haligonian:

> "I think another very great factor to be considered was the publicity campaign conducted over the years by Frank Doyle, who was an editor of the Halifax [*Chronicle-Herald* and *The Mail-Star*].... This resulted in tremendous interest focussed on the...health hazards in the community.... Perhaps the general responsiveness [of Halifax citizens] to the Africville relocation would have resulted largely from this."

12   Clairmont and Magill, *Africville Relocation Report*, p. A25. The proposal to use Africville land for an expressway follows a pattern that critics of American urban renewal programs call "Negro clearance." Anderson points out that the goal of the American renewal schemes is often the preservation

or creation of a white middle-class neighbourhood, and that blacks constitute a very high proportion of the displaced people. Martin Anderson, *The Federal Bulldozer: A Critical Analysis of Urban Renewal, 1949-1962* (Cambridge, Mass.: The M.I.T. Press, 1964).

[13] Anderson has noted that it is not uncommon for urban renewal cleared land to be vacant for a number of years before new construction is begun: "A typical urban renewal project takes a long time. The planning stage for an average project takes approximately three years. The over-all length of time, from start of planning to completion of new construction, needed for an average project is about 12 years." Ibid., p. 229; see also pp. 73-90.

[14] *City of Halifax: Prison Land Development Proposals, Report No. 1, Survey and Analysis,* Vol. 2, *Social Factors,* June 23, 1969, p. 3. This report is on file at city hall, Halifax, N.S.

[15] *City of Halifax: Prison Land Development Proposals. Report No. 2. Area Conceptual Plan,* October 14, 1969. This report is on file at city hall, Halifax, N.S.

[16] Alvin Gouldner describes the liberal establishment in *The Coming Crisis of Western Sociology,* pp. 500-502. He attacks specifically a "new ombudsman sociology" whose very criticism of middle-level welfare authorities and establishments serves as a kind of lightning rod for social discontent, strengthening the centralized control of the highest authorities, and providing new instruments of social control for the master institutions.

[17] "In Search of a Sense of Community," *Time,* April 6, 1970.

[18] Fraser, op. cit.

[19] *Minutes of the Halifax City Council, Halifax, N.S.,* September 14, 1967; see also an interview with the relocation social worker: Sheila Urquhart, "Africville Program Complete in July," *The Mail-Star,* Halifax, N.S., July 5, 1967.

[20] Dexter, op. cit.

[21] See, for instance, Sheila Urquhart, "Ghetto Going on Schedule," *The Mail-Star,* Halifax, N.S., January 3, 1966: and Sheila Urquhart, "Africville Program Complete in July," *The Mail-Star,* Halifax, N.S., July 5, 1967.

[22] "End of Africville," *The Mail-Star,* Halifax, N.S., July 7, 1967.

[23] See, for instance, Jim Robson, "Mayor to Probe Africville Claims," *The Mail-Star,* Halifax, N.S., October 3, 1969; and "Social Worker on Africville: Follow-Up Could Have Averted Relocation Problems," *The Mail-Star,* Halifax, N.S., October 4, 1969.

[24] In addition to interviewing black leaders in the metropolitan area, the researchers and their assistants discussed Africville with a large number of

blacks living in Halifax County and in communities as distant as Guysborough County.

25 See, for instance, the "Letter to the Editor," *The Mail-Star,* Halifax, N.S., August 11, 1962, submitted by B.A. Husbands, President, Halifax Coloured Citizens Improvement League. Mr. Husbands, in putting forward his particular plan, observed, "I feel that where the people of Africville have striven within their means to provide shelter for their families they should be given the...opportunity to better themselves and, at the same time, better the community as a whole."

26 Tape-recorded interviews, August 1969. Two of the leaders alluded to here went into the community after relocation was underway. It should be noted that Africville relocatees did not acknowledge the assistance of local black leaders from outside Africville. Over seventy percent reported that they did not even meet with the black caretakers from the Halifax Human Rights Advisory Committee to discuss their situation or terms of settlement. A mere handful of relocatees reported contact with black leaders for the purpose of receiving assistance to help them cope with the relocation.

27 Two black leaders, who claim to have disagreed with the strategy followed by the Halifax Human Rights Advisory Committee on the grounds that unintentionally its members were being co-opted by the city, reported that they were labelled troublemakers when they attempted to assist Africville residents. Regardless of whether these allegations are true, it is probably true that once a community organization develops it tends to channel and restrict others' participation.

28 White liberal allies are, of course, often useless. James Q. Wilson, discussing politics in the United States, observed that "Negro civic leaders stand on the periphery of power. They hope to needle or prod or anger or humiliate those who can direct the course of affairs into granting concessions to Negro demands. The Negroes themselves are remote from the centers of influence, and this distance gives a certain logic to their views of the public interest and appropriate strategies for action. But those whom they seek to influence are often powerless also, if by power we mean the ability to establish binding public policy. The White civic leaders and politicians are either complacent or caught up in their own conflict of interest, and are severely constrained by their own opinions and fears as to the consequences of any radical change in the racial patterns of the city." James Q. Wilson, *Negro Politics* (New York: The Free Press, 1960), p. 286.

29 Wilson observes that "the bargainer is not as highly committed to specific ends as is the militant, and is correspondingly less willing to alter the mission of an organization to strike out at a target of opportunity not previously agreed upon as being within its purview. To do so would mean a sacrifice in other goals—such as friendly relations with supporters." Ibid., p. 234.

[30] Winks, *The Blacks in Canada,* op. cit., p. 456. Winks is mistaken in reporting that the last building fell to the bulldozers in January, 1967.

[31] See Clairmont and Magill, *Nova Scotian Blacks.*

[32] In most instances, exaggerations refer as much to what might have been as what was.

[33] See Eugene Williams, "The NSAACP and Education," M.A. Thesis, Maritime School of Social Work, Halifax, N.S., 1969, p. 48.

[34] One black leader of this stamp expressed his dissatisfaction with the Africville relocation, and pointed out that his early criticism of the relocation process had resulted in his being labelled a troublemaker. He argued that the price of integration, as exacted by the relocation, was much too high. At the time of relocation his views seemed out of step with the pro-integration and civil-rights oriented younger black leaders. In a later militant and nationalistic period, his views are accepted and influential.

[35] Correspondence with a civil law specialist, Halifax, N.S.

[36] G. Bruce Doern and Peter Aucoin, eds., *The Structures of Policy-Making in Canada* (Toronto: Macmillan of Canada, 1971), p. 5.

[37] The editors of *The Mail-Star* also noted the importance of Africville lands to the city's future growth: "Not only is Halifax short of all types of land many businesses need and demand. Providing suitable docking facilities are built, part of this problem will be met when the demolition of Africville is completed."—Editorial. "Plan to Secure More Waterfront Land," *The Mail-Star,* Halifax, N.S., July 16, 1964.

[38] What the development department might regard as an unusual degree of consideration to social welfare matters would appear insignificant from the point of view of those familiar with the extremely difficult task of effecting significant social change for such a disadvantaged group within existing institutional arrangements.

Deconstructing Africville: 1999

"The past is not dead history; it is living material out of which man makes the present and builds the future."[1]

As Palys has observed, "social constructionism emphasizes the idea that 'reality' does not exist independent of our opinions of it... we actively 'construct' or 'produce' reality through our actions and beliefs about it."[2] Knowledge and beliefs are of course developed, transmitted and maintained in social situations, and a fundamental sociological perspective holds that there are multiple social realities constructed.[3] Accordingly, social reality is negotiated through experiences and is constructed and reconstructed on an ongoing basis. Sometimes there may be a consensus-based social construction of a situation, usually because a dominant group has exercised effective hegemonic influence; more often there is significant 'contested terrain' among diverse, similarly focused, social constructions which share a significant core of beliefs and interpretations. It appears that in the case of 'Africville as a community' there was consensual social constructionism in the pre-relocation and relocation periods, at least apart from community members themselves. On the other hand the current social constructionism with respect to Africville can be characterized as diverse with much common core 'social reality' and much contested terrain. In this chapter we address these phases and highlight the process of transformation whereby Africville has gone from stigmatized to celebrated.

From a social movement perspective successful constructionism appears to depend upon the congruence of three factors, namely interests, pressures and knowledge.[4] Deconstructing 'Africville' essentially entails examining how these factors have shaped past and current social constructions and effected the transformation noted above. It can be argued that in each phase particular facets of Africville and of its relationship to the larger society have been highlighted as a consequence of different pressures and interests and the salience of different knowledge. It is also relevant to inquire as to what the implications of particular social constructions are and here this would mean focusing upon multiple functions such as agenda-setting, mobilization, empowerment. sociality and identity.

Africville's Relocation Social Construction

When Africville was being bull-dozed the Toronto Star referred to its 'slow and welcomed death' and Halifax papers commented that 'soon, mercifully, all would be forgotten'. That was thirty years ago during which time Africville has become more well-known and more celebrated than ever. And the whole domain of sentiments relating to the conception of Africville has drastically changed. As Godfrey has remarked, "the change has been philosophical: ideas about urban renewal, forced integration and orderly city planning have been overshadowed ... by values stressing community bonds, organic development and consensus."[5] In the earlier times the social construction of Africville emphasized the former values and strategies and led to the conclusion that relocation was inevitable and desirable. Integration was the Holy Grail. Africville was for the most part segregated. It was not a neatly laid out community with appropriate services and facilities. Its people were poor and unsophisticated. In a thoughtful newspaper piece entitled 'Africville: What If?', empathetic Charles Saunders asked what would have happened if Africville had been better organized, had had strong internal leadership and more effective resistance tactics? His answer was that it probably could not have resisted the relocation because that really meant resisting the "social forces that were sweeping North America"; thus "the community was fated to serve as an example, both to its own residents and to other black settlements in Nova Scotia."[6] It was too vulnerable on too many other issues to resist these powerful forces. Of course that earlier social construction was partial, biased, unsympathetic to what the residents had achieved in the face of racism, neglect and so forth but just as life is not especially fair so too social constructions are always selective, reflecting the knowledge, pressures and interests of the times. These factors have been discussed at length in this book so perhaps it suffices here to note that interests included the possibilities of alternative land uses and urban renewal opportunities while pressures included housing norms, critical external 'press' and liberal-welfare commitments (and hubris!); knowledge considerations included the emphasis on less attractive aspects of community life and the existence of some transients and squatters rather than on the positive community life and the historic character of its settlement and development.

In the relocation imagery progress was defined by the various categories of officials, politicians, policy-oriented academics and influential, public-spirited citizens. The views of these persons generally held sway throughout society, among both its black and white members. In this definition of the situation Africville was stigmatized and an inappropriate candidate for continuance or refurbishment. It was difficult for even its residents to resist this social construction, a circumstance that explains why they rather quickly came to accept the inevitability of relocation and offered virtually no resistance to the relocation program. As Erving Goffman remarks of stigmatized persons, "the standards he has incorporated from the wider society equip him to be intimately alive to what others see as his failing, inevitably causing him, if only for moments, to agree that he does indeed fall short of what he really ought to be."[7]

Formalizing a New Social Construction

The social constructionism of Africville as a community began to change shortly after most residents had been relocated. It began with the publicity around the 'Pa Carvery case' where this elderly gentleman, a major property owner and scion of one of Africville's oldest families, resisted with great dignity the increasingly crass efforts by city officials to buy him out (their efforts included waving a bag of money in relatively small bills in front of him in a city office). It continued with events surrounding the launching of the research detailed in this monograph, namely the reassembling of relocatees to discuss their post-relocation experiences, the formation of the Africville Action Committee, the publicity given to the plight of some relocatees and the failure on the City's part to deliver on many of its pre-relocation promises, and the formation of the Seaview Credit Union to provide short-term, modest financial relief. These developments helped to undermine the extant social construction of 'Africville as a community' largely by showing how the promises fell so far short of reality and that the actual alternative to life in Africville at least in the short run was not especially attractive for many relocatees. It is interesting to note that the research/evaluation was commissioned by the Government of Nova Scotia on the premise that the relocation program had been a very positive and progressive initiative; as it turned out the thrust of the research/evaluation was to profoundly challenge this perspective and to facilitate relocatees' advocacy.

The more positive dimension of the deconstruction process came largely from the people themselves. In the early 1980s a number of young adult Africvilleans began to reclaim their legacy by returning to the old site for picnics and so forth. With the formation of the Africville Genealogical Society a structure was put in place to organize annual reunions there in the summer and to celebrate the Africville that was and could have been. While there was clearly also an agenda for further negotiations with the City associated with this development, it does appear that the major impetus was to draw upon and secure succour from 'Africville' as family, home and community. These concerns appeared to become more poignant to a generation of Africvilleans coming to grips not only with their own identities (e.g., roots, social ties) but also having a need and desire to deal with their children's similar quests in a modern society increasingly impersonal, atomistic and apparently unable to provide its citizens with a positive, secure sense of themselves. The formation of the Genealogical Society and the activities of the Africvilleans conveyed a quite different and of course much more positive social construction of Africville, one that was congruent with contemporary developments in the larger society such as the revitalization of black subculture, the proliferation of identity movements, and a disillusionment with liberal-welfare priorities and approaches to social change.

In 1989 these deconstructionist strands came together in a formal, almost ceremonial way and there was a 'coming-out-party' as it were, for a new social construction of 'Africville as a community'. In the fall of that year an exhibition entitled 'Africville: A Spirit That Lives On' was successfully launched at Mount Saint Vincent University in Halifax under the co-sponsorship of the National Film Board, the Art Gallery of Mount Saint Vincent University, the Black Cultural Centre and the Africville Genealogical Society. Using photographs, artifacts, tapes and other memorabilia the exhibition aimed at "capturing the essence of Africville, what it was, and why it has not been and should not be forgotten". Associated with the exhibition were a host of activities including a memorial service at the Cornwallis Street Baptist Church (mother church of the African Baptist Association), an official exhibition opening, an evening of music and readings (poetry and dramatized readings) which brought together many of the leading artists and entertainers in the Nova Scotian black community, and a week-end conference highlighting the theme 'The Africville Experience: Lessons For The Future'; this conference featured a panel of several key black and white decision-makers / participants in the Africville Relocation Program, and, later, a day of presentations and remembrances by Africvilleans. All activities were well-attended.

The exhibition program celebrated Africville and signalled a triumphal reconstructionism. Within two years the exhibition had travelled across Canada to very positive critical reviews before being permanently housed at the Black Cultural Centre. An award-winning National Film Board documentary 'Remembering Africville' (1991),[8] and a new Africville book combining scholarly and artistic work, 'The Spirit of Africville' (1992),[9] followed in its wake, as did a slew of radio, television and artistic works. Throughout the exhibition and related events, and reflected in subsequent developments, there were two chief recurring themes. Perhaps the most basic was the affirmation by former residents, relocation decision-makers, artists and others that Africville was a community to be proud of, a fine community with all the positive connotations implied by that term, and even an heroic community since its people struggled against so much racism and neglect. The shortcomings were deemed to have been readily correctable if a sensitive and sympathetic larger society had been in place. The second theme, equally pervasive, was that an Africville relocation today would not be countenanced by anyone whether they be Africvilleans, other Blacks, community activists or City officials. It was agreed by all that what was lost by the destruction of the community far outweighed any benefits the relocation yielded to the former residents.

The two-day conference witnessed a considerable outpouring of emotion, both joy and grief, by Africvilleans. Adults who were young teenagers at the time of relocation recalled enduring friendships, the oneness of the community when it came to sharing food and playing in homes, and the free spaces of fields and ocean frontage. Some particularly stressed how the relocation robbed them of the opportunity to improve the housing and other community amenities as others of their age had done over time in similar 'poor' areas (whether white or black) of metropolitan Halifax / Dartmouth. There was anger too among some of the elderly Africvilleans, one of whom decried the historical pattern of official responses to Africville in the words: "The City is no good. Maybe some of them will rot in hell for some of the dirty deeds they did to Blacks".

Community activists and government officials who had been active in the relocation decision-making generally expressed regret about the relocation program, contending that while their intentions were honourable the circumstances at the time left them little room for manoeuvre. A community activist who had assisted in the establishment of the Human Rights Advisory Committee (HRAC) which formally represented Africville's interests, observed that "Africville people got less than they believed they were entitled to because they lacked the clout to do better". He noted that voluntary and part-time efforts such as contributed by HRAC members are usually inadequate and that effective organization among the disadvantaged "takes hard, gruelling, drudgery work ... it requires money". Black leaders from outside Africville who served on HRAC indicated that, seeing no alternative to relocation that was acceptable to the City, they strove to ensure that the relocation was at least carried out with as much benefit as possible to the Africville residents; one rued, "those who live today do not know the agony we went through. We made decisions because we could not put off decisions any longer. We did what we had to do because it seemed to be the best alternative of the choices before us". Another black HRAC member recalled his shock, upon settling in Halifax, of seeing the physical conditions in Africville, his subsequent concern for helping to remedy the situation, and his sense that he and the HRAC did the best they could given the 'realization' that Africville had to go.

White former governmental officials who participated in the panel were in agreement that, as one said, "we undervalued the importance of a sense of community". One such person, an alderman at the time of relocation who had a strong progressive reputation and collaborated closely with HRAC, contended that the decision to eliminate Africville was an honourable one based on the poor housing conditions, the desire to end segregation and the 'public embarrassment' the City was experiencing because of Africville. He underlined the point that "while hindsight is great ... we accepted staff, outside expert and HRAC advice". The former provincial deputy minister of Welfare during the relocation called attention to the hubris of social planning at the time - the sense among bureaucrats and technocrats that they knew best and knew how, basically within the existing social framework of society, to significantly improve life conditions for the disadvantaged. In his view the major lesson of Africville has been the realization that social and economic change cannot be manipulated but must begin where the people and the community are at, building upon their traditions and preferences. Pointing to the lack of follow-up and the failure of the liberal-welfare rhetoric that accompanied the relocation, he echoed the community activist cited above in reiterating the moral "don't trust long-term commitments in government or otherwise unless you have the money and power and the clout to force government and others to listen to you and not forget that you exist".

Clearly then the 1989 exhibition/conference and its aftermath buried the former consensus-based social construction of Africville. The positive aspects of Africville now were strongly emphasized and the negative ones minimized. Bureaucrats and technocrats went from being potential saviours to imprudent 'heavies' and the relocation program was deemed to be based on inadequate knowledge and an inappropriate prioritization of values and principles. It is interesting to speculate whether such a transformation in social constructions would have happened, and how significant Africville's symbolism would be today, if the promises of better housing, social programs and enhanced life opportunities had been realized by the individual relocatees and their families. Experience suggests that the changes wrought even by a more successful relocation program would likely be modest. And for Africvilleans the price would still have been high in terms of identity, social and physical resources, and sense of belonging. Leaders in the black community of Nova Scotia share this realization with the Africville people. One black pastor in addressing the conference noted that the legacy of relocation "has been an uppermost thought in black consciousness"; in added:

> "Africville could still be a little community on Bedford Basin.
> It could still be a housing development on Bedford Basin.
> There could now be a paved highway through the
> community of Africville on Bedford Basin. There could be
> a transit system through the community of Africville. Yes,
> all those things that we see developing in other parts of
> our area could have been in Africville, but God knows it
> will never, never, never happen again".

The transformation of social constructions of Africville had implications beyond pure symbolism and contribution to the configuration of black mythico-history (see below). It initiated another round of demands for individual and collective reparations channelled by the Africville Genealogical Society and resulting in new negotiations with City officials.

It also contributed to actions taken by the City, either in memory of Africville or fear of protest, to disallow development projects proposed in the early 1990s, which would have encroached upon Seaview Memorial Park - Africvilleans finally won some zoning battles, at least for the park dedicated to their old community.

The Contemporary Social Construction of Africville

What about the current situation, the present social construction? Is there general agreement? Well virtually all City officials, relocation decision-makers and the general public would probably concur with Halifax's mayor who was recently quoted as saying that "the Africville relocation was a terrible experience that should not be repeated."[10] The city manager commented at a 1994 public meeting with many angry former Africville residents that "It was urban renewal. It was done in an unacceptable fashion. It happened in virtually every city in Canada. I'm not defending this; it's historical fact."[11] The view that the Africville relocation program was unwise, unacceptable and not-to-be repeated is the core of the present definition of the situation. This core also contains views and perceptions that Africville was a valuable community providing identity and support to its members and that its people had coped with much adversity. There is some contested terrain between officials, 'white' commentators and the majority of Nova Scotian people on the one hand, and Africville relocatees and their offspring and black leaders and ordinary black citizens on the other hand. The contested terrain relates to two main points, namely whether the Africville relocatees were fairly compensated for their property, and the degree of culpability on the part of City officials and the larger society. Among the former the view appears to be that compensation at least in the narrow sense was fair, that other disadvantaged citizens were treated no better under similar conditions and that in the words of one commentator "we can't judge those who destroyed it [Africville] by our 1990 values."[12] Among former Africville residents and many Nova Scotian blacks the social construction of Africville includes ideas that the property compensation was not fair, that 'whites' would have been treated differently, and that racism and greed, as much as simply different, acceptable-in-themselves values and principles such as racial integration, accounted for the Africville experience.[13]

The contested terrain may also be seen at the level of policy or solutions. Among former residents and many black leaders, if not ordinary black citizens, the view appears widespread that there should be, if not some direct individual level compensation, then at least some housing development in the old Africville area where the relocatees and their offspring are given priority though not perhaps exclusive rights. Such views are generally not accepted by City officials or the general public where the emphasis is on more commemorative actions and symbols.

The new core social construction of Africville is of course still a social construction. It is a selective presentation of a community's experiences and quality of life. Clearly though it is constructed upon a strong knowledge base (e.g, the historical settlement, the generational recreation of communitarian sentiments even in the face of adversity and significant out-migration), and it is congruent with post-modernist cynicism concerning bureaucratic/technocratic values and leadership, and its preoccupation with identity and diversity. Perhaps most significantly it is much more grounded than its predecessor in the voices and experiences of the Africville people themselves. It appears to be also much more empowering for them and for Nova Scotian blacks in general, not an unimportant consideration for a small minority whose culture, in the larger sense of history and identity, has been traditionally disparaged and neglected. The new social construction of Africville may be seen as a re-claiming of a group's social heritage. As one local black politician observed "when you're a minority you need to stick together ... [because of relocation] the Africville people lost that."[14]

Collective memories are social constructions[15] which configure a group's mythico-history.[16] In total they lay out a social heritage which not only provides an historical accounting but also provides heroes and myths that may be likened to the directional statements and philosophies that organizations often strive to effect. Here is the stuff from which the poets, artists and political leaders draw in their creativity. It is also the stuff that group members can draw upon for strength and meaning in their everyday lives. Certainly the current social construction of Africville can be very valuable in these regards. Already Africville has been a reservoir for creative impulses; as Saunders notes "Wondering what it might have been and remembering what it was ... that's the soil from which creativity springs. The Africville experience has been a major source of inspiration for artists with roots inside and outside the community."[17] It appears fair to say that Africvilleans have been empowered by the new social construction even if, as appears likely, the current and possibly last round of negotiations with the City will yield minimal material benefits for them. Africville will have been commemorated through the Seaview Park, the monument there to the Africville families and presumably the replica of the old Africville church. The people have reclaimed their social heritage and can carry with them and pass along to their descendants an uplifting sense of their community and their roots. For others, non-Africvilleans and non-Blacks, the current social construction of Africville may well be, as Silver Donald Cameron writes in his article 'Irrepressible Africville,' a major marker for "the importance of culture and community and the understanding that a real democracy aids people in doing what they want to do themselves".[18]

Notes

1   Rene Dubos, *So Human an Animal* (New York: Scribner, 1968), p. 270.
2   Ted Palys, *Research Decisions: Quantitative and Qualitative Perspectives* (Toronto: Harcourt Brace Jovanovich Canada Inc., 1992) p. 414.
3   Peter Berger and Thomas Luckman, *The Social Construction of Reality* (Garden City: Doubleday, 1966).
4   See Clairmont, "Community-Based Policing: Implementation and Impact," *Canadian Journal of Criminology*, July-October 1991, pp. 469-484.
5   See J. Godfrey, *Toronto Globe and Mail*, October 12, 1990.
6   See Charles Saunders, *The Daily News*, Halifax, November 15, 1989.
7   Erving Goffman, *Stigma* (Englewood Cliffs, New Jersey: Prentice Hall, 1963), p. 7.
8   Shelagh Mackenzie, *Remembering Africville* (Ottawa: National Film Board).
9   Africville Genealogy Society (ed.), *The Spirit of Africville* (Halifax: Formac Publishing Limited, 1992). Many of the quotations in Chapter Nine are taken from this book.
10 *Toronto Globe and Mail*, May 8, 1995.
11 *Halifax Mail Star*, August 28, 1994.
12 Brian Fleming, "Compensation for Africville," *Halifax: The Daily News*, March 29, 1995.
13 *Daily News*, August 28, 1994.
14 *Daily News*, July 25, 1996.
15 See Maurice Halbwachs, *On Collective Memory* (Chicago: The University of Chicago Press, 1992).
16 See Liisa Malkki, *Purity and Exile* (Chicago: The University of Chicago Press, 1995).
17 *The Daily News*, July 24, 1994.
18 See Silver Donald Cameron, "Irrepressible Africville" (Toronto: Canadian Living, 1993).

Epilogue

On Saturday, August 19, 1972, shortly after the official release of the authors' *Africville Relocation Report*, delegates to the 119th session of the African United Baptist Association of Nova Scotia passed a motion expressing their dissatisfaction with the "methods, strategies and attitudes used to sever the residents of Africville from their land." Thirteen days earlier the Africville Action Committee, with the assistance of the pastor of the Cornwallis Street Baptist Church (the mother church of the African United Baptist Association) had arranged for a fitting burial of the Africville community; on Sunday, August 6, 1972, twelve hundred people, young and old, gathered on the site of the former Africville community for a spiritual revival and memorial service. It was an honourable ending for a unique community.

Plate 8.1 MEMORIES OF AFRICVILLE. Billed as a spiritual revival and memorial service at the site of the former Africville community in northend Halifax. Twelve hundred persons, young and old, gathered on the shore of Bedford Basin for the weekend memorial service sponsored by the Cornwallis Street Baptist Church. In this gathering were scores of people from the families who had been relocated from this area of the city in recent years.

Foreword to the 1974 Edition

This account of the life and death of Africville is a landmark in the scanty literature of relocation. It is both a study in political decision-making affecting a Canadian black community and an important document in our social history.

Relocation of people, forced or induced by governments to move from their homes and often their places of work, has become a regular occurrence in contemporary society. Public works, urban renewal, large resource development enterprises, hydroelectric developments, national parks, and anti-poverty programs have, in the name of progress and in the hope of social and private affluence, been dismantling and restructuring significant parts of Canadian society. Such projects have often exacted a heavy toll among those supposedly benefiting from the "progress."

Something different and historically new in relocation policy has emerged in the modern liberal-democratic state, namely the compulsory removal and resettlement of people "for their own good." While the most dramatic versions of this process have been played out in rural hinterland areas, in sheer quantity the policy has been associated especially with slum clearance and the urban scene. The Africville relocation is a classic illustration of this purportedly liberal-humanitarian objective and of its limitations in practice.

Relocation is a class process, with so few exceptions as to prove the point. It is not unknown but rare, that affluent people are required to move, either for the sake of societal progress or "for their own good." In such cases, usually the people themselves are able to defend their interests and to command the help of well-paid professional advocates. They possess personal aptitudes and skills, as well as material resources, enabling them to re-establish in a similar friendly cultural environment. Their rights are understood and likely to be respected by their peers in government, industry, and the general community.

By contrast, the fate of the uprooted poor is inevitably harsh, whether they are whites in slums, blacks in ghettos, native people in their own territories, or other minority and stranded groups in society. Application of the concept of effective human rights and dignity for deprived peoples is still new. The methods of applying the concept when such people are uprooted are of necessity still experimental and likely to be faulty. The means of enabling them to safeguard their own values and precious elements of lifestyle, and to avoid being overwhelmed by commercial-industrial culture, may be unclear. Nevertheless, the difficulties offer no excuse for continuing majority shortsightedness, greed, haste, and, in short, selfishness in pursuit of majority self-interest.

While every relocation must turn on its own facts, each case tends to be addressed as though it were unique, to be worked out in practical ways by administrators as power figures, without confrontation if possible or with confrontation if necessary in the light of political and economic expediency. Practicality and conventional wisdom will continue to govern relocation decisions and the way they are carried out. Yet a thorough historical and analytical study such as the present one, with careful attention to the political administrative procedures as well as to the experience of the people relocated and the consequences for them in the years afterwards, can have solid value both for administrators responsible for future relocations and for leaders acting on behalf of the people involved in them.

Here the authors have set out alternative models of the relocation process, and their treatment of the subject (along with extensive discussions of modes of relocation in the official report) breaks new ground. It will no doubt receive attention from public administrators, social scientists, and concerned citizens, as well as from people being relocated and those acting on their behalf.

Greatly to their credit, those having administrative and professional responsibility for the Africville relocation wished, as relocation neared completion, to have an historical description and critical evaluation. The Institute of Public Affairs, Dalhousie University, agreed to undertake the task, which was in keeping with its tradition of involvement in social change and in investigating public policy problems. Professors Clairmont and Magill, sociologists having a record of research and concern in social policy, were co-directors of the study. Financial support was provided by the Nova Scotia Department of Public Welfare (now Social Services) and by the Canada Department of Health and Welfare. The full cooperation of officials of the City of Halifax and of the Nova Scotia Department, in the best spirit of modern public administration, is gratefully acknowledged. It will be clear from the text that a critical evaluation of roles of individuals, acting on behalf of the community, implies no criticism of a personal nature.

Guy Henson
Director, Institute of Public Affairs
Dalhousie University
February, 1974

Foreword to the 1987 Edition

It is appropriate that this revised edition should appear at this time some twenty years after Africville was first thrust into the limelight as a local, provincial, and national issue. At the local level, the 1974 book drew attention to the plight of neglected Africville residents whose former locality became the dumping ground of city garbage as well as the victim of the indifferences of a city council to the needs of black city residents. At the provincial level, the plight of these Africville residents living less than ten kilometres from Province House did little to bring comfort to a provincial government which was working towards the creation of a more just society by giving expression to fair employment, fair accommodations, and human rights legislation. At the national level, the issues of Quebec nationalism, bilingualism, biculturalism, and, eventually, multiculturalism at the time would amount to hollow piety in their respective contexts while in the very heart of the eastern gateway to Canada some of the earliest founders and residents of the capital city of Halifax were being removed involuntarily from their homes in the name of "progressive" relocation.

When the relocation was completed a generation ago, the physical destruction that was wrought failed to wipe out the episode. Over the years, Africville residents who were born there, who settled there, who once lived there, recall and revere their memories. For them, as one Africville relocatee said with candid emotion in a February 1987 CBC television show entitled "Memories of Africville," **"There will always be an Africville."**

Both young and old, blacks and whites continue to discuss and debate the merits and demerits of Africville. And that is as it should be. Africville is a part of Canada's past. It is also an important part of Canada's present for it has many lessons for all Canadians whether of minority or majority affiliations.

In the twenty-odd years since the demise of Africville, Nova Scotia blacks remember Africville not only because of what happened to the residents and to the settlement but because of what has happened since then to the rank and file of Nova Scotia blacks. It is true, they would say, that a few black professionals are in good places. They would be in a position to say that the first black judge was sworn in in Halifax on March 25, 1987. But for as long as some fifty to seventy percent unemployment rates apply to many of the predominantly black settlements of Nova Scotia, Africville will also be a symbol of the difficulties facing blacks in Nova Scotia.

But the memories are not limited to despair and disgust. There is the unflagging determination, too, of old and young alike to get on with their lives and show that even if painful memories remain, disappointments could be turned into opportunities to recall a rich and vivid history. One such effort is exemplified in the oral testimonies of former Africville residents who gave detailed accounts of their experiences. On September 13, 1986, at the North Branch Public Library, Gottingen Street, individually, collectively, and spontaneously they spoke of communal bonds, of religious bonds, of mutual self-help, of their well-kept homes and gardens, of their homecrafts and of their strength in music, of their church and school and of their ministers, deacons, teachers, and elders.

Another effort is exemplified in the work of the Africville Genealogy Society, which was founded in 1982 by three young former residents of Africville. Two of the founders gave their testimonies at the September 13 meeting. They were young adults when the relocation of Africville took place. Now they and the other members of the Society organize an annual reunion during the last weekend of July every year to remember Africville, to pray on the hallowed grounds which once housed their Seaview Baptist Church and to celebrate the scenic beauty of what was once their home. The grounds on which this annual reunion takes place are now called Seaview Memorial Park, which extends over twenty-five acres overlooking Bedford Basin. That is the new name of Africville. When the offical opening took place on June 23, 1985, many former Africville residents were there. While the city of Halifax now has plans to build a swimming pool and a canteen on the site, as well as such tourist attractions as a point for boat rides, former Africville residents who attended the official opening could not hide their feelings. One Africville relocatee summed up their feelings when she said: "If they could spend all this money on a park, why couldn't they bring the water down here [when Africville residents lived in the community]."

For Africville relocatees, for their children, and for their children's children, *Africville: The Life and Death of a Canadian Black Community* will always serve the salutary function of explaining how, when, and why things happened as they did. Donald H. Clairmont and Dennis William Magill have, through a skilful combination of scholarship and compassion, produced a valuable book on a much neglected field in Canadian Studies.

Bridglal Pachai, Ph.D.
Executive Director
Black Cultural Centre for Nova Scotia
Halifax, Nova Scotia
March, 1987

Bibliography

Books, Articles and Theses

Africville Genealogy Society (ed.), *The Spirit of Africville*. Halifax: Formac Publishing Limited, 1992.

Alinsky, Saul. *Revielle for Radicals*. Chicago: University of Chicago Press, 1946.

Anderson, Martin. *The Federal Bulldozer: A Critical Analysis of Urban Renewal, 1949-1962*. Cambridge, Mass.: The M.I.T. Press, 1964.

Banfield, Edward C. and James Q. Wilson. *City Politics*. Cambridge, Mass.: Harvard University Press, 1963.

Beaton, Sarah M. "Effects of Relocation: A Study of Ten Families Relocated from Africville, Halifax, Nova Scotia," Master of Social Work Thesis, Maritime School of Social Work, Halifax, N.S., 1969.

Benedict, R. *Patterns of Culture*. London: Mentor Books, 1934.

Berger, Peter and Thomas Luckman. *The Social Construction of Reality*. Garden City: Doubleday, 1966.

Blau, Peter M. *Exchange and Power in Social Life*. New York: Wiley, 1964.

Brand, G. *Interdepartmental Committee on Human Rights: Survey Reports*. Halifax, N.S.: Nova Scotia Department of Welfare, Social Development Division, 1963.

Brookbank, C.R. "Afro-Canadian Communities in Halifax County, Nova Scotia." Unpublished M.A. Thesis, University of Toronto, 1949.

Cameron, Silver Donald. "Irrepressible Africville." Toronto: Canadian Living, 1993.

Clairmont, Don. "Community-Based Policing: Implementation and Impact," *Canadian Journal of Criminology*, July-October 1991, pp. 469-484.

Clairmont, Donald H. in collaboration with K. Scott Wood, George Rawlyk, and Guy Henson. *A Socio-Economic Study and Recommendations: Sunnyville, Lincolnville and Upper Big Tracadie, Guysborough County, Nova Scotia.* Halifax, N.S.: Institute of Public Affairs, Dalhousie University, 1965.

_____. and Dennis William Magill. *Nova Scotian Blacks: An Historical and Structural Overview.* Halifax, N.S.: Institute of Public Affairs, Dalhousie University, 1970.

_____. and Dennis William Magill. *Africville Relocation Report.* Halifax, N.S.: Institute of Public Affairs, Dalhousie University, 1971.

_____. and Fred Wein. "The Nova Scotia Race Relations Experience," *Banked Fires—The Ethnics of Nova Scotia.* Douglas F. Campbell (ed.), Port Credit: The Scribbler's Press, 1978.

Clark, Terry N. *Community Structure and Decision-Making: Comparative Analyses.* Chandler Publications in Anthropology and Sociology. San Francisco: Chandler, 1968.

Commission Report on Relocation. Washington, D.C.: United States Department of Health, Education and Welfare, 1965.

Craig, Kenneth. "Sociologists and Motivating Strategies." Unpublished M.S. Thesis, University of Guelph, Department of Sociology, Guelph, Ontario, 1971.

Dexter, Susan. "The Black Ghetto That Fears Integration," *Maclean's Magazine,* July 25, 1965.

Doern, G. Bruce and Peter Aucoin (eds.). *The Structures of Policy-Making in Canada.* Toronto: Macmillan of Canada, 1971.

Dubos, Renee. *So Human An Animal.* New York: Scribner, 1968.

Durkheim, E. *The Elementary Forms of the Religious Life.* Collier Books edition. Galt, Ont.: Collier-Macmillan, 1961.

Ferguson, C.B. *A Documentary Study of the Establishment of the Negroes in Nova Scotia.* Bulletin No. 8. Halifax, N.S.: Public Archives of Nova Scotia, 1948.

Fraser, Graham. *Fighting Back: Urban Renewal in Trefann Court.* Toronto: Hakkent, 1972.

Fraser, Sylvia. "The Slow and Welcome Death of Africville," *Star Weekly, Toronto,* January 1, 1966, pp. 1-7.

Fromm, Erich. *The Sane Society.* New York: Rinehart, 1955.

Gans, Herbert J. *The Urban Villagers: Group and Class in the Life of Italian Americans.* New York: The Free Press, 1962.

Goffman, Erving. *Stigma.* Englewood Cliffs, New Jersey: Prentice Hall, 1963.

Gouldner, Alvin W. *The Coming Crisis of Western Sociology*. New York: Basic Books, 1970.

Greaves, Ida. *The Negro in Canada: National Problems of Canada*. McGill University Economic Studies, No. 16. Montreal: McGill University, Department of Economics and Political Science, n.d.

Groberg, Robert P. *Centralized Relocation*. Washington, D.C.: National Association of Housing and Redevelopment Officials, 1969.

Halbwachs, Maurice. *On Collective Memory*. Chicago: The University of Chicago Press, 1992.

Haliburton, Thomas C. *An Historical and Statistical Account of Nova Scotia*. Vol. II. Halifax, N.S.: Joseph Howe, 1829.

Henry, Francis. *Forgotten Canadians: The Blacks in Nova Scotia*. Toronto: Longman Canada, 1973.

Homans, George Casper. *Social Behavior: Its Elementary Forms*. New York: Harcourt, Brace and World, 1961.

Hunter, Floyd. *Community Power Structure: A Study of Decision Makers*. New York: Doubleday and Co., 1963.

Iverson, Noel. *Communities in Transition: An Examination of Planned Resettlement in Newfoundland*. St. John's, Nfld.: Institute of Social and Economic Research, Memorial University of Newfoundland, 1967.

Jacobs, Jane. *The Death and Life of Great American Cities*. New York: Random House, 1961.

Kaufman, Arnold S. *The Radical Liberal: The New Politics: Theory and Practice*. New York: Simon and Schuster, 1970.

Key, William H. *When People Are Forced to Move*. Topeka, Kansas: Menninger Foundation, 1967. Mimeographed.

Kramer, Ralph M. *Participation of the Poor: Comparative Community Case Studies in the War on Poverty*. Englewood Cliffs, N.J.: Prentice Hall, 1969.

Krauter, J.F. "Civil Liberties and the Canadian Minorities." Unpublished Ph.D. Dissertation, University of Illinois, 1968.

Lotz, Jim. "Resettlement and Social Change in Newfoundland," *The Canadian Review of Sociology and Anthropology*, VIII (1971) pp. 48-59.

MacDougall, Bernard. "Urban Relocation of Africville Residents." Master of Social Work Thesis, Maritime School of Social Work, Halifax, N.S., 1969.

Mackenzie, Shelagh. *Remembering Africville*. Ottawa: National Film Board, 1991.

MacKerrow, P.E. *A Brief History of the Coloured Baptists of Nova Scotia, 1832-1895*. Halifax, N.S.: Nova Scotia Printing Co., 1895.

Malkki, Liisa. *Purity and Exile*. Chicago: University of Chicago Press, 1995.

Martell, J.S. "Halifax During and After the War of 1812," *The Dalhousie Review*, XXIII (1943-44).

Mattiasson, John. "Forced Relocation: An Evaluative Case Study." A paper presented at the annual meeting of the Canadian Sociology and Anthropology Association, Winnipeg, 1970.

Merton, Robert K. *Social Theory and Social Structure*. Glencoe, Ill.: The Free Press, 1949.

Morrison, William. *A Study on Some of the Social Aspects of Urban Renewal*. Winnipeg, Man.: Community Welfare Planning Council, 1967.

Niebank, Paul L. and M. Yessian. *Relocation in Urban Planning: From Obstacle to Opportunity*. Philadelphia: University of Pennsylvania Press, 1968.

Oliver, Pearleen. *A Brief History of the Colored Baptists of Nova Scotia, 1782-1953*. Copyright of text material, Pearleen Oliver, 1953.

Oliver, W.P. *The Advancement of Negroes in Nova Scotia*. Halifax, N.S.: Nova Scotia Department of Education, 1949.

Palys, Ted. *Research Decisions: Quantitative and Qualitative Perspectives*. Toronto: Harcourt Brace Jovanovich Canada Inc., 1992.

Pickett, Stanley H. "An Appraisal of the Urban Renewal Programme in Canada," *Urban Renewal*. Toronto: Centre for Urban and Community Studies, University of Toronto, 1968. Reprinted from *University of Toronto Law Journal*, XVIII, 3 (1968).

Pivin, Francis Fox and Richard A. Cloward. *Regulating the Poor: The Functions of Public Welfare*. New York: Random Vintage Books, 1972.

Rainwater, Lee. *Behind Ghetto Walls: Black Family Life in a Federal Slum*. Chicago: Aldine Publishing Co., 1970.

_____. "Crucible of Identity: The Negro Lower-Class Family," *Daedalus*, XCV, 1 (1966), pp. 172-217.

_____. "Poverty and Deprivation in the Crisis of the American City." Occasional Paper No. 9., Mimeographed. St. Louis, Mo.: Washington University, 1966.

Rose, Albert. "The Individual, the Family and the Community in the Process of Urban Renewal," *Urban Renewal*. Toronto: Centre for Urban and Community Studies, University of Toronto, 1968. Reprinted from *University of Toronto Law Journal*, XVIII, 3 (1968).

_____. *Regent Park: A Study in Slum Clearance*. Toronto: University of Toronto Press, 1958.

Rossi, Peter Henry. *Why Families Move*. Glencoe, Ill.: The Free Press, 1955.

Ryerson, Stanley B. *Unequal Union: Confederation and the Roots of Conflict in the Canadas, 1815-1873*. Toronto: Progress Books, 1968.

Seeley, John R. "The Slum: Its Nature, Use, and Users," *Journal of the American Institute of Planners*, XXV (1959), pp. 7-14.

Seeman, Melvin. "On the Meaning of Alienation," *American Sociological Review*, XXIV (December 1959), pp. 783-91.

Silberman, Charles. *Crisis in Black and White*. New York: Vintage, 1964.

Smith, T. Watson. *The Slave in Canada, Vol. X of Collections of the Nova Scotia Historical Society*. Halifax, N.S.: Nova Scotia Printing Company, 1899.

Smith, W.F. *Preparing the Elderly for Relocation*. Philadelphia: University of Pennsylvania, 1966.

Spiegel, Hans B. "Human Considerations in Urban Renewal," *Urban Renewal*. Toronto: Centre for Urban and Community Studies, University of Toronto, 1968. Reprinted from *University of Toronto Law Journal*, XVIII, 3 (1968).

Staebler, Edna. "Would you Change the Lives of These People?" *Maclean's Magazine*, May 12, 1956.

Stein, David Lewis. "The Counterattack on Diehard Racism," *Maclean's Magazine*, October 20, 1962.

Stephenson, Gordon. *A Redevelopment Study of Halifax, Nova Scotia*. Halifax, N.S.: City of Halifax, 1957.

Stevens, G.R. *Canadian National Railways. I: Sixty Years of Trial and Error (1836-1896)*. Toronto: Clarke, Irwin & Company, 1960.

_____. *Canadian National Railways. II: Towards the Inevitable (1896-1922)*. Toronto: Clarke, Irwin & Company, 1962.

Sumner, G. *Selected Essays*. New Haven, Conn.: Yale University Press, 1924.

Thurz, Daniel. *Where Are They Now?* Washington, D.C.: Health and Welfare Council of the National Capitol Area, 1966.

Tönnies, Ferdinand. *Community and Society (Gemeinschaft und Gesellschaft)*. Translated and edited by Charles P. Loomis. New York: Harper and Row, 1963.

Urban Renewal. Toronto: Centre for Urban and Community Studies, University of Toronto, 1968. Reprinted from *University of Toronto Law Journal*, XVIII, 3 (1968).

Vallee, Frank G. *Kabloona and Eskimo in the Central Keewatin*. Ottawa: Northern Co-ordination and Research Centre, Department of Indian Affairs and Northern Development, 1962.

Wadstrom, C.B. *An Essay on Colonization, II*. London: Darton and Harvey, 1794.

Wallace, David A. "The Conceptualizing of Urban Renewal," *Urban Renewal*. Toronto: Centre for Urban and Community Studies, University of Toronto, 1968. Reprinted from *University of Toronto Law Journal*, XVIII, 3, (1968).

Walker, James W. "The Establishment of a Free Black Community in Nova Scotia," *African Diaspora*, R. Rotberg and M. Kilson (eds.). Boston: Harvard University Press, 1974.

_____. *A History of Blacks in Canada.* Ottawa: Canadian Government Publishing Centre, 1980.

Williams, Eugene. "The NSAACP and Education." Master of Social Work Thesis, Maritime School of Social Work, Halifax, N.S., 1969.

Willson, Beckles. *Nova Scotia: A Province That Has Been Passed By.* London: Constable & Co., 1911.

Wilson, James Q. *Negro Politics.* New York: The Free Press, 1960.

_____. "Is Urban Renewal A Class Struggle," *Current* (1964).

_____. "Planning and Politics: Citizen Participation in Urban Renewal," *Citizen Participation in Urban Development. I: Concepts and Issues*, Hans B.C. Spiegel (ed.). Washington, D.C.: Center for Community Studies, National Institute for Applied Behavioral Science, 1968, pp. 43-60.

Winks, Robin W. *The Negro in Canada: An Historical Sketch. Draft for The Blacks in Canada.* New Haven: Yale University Press, 1971.

_____. "The Canadian Negro: A Historical Assessment. Part I: The Negro in the Canadian-American Relationship," *The Journal of Negro History*, LIII, 4 (1968).

Newspaper Articles (Chronological)

Slade, Ron M. "Project to Cost $106,200," *The Mail-Star*, Halifax, N.S., August 20, 1954.

"Africville Families Poisoned," *The Chronicle-Herald*, Halifax, N.S., January 28, 1958.

"Africville, Too, Needs a Playground," *The Mail-Star*, Halifax, N.S., July 15, 1961.

"Africville Cleanup Set for Spring," *The Mail-Star*, Halifax, N.S., November 22, 1961.

"Get Step Closer to Expressway," *The Mail-Star*, Halifax, N.S., February 17, 1962.

"Africville District Takeover Being Viewed as Necessary: Halifax Planning Board Considers Report Tuesday," *The Mail-Star*, Halifax, N.S., August 1, 1962.

Husbands, B.A., "Letter to the Editor," *The Mail-Star*, Halifax, N.S., August 11, 1962.

"Residents Want to Keep Homes in Africville," *The Mail-Star*, Halifax, N.S., August 9, 1962.

"Local Negroes Need Help: Far Sighted Policy Needed, Says Dalhousie Report," *The Mail-Star*, Halifax, N.S., October 4, 1962.

"Africville Ruling: Area Residents Anxious to Have Rights Honored," *The Mail-Star*, Halifax, N.S., October 16, 1962.

"Africville: Early Action Urged," *The Mail-Star*, Halifax, N.S., October 25, 1962.

Doyle, Frank. "Dwellings at Dump Not Very Historic," *The Mail-Star*, Halifax, N.S., January 18, 1963.

Shaw, Alexa. "Two-Week Project a Big Success at Africville Church," *The Mail-Star*, Halifax, N.S., July 18, 1963.

"Africville: Time For Action Is Now," *The Mail-Star*, Halifax, N.S., December 23, 1963.

"37 Africville Residents Approve of Rose Report," *The Mail-Star*, Halifax, N.S., January 10, 1964.

"City to Make Africville Move As Painless as Possible, Mayor Says," *The Mail-Star*, Halifax, N.S., January 17, 1964.

"Plan to Secure More Waterfront Land," *The Mail-Star*, Halifax, N.S., July 16, 1964.

Doyle, Frank. "Africville's Shackdom Shows Lack of Action," *The Mail-Star*, Halifax, N.S., February 10, 1965.

"Africville to Get Water Tanks," *The Mail-Star*, Halifax, N.S., April 9, 1965.

"Says City Falling Down on Africville Project: Welfare Director Says Relocation Not Necessary," *The Mail-Star*, Halifax, N.S., April 26, 1965.

Urquhart, Sheila. "Ghetto Going on Schedule," *The Mail-Star*, Halifax, N.S., January 3, 1966.

"Africville May Disappear by Year's End," *The Mail-Star*, Halifax, N.S., January 5, 1966.

"Woman Fined for KKK-Type Threat," *The Mail-Star*, Halifax, N.S, February 22, 1966.

"Africville Deaths: Fatal Level of Wood Alcohol Discovered," Halifax, N.S., May 27, 1966.

The Free Press, Dartmouth, N.S., December 8, 1966.

Urquhart, Sheila. "Africville Program Complete in July," *The Mail-Star*, Halifax, N.S., July 7, 1967.

"End of Africville," *The Mail-Star*, Halifax, N.S., July 7, 1967.

Westell, A. "Shocking Poverty in Nova Scotia," *Detroit Free Press*, June 1969.

Robson, Jim. "Mayor to Probe Africville Claims: Seeks Way to Help," *The Mail-Star*, Halifax, N.S., October 3, 1969.

"Social Worker on Africville: Follow-Up Could Have Averted Relocation Problems," *The Mail-Star*, Halifax, N.S., October 4, 1969.

Robson, Jim. "Last Africville Resident: If I Had Been a Little Younger City Would Never Have Gotten My Land," *The Mail-Star*, Halifax, N.S., January 12, 1970.

"Ward Replies to NSAACP Charge," *The Mail-Star*, Halifax N.S., January 24, 1970.

O'Brien, John. "Council Closes [Miller] Case: Error in Judgement Recognized," *The Mail-Star*, Halifax, N.S., January 30, 1970.

"People Moved Out in Garbage Trucks," *The Mail-Star*, Halifax, N.S., February 26, 1970.

"In Search of a Sense of Community," *Time*, April 6, 1970.

Saunders, Charles. *The Daily News*, Halifax, November 15, 1989.

Godfrey, J. *Toronto Globe and Mail*, October 12, 1990.

Saunders, Charles. *The Daily News*, Halifax, February 4, 1994.

The Daily News, July 24, 1994.

Halifax Mail Star, August 28, 1994.

Toronto Globe and Mail, May 8, 1995.

Fleming, Brian. "Compensation for Africville," *Halifax: The Daily News*, March 29, 1995.

Daily News, July 25, 1996.

City of Halifax (Chronological)

Halifax, City of. *Minutes of the Halifax City Council, 1852-1970, passim.*

_____. *Report of the Halifax School Commissioners*, 1883.

_____. *The Master Plan for the City of Halifax as Prepared by the Civic Planning Commission*, Ira P. MacNab, Chairman. Halifax, N.S., November 16, 1945.

_____. *Report by the City Manager to the Mayor and City Council*, August 19, 1954.

_____. *Report of the Housing Policy Review Committee*, Alderman Abbie Lane, Chairman. Halifax, N.S., August 8, 1961.

_____. Memorandum from D.A. Baker, Assistant Planner, to K.M. Munnich, Director of Planning, City of Halifax, January 2, 1962. Industrial Mile File, Development Department.

_____. Memorandum from the City Manager to the Mayor and Members of the Town Planning Board, February 20, 1962. Industrial Mile File, Development Department.

_____. Planning Office. Map P500/46, Industrial Mile-Africville Area: Land Ownership and Buildings, July 26, 1962.

_____. Letter from Dr. Allan R. Morton to the Mayor of Halifax and Members of the City's Health Committee, August 9, 1962. Africville File, Social Planning Office.

_____. Report by Dr. A.R. Morton, Commissioner of Health and Welfare, August 28, 1962, Mimeographed.

_____. Report by G.F. West, Commissioner of Works, September 6, 1962, Mimeographed.

_____. Report by J.F. Thompson, City Assessor, September 7, 1962, Mimeographed.

_____. *Minutes of City Council's Africville Sub-committee, 1966-1967, passim.*

_____. *City of Halifax: Prison Land Development Proposals, Report No. 1, Survey and Analysis, Volume 2, Social Factors,* June 23, 1969.

_____. *City of Halifax: Prison Land Development Proposals, Report No. 2, Area Conceptual Plan,* October 14, 1969.

Other Government Sources

Halifax, County of. *Registry of Deeds,* Books 10 to 1654, passim.

Nova Scotia Legislative Assembly. *Journal and Proceedings of the House of Assembly, 1849-1855, passim.*

Nova Scotia. Public Archives of Nova Scotia, Vols. 77 and 451.

_____. Public Archives of Nova Scotia, Assembly Petitions (Education, 1860) File on Africville.

_____. Public Archives of Nova Scotia, Census, City of Halifax, 1851.

_____. Public Archives of Nova Scotia. Census of 1871.

Other Sources

Blum, Sid. Correspondence with Mrs. Nancy Edwards (pseudonym) September 6, 1961, April 19, 1962 and August 9, 1962.

_____. Letter from Sid Blum, National Committee on Human Rights, Canadian Labour Congress, to F.C. Brodie, Human Rights Committee, Halifax-Dartmouth District Labour Council, October 17, 1961.

Communication from Miss Phyllis R. Blackeley, Assistant Archivist, Public Archives of Nova Scotia, Halifax, April 1970.

Correspondence between the Halifax Human Rights Advisory Committee and His Worship the Mayor and Aldermen, City of Halifax, September 6, 1963.

Halifax Human Rights Advisory Committee. *Minutes of Meetings,* September 21, 1962 to January 23, 1967, passim.

Letter from Mrs. Alexa McDonough, Special Projects Supervisor, Office of the Social Planner, City of Halifax, May 6, 1970.

Memorandum from A. Alan Borovoy, Executive Secretary, Toronto and Disrict Labour Committee for Human Rights, August, 1962.